THE
Andy
Griffith
Show

THE
Andy
Griffith
Show

by RICHARD KELLY

JOHN F. BLAIR, PUBLISHER
WINSTON-SALEM, N. C.

Seventh Printing, Revised Edition, 1989

Library of Congress Cataloging in Publication Data

Kelly, Richard Michael, 1937–
  The Andy Griffith show.

  Includes index.
  1. Andy Griffith show (Television program) I. Title.
PN1992.77.A573K4 1984   791.45'72   84–24597
ISBN 0–89587–043–6

To Barbara

Contents

Preface

Twenty-five years have passed since Americans were first introduced to Mayberry's sheriff without a gun. At the time I was involved in graduate study at Duke University in Durham, North Carolina, and was amused at the local references made on the show to Raleigh, Mt. Pilot (Pilot Mountain), and Siler City. I quickly became a faithful viewer and eventually found myself a more knowledgeable citizen of Mayberry than I was of the city I lived in. As the seasons passed I grew familiar with all of Mayberry's townspeople and soon got to know their habits better than those of my actual associates. It wasn't long before I knew the Mayberry Union High theme song, Barney's middle name, and Andy's favorite meal. When the show went off the air in 1968, I was able to see it all over again in reruns and can do so to this day. My involvement with the series has finally led me to write this book. It is my hope that in the process of explaining how the show was produced and developed I will provide not only an entertaining and informative account of how a television program is created and grows into a national and international success but also an answer to how a fictitious group of people can arrest and delight the imagination.

A casual viewer of *The Andy Griffith Show* might well wonder why anyone would choose to write a book about it, indeed, about *any* television program. Outside of *The Making of Star Trek* (1968), there have been few serious, extended studies of particular television shows. *Lucy & Ricky & Fred & Ethel: The Story of I Love Lucy* (1976) and *M*A*S*H: the Inside Story of TV's Most Popular Show* (1981) present thorough accounts of the programs but focus more upon the actors' personalities than upon the craft and artistry of the series. A prevalent attitude among intellectuals is that television is throw-away entertainment, not art. Some publishers have a standing policy not to accept studies of television programs or motion pictures. One is reminded of the nineteenth-century attitude towards novels—that they were throw-away entertainment.

In Shakespeare's day plays were considered ephemeral and most were not published. Obviously, there are thousands of plays, novels, and television programs unworthy of study. The medium of television, however, does not prevent a show from being a work of art, although because of pressures of time and money, a television program is more likely to be compromised than a novel or play. *The Andy Griffith Show*, for example, appeared for about thirty-two consecutive weeks each year for eight years. With a schedule like that, there inevitably will be poor shows and repetition of themes. In fact, it is a wonder that any artistry whatsoever could be achieved and maintained. And yet it was. Unlike so many programs today that begin with a slick pilot and then degenerate, the *Griffith Show* actually improved with time. Beneath its simple rustic setting lies a high degree of sophistication. The acting, writing, production, directing, and scoring were painstakingly worked out and blended to produce one of the more popular *and* artistic creations of the 1960s.

Ideally one should plan to write about a show that is in production. My task was complicated by the passage of time since the show went off the air. The Desilu Studio, where the series was filmed, is now a warehouse; the sets have all been auctioned or destroyed; shooting schedules and production details have been discarded; two of the actors, Paul Hartman (Emmett the fix-it man) and Howard McNear (Floyd the barber), are dead; and Frances Bavier (Aunt Bee) has retired to Siler City, North Carolina, and declines to be interviewed. But many riches remain. Andy Griffith has a bound set of all the scripts from the show, which he made available to me. Ron Jacobs provided me with a print of the pilot for the series, "Danny Thomas Meets Andy Griffith." Jack Dodson preserved several working scripts, which he gave to me. And Don Knotts, Frances Bavier, and Viacom have sent me many photographs that were taken during the filming of the show. Finally, I made several trips to Los Angeles to make extensive tape-recorded interviews with the people chiefly

responsible for the series: Andy Griffith, Don Knotts, Jack
Dodson (Howard Sprague), Sheldon Leonard (Executive
Producer), Aaron Ruben (Producer-Writer), Richard O.
Linke (Associate Producer), Ron Jacobs (Associate Pro-
ducer), and Earl Bellamy (Director).

In Part One I have allowed these people to unfold the
story of *The Andy Griffith Show* in their own words. Their
various convictions and perspectives, sometimes at odds
with those of other members of the company, reveal the
dynamic and complex nature of a production company
dedicated to two sets of goals: financial success and high
ratings on the one hand, and the creation of wholesome
comedy with a high level of artistic integrity on the other.
Amazingly, these seemingly contradictory goals were realized, and that is an extraordinary event in television history.

After tracing in Part One the development of the show
from its conception to its conclusion, I have in Part Two
examined the artistic qualities of the series that made it a
television "classic." This revised edition carries a new chapter in Part Two in which I have discussed the contributions
made to the series by two of its best writers, Harvey Bullock and Everett Greenbaum.

Part Three contains completely new material that ex-
amines what has happened since this book was first published in 1981. The chapter entitled "Don't Look Back"
provides updates on the careers of various cast members
and features excerpts from recent interviews with members of the cast who were not available during the writing
of the first edition. "Mayberry in the 1980s" discusses the
phenomenal growth of interest in the show that is currently taking place. This chapter also includes information
on two organizations that were founded to celebrate *The
Andy Griffith Show* and to promote the airing of the show in
local communities.

Parts Four and Five are comprised of supplemental material for the serious student of the show. A second script
has been added to Part Four. The new script is entitled

"The Wandering Minstrel" and, although it contains many of the classic elements of the series, it was never filmed. Part Five contains a listing and summary (with some revision of details) of all 249 episodes of the show, arranged according to the dates of their original presentation.

I want to thank the many people who helped me in writing this book: Andy Griffith, Richard Linke, Don Knotts, Jack Dodson, Aaron Ruben, Sheldon Leonard, Earl Bellamy, and Ron Jacobs for their generosity in granting me extended interviews and for responding to my subsequent letters requesting further information and materials. I am particularly indebted to Richard Linke for his strong and continued support of my project and for opening a number of doors otherwise closed to me. I want to thank Barbara Matchett, Don Knotts' secretary-manager, for getting Don and me together despite some last-minute problems in our schedules. I owe a debt of gratitude to Thomas Wheeler and Richard Goode for their helpful critical observations about the show. My wife Barbara I thank for her careful reading of the manuscript and for her many good suggestions for its revision. Special thanks go to Becky Caldwell, Ernest Lee, and Les White for their invaluable assistance with the plot summaries. I would also like to acknowledge both the support and criticial suggestions given to me by George McDaniel and my publisher, John F. Blair. I also thank the trustees of the John C. Hodges Better English Fund at the University of Tennessee for a travel grant that allowed me to make two trips to Los Angeles, where I interviewed most of the principals of the show.

In preparing this edition I have received help from many people around the country who love *The Andy Griffith Show* as much as I do. I especially want to thank Jim Clark for sharing with me his rich knowledge of the show. I owe a debt of gratitude to Paul Gereffi, David McDaniel, and Tommy Ford for their aid in correcting details in the summaries. Thanks also to John Meroney for allowing me

PREFACE xiii

to use his interviews with Aneta Corsaut, Betty Lynn, and Hal Smith.

My warm appreciation goes to Harvey Bullock and Everett Greenbaum for supplying me with scripts and photographs as well as for their enthusiasm and helpful comments, and to George Lindsey for his gracious interview.

Finally, my thanks again to Andy Griffith, Don Knotts and Jack Dodson for their help in updating this book and for their continued support of this study.

Richard Kelly

Knoxville, Tennessee

PART

1

(Preceding page)
Andy Griffith with Richard O. Linke, his Personal Manager and business
partner since 1954.

CHAPTER 1

A Small Town Makes It Big

I Mayberry

The Andy Griffith Show was one of the most successful long-running series in television history. It ranked among the top ten shows in the nation during its entire eight prime-time seasons, from 1960–61 through 1967–68. In fact, it was the number one program in the national ratings in its last year when Andy Griffith left the show. The sponsor, General Foods, refused to relinquish the series, and a version of the show entitled *Mayberry, R.F.D.*, with Ken Berry as Andy's replacement, ran for three more years and also commanded ratings in the top ten. The reruns of *The Andy Griffith Show*, which began in 1964, are still among the most watched daytime shows in the country. It is astonishing to think that a series with no sex and no violence has captured the hearts and imaginations of millions of viewers during the past twenty years.

Anyone who has watched the show will remember some of its classic moments: Andy limiting Deputy Barney Fife to one bullet, which he must carry in his shirt pocket; Aunt Bee churning out pickles for the county fair that taste like kerosene; Floyd daydreaming about expanding to a two-chair barbershop; Gomer wondering if his suit is plain enough during one of Barney's "plain clothes" operations; Otis trying to jump into the jailhouse bed that had been laid on its side against the wall ("Now I know I must be drunk. I never fell onto the wall before!"); and Barney's disguising himself as a department-store dummy in an attempt to catch a shoplifter.

One of the most memorable of all scenes—Andy Griffith's favorite—and one that captures the essence of Mayberry is that in which Andy and Barney are sitting on the front porch on a drowsy afternoon. Barney stretches and says: "Know what I'm gonna do?" Andy half acknowledges the question with a grunt. Barney continues: "I'm gonna go home, take a nap, go over to Thelma Lou's, and watch a little TV." Several seconds of silence pass and then Barney slaps his stomach: "Yep, that's what I'm gonna do—go home, take a nap, go over to Thelma Lou's, and watch a little TV." Several more seconds of silence elapse and then Barney continues: "That's it—home, nap, over to Thelma Lou's . . ." and Andy comes in with "watch a little TV?" The brilliant use of repetition and timing, the nostalgic front porch, the leisure and carefreeness of a simpler world we all think we once shared—make this scene a hallmark of the show.

Another classic exchange takes place between Andy and Floyd on the bench outside the courthouse. After complaining about the heat, Floyd exclaims, "You know, everybody complains about the weather but nobody does anything about it. Calvin Coolidge said that." Andy: "No, Floyd, that wasn't Calvin Coolidge that said that, it was Mark Twain." Floyd looks stunned and confused by Andy's correction and after a few moments of silence asks, "Then what *did* Calvin Coolidge say?"

Because the war in Southeast Asia and the racial and student riots of the sixties were running simultaneously against the *Griffith Show*, it is little wonder that a town like Mayberry was so appealing. The former mayor of Raleigh, North Carolina, Jyles J. Coggins, comments on the believability and the human values found in the show: "I have seen and enjoyed *The Andy Griffith Show* many times. Although I believe the shows are somewhat exaggerated in reflecting the naiveté and hickishness of small-town Southern people, especially today, they do show the imaginative life-style of twenty or thirty years ago. The basic qualities of goodness of the people and genuine concern for one another and the community are still true to North Carolina." As an aside, the mayor also notes that "our tourist industry has climbed steadily, and *The Andy Griffith Show* may be partially responsible in helping put North Carolina on the map."

The mayor's comment about the goodness of the people and the genuine concern for one another and the community is a relevant perception of the basic reason for the enormous appeal of the series. All of the characters of Mayberry—Sheriff Andy Taylor, Aunt Bee, Opie, Barney Fife, Floyd the barber, Gomer Pyle, Cousin Goober, Sarah the telephone operator, Thelma Lou, Helen Crump, Juanita from the diner, Otis Campbell, Clara Edwards, Emmett the fix-it man, Howard Sprague, Ernest T. Bass, the Darling family, Mayors Stoner and Pike, to name the most familiar—care about each other. Love and respect are two qualities that are always in the background of Mayberry's comic community. Many of the characters may be stereotypes, but they come across as people with genuine feelings. They move into one another's lives as human beings, uncomplicated by greed, violence, or sex—and the town reflects their collective comic innocence. *The Andy Griffith Show*, unlike other "rural" shows such as *Beverly Hillbillies*, *Petticoat Junction*, and *Green Acres*, is unique in its innovative presentation of character and atmosphere.

After the show had been running a few years, Sheldon Leonard remarked to Andy Griffith that the series was misnamed; "it should have been called *Mayberry*." The real hero of *The Andy Griffith Show* is the town of Mayberry, presided over by the sheriff without a gun, Andy Taylor. It is a small world, one that, ironically, is more colorful on simple black-and-white television sets. It is filled with wonderful characters we can all understand and care about. It is nostalgic and funny, and most important, it is timeless. The great North Carolina novelist Thomas Wolfe suggested that we can't go home again. That unpleasant truth can be tempered by a visit to Mayberry.

As the series progressed and new characters were introduced and developed, the believability of this ageless town increased. Numerous specific details fleshed out its character. Aunt Bee's favorite section of the newspaper, for example, was a gossip column called "Mayberry after Midnight." The perimeter of the Mayberry mind extends to Siler City and Raleigh, and seldom further. The fact that Mayberry is the center of the universe is made wonderfully apparent in the title of a motion picture that Barney mentions, "The Monster from Out of Town." Small-town activities abound and set the life-styles of all the inhabitants: the annual fair (at which Aunt Bee enters her kerosene pickles), the Founders' Day ceremony (for which Floyd writes the fetching song "Hail to thee, Lady Mayberry"), the annual band contest, the ladies' garden club meetings, the Sunday morning church services, the choir practices, the picnics, fishing at Myers' Lake, and the high school reunions (where Andy and Barney sing in harmony "Mayberry Union High"). Mayberry not only acquired its own character but quickly established its own history. Besides the Founders' Day episodes, which always conjured up Mayberry's past—once with Floyd playing the part of Captain John Mayberry in the pageant—there were several other shows that delved into the rich fictional past of the town. Usually the legends of Mayberry, under close scrutiny, turned out to be rather exaggerated. Everyone in town, for example, believed his ancestors were the central figures in the great Battle of Mayberry fought in the 1700s, during which the settlers bravely destroyed a savage horde of Cherokees. Opie, who is writing an essay on the subject for class, goes to the Raleigh library, discovers the true account in a old newspaper, and bursts the town's bubble of pride. It turns out that a handful of settlers encountered a handful of Indians. They both became so frightened that they started drinking, and the great battle of Mayberry consisted of a farcical drunken brawl, the only casualties being several unlucky farm animals.

Like its inhabitants, the town had a distinctive character and a past, and it was guided by its traditions. Mayberry could no more change than Barney or Andy could change. Ruben, Griffith, and others took pains to protect its character and identity. Central to this character was the pace of the town—and of the show. The small talk between Andy and Barney sitting on the front porch or between Andy and Floyd in the barbershop conveyed an authentic atmosphere of village life. They would discuss the luncheon special at the diner, or the radio show of the singer Leonard Blush, or reminisce about the Apricot Queen who once passed through town. A typical scene is the one in which Barney explains to Andy what it was like out on the town, at Morrelli's Italian Restaurant:

Barney: I remember I went overboard with Thelma Lou on her last birthday.
Andy: Did you get her something nice?
Barney: Nicest present I ever gave her. Know what I did? Took her out to dinner.
Andy: Took her out to *dinner?*
Barney: Well, yeh, you know we usually go dutch. Took her to Morrelli's.
Andy: Oh, *Morrelli's!*
Barney: Now *there's* a place to take a girl. Out on the highway like that, nice and secluded. Red checkered tablecloths.
Andy: Fancy, fancy.
Barney: You know, they'll let you take a bottle in there.
Andy: You don't drink, though.
Barney: Noooo, ha, ha!
Andy: What did you have to eat?
Barney: The Deluxe Special. You know you can hold it down to $1.85 out there, if you don't have the shrimp cocktail.
Andy: Did you have shrimp cocktail?
Barney: Well, no, I told Thel let's not fill up. Minestrone was delicious, though.
Andy: Oh, yeah. When that's made right that's really something.
Barney: And for the main dish, pounded steak à la Morrelli.
Andy: Oh?
Barney: It's really pounded, too. No question about it. They have one of these open kitchens and you can look right in there and watch them pound it right with your own eyes.

Andy: Oh, yeah. Kinda see what you're gettin'.
Barney: I tell ya, Andy, when that meal was finished I did something I rarely do. I sent my compliments back to the chef. They appreciate them things. He kinda looked up from his pounding and sort of waved at me.
Andy: I'm gonna have to take Helen over there one of these days.
Barney: Oh she'd *love* it, *love* it! It's not only the food either. It's the atmosphere. Well, they have the candles on the table and the music. They got a gypsy violinist out there. He must have played six or eight songs standing over our table. Of course, you got to slip him a quarter.
Andy: Yeah, those fellows work on tips.
Barney: One thing about gypsies, though, they're moody.

Sometimes the show would open with Barney humming while he was sweeping the courthouse floor, and Andy would be quietly repairing the gooseneck lamp. The camera would leisurely and lovingly record these seemingly insignificant sounds and activities. One never had a sense that the producers and actors were aware of the thousands of dollars of air time they were rapidly consuming. Their scenes were truly innovative, but they did not happen at once. Knotts explains the evolution of those scenes:

Of course, in the beginning they didn't write that into the scripts. In the beginning the feeling was that, as in all television shows, the story should go from point A to point Z, plot all the way. During the readings I would sit in with Aaron, Bob Sweeney, Andy, and usually Sheldon and we would pick the script apart. Andy would begin to tell how people talked back home. We got a little static at first because they'd say, "We can't stop the story," but the more we did it, the more they liked it. Soon they began to write it into the scripts, and that turned out to be one of the things in the show that people identified with the most . . . .

Knotts explains that his and Griffith's rural background provided much of the material and tempo of those scenes:

All of my family in West Virginia were rural people. Although we lived in town, my father was a farmer and all my relatives

were farmers. And Andy's people were all very country, as we
would call them. So we had experienced all these years in our
childhood sitting around on a farm and everybody having dinner—and the farmers don't talk much, you know. Finally someone would say, "You want to go down to the gas station and get
a bottle of pop?" Everyone would sit there and say, "That might
be a good idea." A few minutes later he'd ask it again. We both
remembered moments like those and they cracked us up. So we
put them in the show. Andy was a great one for calling the writers when they had written something that didn't ring true. He
would say, "I have an uncle in North Carolina who's just like this
guy and he wouldn't say that." "Well, what would he say?" He'd
tell them and they'd write it down.

Another feature of the town was its imaginary characters: Sarah, the telephone operator, and Juanita, Barney's
other girlfriend who worked at the Bluebird Diner. These
two characters, though never seen and never heard, acquired a credibility comparable to that of all the other
characters—perhaps they were even more colorful because one's imagination could play with them. When Barney would place a personal phone call to Thelma Lou or
to the diner, he invariably had to answer to that watchdog
of all telephone conversations, Sarah. Aaron Ruben, who
created the characters, said: "I don't know why, but I particularly like unseen characters. I also had one on *C.P.O.
Sharkey* named Natalie. These characters create curiosity."
They reminded Andy Griffith of the old radio show *Vic
and Sade*: "They had originally only three characters—
later four—but they talked about their town and other
towns nearby, and you never met any of those people. But
their talk about them made you believe they were there."
Concerning Sarah and Juanita he said: "If you ever saw
them, it would be a disappointment; they're too colorful
in your mind."

Still, Don Knotts did have a clear sense of what Juanita
was like:

I saw her as a conglomeration of every diner waitress I've ever
seen that you try to make when you're in there at one o'clock in

the morning for a little coffee. I think every guy has thought of that one time or another. She was easy and Barney got a little on the side.

When Knotts made *The Ghost and Mr. Chicken*, his first motion picture after leaving the series, the writers (Fritzell and Greenbaum, who wrote for the *Griffith Show*) had an invisible character who cried out during one of Knotts' nervous speeches, "That a boy, Luther!" During the rewriting of the script Griffith suggested that the invisible shouter be kept as a running gag throughout the film. He was, and it worked very well. For years, Knotts recalls, people would yell at him, "That a boy, Luther!"

Sometimes even Barney Fife would become an unseen character. As the series progressed, the writers gave Barney larger and larger parts, and the thirty-two shows a year began to tell on Knotts. Finally he asked to be written out of four scripts a year so that he could catch his breath. Even in his absence, however, Barney's character was present. In one episode, for instance, Andy receives a letter from Barney, who is on his vacation in Raleigh. In it he explains he got his favorite corner room in the "Y," remarks how a quarter goes "just like that" in the big city, and how he has a pick-me-up snack before going to the "Y's" evening movie. Floyd, who is listening with all the eagerness of a child to Andy reading the letter, remarks, "Gee, that Barney writes a good letter!" And thus Barney maintains his presence even when he is off the show.

II Mayberry Watchers

The sort of people who have been attracted to the world of Mayberry has been examined by pollsters, and their findings are interesting. According to the A. C. Nielsen ratings for a six-week period from October 23 to December 3, 1967 (the last year of *The Andy Griffith Show*), the top ten shows in the nation were:

    1. Lucy Show

2. Andy Griffith (rose to #1 by end of season)
3. Bonanza
4. Red Skelton
5. Gunsmoke
6. Family Affair
7. Jackie Gleason
8. Gomer Pyle (a spin-off of *The Andy Griffith Show*)
9. Saturday Movies
10. Beverly Hillbillies
    Friday Movies

In the South, *Andy Griffith* ranked third for the six-week period, following *Gunsmoke* and *Bonanza*. In the Northeast, however, *Andy Griffith* completely fell out of the top ten, where the leading shows were *Jackie Gleason, Smothers Brothers*, and *Dean Martin*, all variety shows. A breakdown of the income of the audience revealed *Andy Griffith* to be third for people making under $5,000 (*Lucy Show* and *Gunsmoke* being one and two). *Andy Griffith* was number four for those with incomes of $10,000 and over (*Saturday Movies, Dean Martin*, and *Friday Movies* being the top three). Finally, among blue-collar workers *Andy Griffith* ranked first, followed by the *Lucy Show* and *Bonanza*; and among white-collar workers *Andy Griffith* ranked third, led by *Saturday Movies* and *Dean Martin*. These statistics may be misleading, for they indicate a small sampling of viewers during a short period of time at the beginning of the last year of *The Andy Griffith Show*. Nevertheless, one could generalize that for that period the show was primarily watched by southern and rural audiences earning less than $5,000 a year, the majority of whom were blue-collar workers. On the other hand, for the entire year the show went into 15,460,000 homes weekly during its last season and ranked number one in the nation. That represents a 42% share of the total viewing audience, a figure that suggests the broad national appeal of the show. In fact, one episode of the series (the one in which Barney returns to host a summit meeting in Mayberry) ranked eleventh among single comedy programs most watched in television from 1960 to the present, with an audience of thirty-three and a half million.

The Andy Griffith Show appears to be winning a more thoughtful appreciation in its reruns, where, because of its continuous appearance day by day throughout the country, one may more readily become involved in the ongoing life of the town. A national survey of daytime television that was taken in 1970 revealed that the series continued its popularity even in reruns. By this time it rated a greater share of the audience in the East than in the Southeast (the "location" of Mayberry). It ranked number five in New York City and Washington, D.C., nine in Knoxville, and eight in the Raleigh-Durham market. Its highest rating that year was in Los Angeles, where it ranked third. In most of the large urban centers of country it was among the top ten. During the next decade the show continued to be rerun in almost every major city in the country, and now, with the growth of cable television, it may be seen in some cities as many as three times a day. Mayberry appears to have charmed the imagination of those people living in complex metropolises where the pastoral view of the small town, with its affection, warmth, and honesty, provides a comforting illusion of society and human nature.

A whole generation has grown up with The Andy Griffith Show, and now, like Ronny Howard (Opie) in his late twenties, they can watch the reruns with "nostalgia." There were 249 episodes of the show produced, averaging about thirty episodes a season, by today's standards (fifteen shows being the norm) an extraordinarily long season. For the past twenty years, then, The Andy Griffith Show has continuously appeared on television throughout the nation and promises to continue for years to come. The principal owners of the series, Andy Griffith, Richard O. Linke, Sheldon Leonard, and Danny Thomas, have collectively earned millions of dollars from the reruns. The producers, directors, actors, and writers for the show also still share in the profits. Many of them, having served their apprenticeship on *The Andy Griffith Show*, later extended their talents in new directions.

Aaron Ruben produced *Gomer Pyle, U.S.M.C.*, *Sanford and Son*, and *C.P.O. Sharkey*. He is currently producing *Wendy Hooper, U.S. Army*. Director Gene Reynolds became the executive producer of *M*A*S*H*. Jim Fritzell and Everett Greenbaum, who together wrote some of the best scripts for the *Griffith Show*, continued their high level of writing for *M*A*S*H*. A writer who came later in the series, Pat McCormick, wrote for Johnny Carson and became a comic television personality in his own right. Some of the minor characters from the show, ones who appeared on an occasional basis, also went on to achieve considerable success in television and motion pictures. These include Jack Nicholson (two appearances), Don Rickles, Burt Mustin, Michael J. Pollard, Buddy Ebsen, Alan Hale, Bill Bixby, Barbara Eden, Ellen Corby, George Kennedy, Frank Sutton, Gavin MacLeod, Jerry Van Dyke, Jack Burns, and Ken Berry. Jim Nabors, of course, got his own show, *Gomer Pyle*, the pilot for which appeared as part of *The Andy Griffith Show*, depicting Andy helping Gomer to adjust to his first day in the Marines. George Lindsey, who replaced Nabors, has been successful in the raucous *Hee Haw*, where he plays an even more rustic character than Goober. Ron Howard sprang to stardom in *American Graffiti* and later in *Happy Days*. After returning to study the art of film-making at USC, he starred in *Eat My Dust* and made his own feature films, such as *Grand Theft Auto*. Don Knotts has been making "family entertainment" films since leaving the show in 1965 and has become identified with Walt Disney Productions. After Andy Griffith left the show in 1968, he attempted two television series—*Headmaster* and *The New Andy Griffith Show*—both of which were soon canceled. He starred in the innovative western *Hearts of the West* and such popular television movies as *Savages*, *Winterkill*, *Washington: Behind Closed Doors*, *Centennial*, and *Murder in Texas*. Although Frances Bavier retired to Siler City, North Carolina, after *Mayberry, R.F.D.* was cancelled, she appeared in the popular motion picture *Benji* and has made a few television commercials. She is the only member of the original cast to remain on the show for more than ten years, from the pilot film in 1960, through several episodes of *Mayberry, R.F.D.* in the 1970s.

There is justice in the success of the series and in the subsequent prominence it helped to win both for the cast and for the people behind the scenes, for in Sheldon Leonard's words, "*The Andy Griffith Show* was one of the best written, best acted, and best produced shows in television history." A close look at the production of the series will support Leonard's appraisal.

CHAPTER 2

Beginning:
The Notion

The Andy Griffith Show began with a notion. Sheldon Leonard, who was producing *The Danny Thomas Show*, and a writer by the name of Arthur (Artie) Stander, came up with the idea of making an episode of *The Danny Thomas Show* that would revolve around a character who was to be a sheriff, justice of the peace, and editor of the paper in a small town. The William Morris Agency informed Leonard that an actor by the name of Andy Griffith was interested in attempting a role in television and that because of his rural background and previous rustic characterizations he would be well suited to the part. Andy Griffith explains his initiation into television, a significant though tentative first step that ultimately led into the development of *The Andy Griffith Show*:

I was in a play called *Destry* [*Destry Rides Again*], and had told the William Morris Agency that I was now ready to try television. I'd always been afraid of it because I figured if you strike out there, that's it. But I was in this play and one night Sheldon came to see me. I was always pretty stupid—I knew the name Sheldon Leonard and I knew the face of this man that I saw as I went up to my dressing room, but didn't put the two together until somebody came up and said, "Sheldon Leonard is here to see you." Then I knew who he was. We went out and talked— and he had this notion. And to be honest with you, I didn't care too much for this notion, but I liked *him*. The next time he was in town we talked again. Dick Linke, my agent, was with me. And still I didn't care for the notion all that much but I liked him a lot and I agreed to do the show.

Sheldon Leonard, the creator of *The Andy Griffith Show* and its executive producer for all eight years, recalls the fortuitous beginning as follows:

The conception of the show was founded on the availability—sudden availability—of Andy Griffith, who at this time had become a client of the William Morris Agency. I was approached by the top echelon of the Agency to see if I could come up with an idea for Griffith, who had expressed an interest in going into television. The idea that I designed put him in a rural setting and surrounded him with characters who would, we hoped, create the comedy that Andy could react to. I then went to New York and had a series of meetings with Dick Linke and Andy, during which we explored the idea and refined it to suit Andy's requirements. And I then asked the writer, Artie Stander, since deceased, to construct an episode of the *Danny Thomas* series, of which I was then producer-director.

Griffith went to Los Angeles to the Desilu Studios to film the pilot episode, directed by Sheldon Leonard.

I had a week off from the play. I came out here, did the pilot—and I remember a lot of that, too, because Danny Thomas made me very nervous (and I'm a slow starter as well). So when we started the show a lot of people (the script clerk told me this later) were talking and wondering why they had me out here. What is this magic they're talking about? This will never work, they said, because I was wooden, very wooden. And as the show progressed I got looser and looser and when they brought the audience in, I was on top of it, and whatever I bring happened. And the show, in fact, did sell.

The pilot, entitled "Danny Meets Andy Griffith," was aired toward the end of the 1960 season. The plot was a simple one: Danny Thomas drives through a small town called Mayberry and is arrested for speeding by the local sheriff, played by Andy Griffith. The show introduced Ronny Howard and Frances Bavier, although the latter did not appear as Aunt Bee until the first episode of the series. In the pilot she plays a town widow who visits the sheriff to report that a department store is harassing her for the unpaid suit in which her ne'er-do-well husband was buried. The role of the town drunk who regularly locks himself up in a jail cell in order to sober up was also introduced, but the part was played by Frank Cady (who later played the storekeeper, Sam Drucker, in *Green Acres*) instead of by Hal Smith. All in all, it was a fast-paced, cleverly organized, and well-written show that highlighted Griffith's talent as a comic actor. His diction, intonation, and down-home anecdotes were something refreshingly new on television, and the audience welcomed the change.

Leonard explains the purpose and subsequent success of the pilot:

> It was the first spin-off within the framework of *The Danny Thomas Show*. We showed all of the components of the new character—what he would be like and who would be working with him, and it worked very well. As a matter of fact, the sponsor of *The Danny Thomas Show* [General Foods] had first access to the new spin-off and immediately was committed to it. And we were in business, as it were.

An important figure in Griffith's move to television was Richard Linke, who became associate producer during the first few years of the *Griffith Show*. Formerly an executive with Capitol Records in New York, Linke first discovered Griffith in the 1950s while listening on his car radio to Griffith's recording, "What It Was Was Football." Intrigued by the humor of the piece, Linke visited Griffith in Chapel Hill, North Carolina, and, in essence, became his manager—a working relationship that has lasted to this day. Instrumental in Griffith's success in plays and motion pictures, Linke now helped Griffith to negotiate his contract with CBS and acquired the role of associate producer to protect himself and Griffith in the significant move:

> That was part of my deal. In New York I was a big gun. I knew everyone. I had all the contacts, whether it was a restaurant or a network or whatever. Out here, now, I could have been gobbled up. This is a funny city. So I was determined to come

out here and do what I did back there, you know, with contacts and this and that. And I knew that if I didn't have a title to protect Andy, he might be gobbled up or I might be thrown out. So, it started as a protection measure. Then I got busy with Ronnie Jacobs, who incidentally taught me the business the first year, and I did many things an associate producer should do.

While Griffith was free to ponder the new complexities of television and his forthcoming series, Linke was busy making important financial transactions. He took pains to establish a name for Griffith and himself not only with the industry but with the banks. He recounts:

I chose to go with Bank of America. A man by the name of Wallace Sharper was a very big executive for the bank downtown and he helped me considerably. We wanted the biggest share of the ownership, and for that you got to put up. I went and got what is called interim financing, since you don't get paid until you go on the air. Once you go on the air, the money flows in. The risk is, if you have a bomb, if you have a loser, yes, you can lose a lot. They gave us $600,000 for each show—or $800,000, I forget which. Luckily, we were a smash, we paid everything back, and our credit was AAA with the Bank of America. Today, I'm sure, if we needed two million we'd get it.

The owners of the show finally included Andy Griffith (who owns more than half), Sheldon Leonard, Danny Thomas, and Richard Linke (through Griffith). Aaron Ruben owned only one year of the show, an important factor in his taking over the *Gomer Pyle* show, of which he owned a large share.

Despite Griffith's success with his first attempt at television, he was far from comfortable with the concept of his new role:

At that point I was supposed to be the sheriff, the justice of the peace, and the editor of the paper in this small town. I would put on a robe when I was to be the justice. I had a uniform when I was the sheriff, and I would put on one of those little green visors when I was editor of the paper. I always hated

that. I hated it from the beginning. I didn't have any knowledge
of script or how you do things in the beginning. I only had a
feeling and an instinct.

Griffith's background and style of acting were in conflict
with this role, for it emphasized comic lines and situations
at the expense of sustained, believable characterization.
He had begun his acting career playing Sir Walter Raleigh
in Paul Green's famous outdoor drama, *The Lost Colony*, in
Manteo, North Carolina. His recorded monologues, "What
It Was Was Football" and his down-home version of *Romeo
and Juliet*, had won him an appearance on *The Ed Sullivan
Show*. A short time later he was cast in the leading role of
Will Stockdale in the Broadway hit, *No Time for Sergeants*.
He also appeared in the motion picture and television ver-
sions of the play. From there he went on to star in two
excellent motion pictures, *A Face in the Crowd* and *Onionhead*. His last leading role before venturing into television
was in the Broadway musical, *Destry Rides Again*. Considering the quality of his previous acting engagements
and the demanding roles, such as that of the vicious, self-
seeking guitar player in *A Face in the Crowd*, directed by
Elia Kazan, it is little wonder that Griffith hated the farce
into which he had gotten himself.

Leonard explains still another side of Griffith's discom-
fort:

Andy had some early misgivings about the frantic atmosphere
in which television comedy was created in those days because it
wasn't written so much as rewritten since the writers for television comedy had not yet developed the finesse that they now
have. For the most part their background experience had been
in radio, the time of the spoken joke and the whole audio medium. Now we had to convert their comedy into something
which had visual components as well as jokes. So this—the need
for constant readjustment, change, revision—was foreign to
Andy's theatrical experience. When you have a play on Broadway, or a piece of material of that kind, you polish it and you do
it, but you don't change it. That year [1960] he was in an envi-

ronment of constant change, and he was not quite sure whether he could adapt to it, but naturally the adaptation was singularly successful and started a career that kept us together for some eleven years.

In any event, Griffith was an adventurous young man, and television was a new frontier that continued to hold a fascination for him, albeit a dangerous one, as he acknowledges. The next development was more to his liking. Having to sit out of *Destry* for ten days with a back problem, Griffith had time to think about the prospects of a new career. During this time Sheldon Leonard and two writers named Jackie Elinson and Charles Stewart visited Griffith at his home in Rye, New York, to discuss the series that General Foods had agreed to sponsor. Griffith recalls the meeting:

> Chuck, Sheldon, and Jackie came and talked to me about some stories, and we came up with four or five story lines. One of them turned out to be called "Manhunt." It was the story of a guy who escaped from a state prison or a road farm—and he escaped into our vicinity, and it was up to us to find him. (Chuck and Jack wrote that episode.) It was the second show we shot. In the beginning [the pilot] I was supposed to tell funny stories about people around the town and be very southern, very rural, and very mountain—rural was the vogue then.

The story lines for some of the early episodes of *The Andy Griffith Show*, beginning with "Manhunt," removed the gimmick of the three roles—sheriff, justice of the peace, and editor. Griffith would simply play Andy Taylor, sheriff of Mayberry. Of course, in the very first episode, entitled "The New Housekeeper," which opens with Andy performing the marriage of his former housekeeper (thereby introducing Aunt Bee as the new housekeeper), Andy is acting as justice of the peace, but only rarely did he revert to that role as the series progressed. The pilot sold the series, introduced the idea of a sheriff in a small town, and brought together Sheldon Leonard, Andy Griffith, Artie Stander, Jackie Elinson, and Charles Stewart. A master of organization, Sheldon Leonard then brought Aaron Ruben from New York to produce the series and employed Ronny Howard, Frances Bavier, and Don Knotts to act in it.

Having secured his stars, Leonard acquired Bob Sweeney as director and a group of talented writers for the first season, including Jack Elinson, Charles Stewart (who wrote the first three shows), Arthur Stander (who wrote the next two) and David Adler, Benedict Freedman and John Fenton Murray, Ben Gershman and Leo Solomon, and Jim Fritzell and Everett Greenbaum. Many of the writers worked in pairs and quickly learned to shape their plots and dialogue to suit the characters and the pace of life in Mayberry. The emphasis was always upon character over action or comic lines. The humor had to flow from the characters and not from jokes.

From the very beginning Leonard was careful to build the show around Griffith's character. He compares his role of producer to that of a decorator:

> When an interior decorator comes into your house to furnish it, he designs the decor to fit the surroundings. In this case, Andy's North Carolina background naturally conditioned the show we were developing for him. I could not very well have made him a New England Yankee or a tobacco-chewing westerner. I had to adapt the material to the qualities that were built into his personality on which we hoped to capitalize.

It sounds easy, but not many producers have the good judgment and perception of a Sheldon Leonard and they force an actor into an environment that is foreign to his talents and character. Such shows, of course, usually fail and give the actors poor exposure. One need only compare Don Knotts as Barney Fife with Don Knotts as a comic clown on *Three's Company* to see Leonard's point.

Linke noted that Leonard had a genius for management: "He is a great organizer—great in putting teams together." An essential part of the Griffith team was the writer. Leonard explains how he secured some of the best writers in the business:

You acquired writers then the same way you acquire writers for any show today, and the way you'll do it far into the distant future. You secure your writers by giving test assignments to writers you believe have an aptitude for the show. Sometimes you're right; sometimes you're wrong. When you're right, you give them further assignments, and you gradually build up a pool of writers upon whom you draw for the kind of material you need.

Keeping one's eyes and ears open to available talent is a necessity for a producer:

You see something on the air that you like; you think it's well written. You call up the producer of that show and you ask how much of it was the contribution of the writer, how much of it was the result of his own editing, and how much of it was the result of general reconstruction. If the answers are satisfactory, you set up an appointment, talk, see if the writer has any ideas that fit your show, then commission the development of one or more of them.

Nevertheless, there is much costly trial and error in the process of acquiring good scripts. Leonard continues:

Much of the time the material turns out to be unsuited to your show and, well, it's been an investment—a losing investment, but still an investment which pays off when a writer does come through for you and supplies you with material for the succeeding year.

Eventually even the good writers disappear, for, as Leonard observes, "The more successful writers become entrepreneurs on their own, or become producers or executives in other areas." A case in point is Aaron Ruben, who both produced and wrote for the *Griffith Show* for its first five years. His success led him from his position of writer to that of executive producer of several shows of his own.

Leonard and Griffith had quickly gathered together some of the most capable people in the business. They did not, of course, know at this time exactly how talented a crew they had assembled, and they would not know for several months, after filming many of the episodes for their first season, how the public was going to respond to their adventure. Now they were facing weeks of hard work and long, long hours to turn the "notion" into a reality.

CHAPTER 3

The Production

I The Routine

The crew of *The Andy Griffith Show* was remarkable for its ability to work together in harmony. Linke says that it was "the happiest, most contented cast and crew, I think, probably in the history of television." Griffith compares the company with that of *The Mary Tyler Moore Show*:

> We shared something—her show and ours. I think we shared something that was unique, because here was a group of people who could all work together with no ego problems; nobody cared who had the joke or who came up with it. It was the best time that I expect I will ever have.

Griffith was very animated when he was recalling these early days, and apparently was saddened by the loss of such a rich and harmonious enterprise. He went on:

> Out in our town [he carefully avoided saying Hollywood], you'll find it's a tough town, and people have to fight for identity. Often people will be working on a script or a scene or a sketch, four or five of them working on it, and somebody will say something funny, and someone else will say, "I said that ten minutes ago." We never had that. If somebody had said something funny ten minutes ago, it didn't matter. The only thing that did matter was: did it work in the script, did it work in the scene, was it funny, and did it play right, was it right for the character?

A typical week preparing a new episode of the show was a complicated but routine affair. In barest outline it went

as follows: on Thursday the entire company would read
two scripts—one to be shot the following week and one
which they had already examined the previous Thursday;
on Friday the company continued to scrutinize the latter
script and then rehearsed it on stage; on Monday, Tuesday,
and Wednesday it was filmed. The cycle began over again
on Thursday. Griffith explains the painstaking process in
detail:

Now, the evolution of a show would come this way: Aaron and
Sheldon and myself and three or four or five writers would all
sit down together for three, four, five days—several hours in the
morning, several hours in the afternoon. Sometimes a writer
would come and stay in the morning and not be there in the
afternoon; sometimes he would be there in the afternoon and
not in the morning. In other words, the only ones that were
there all the time were Sheldon, Aaron, and myself. And we
would sit there and toss story lines back and forth. Say, for instance, you were a writer and you came up with "Convicts at
Large," as it turned out to be called, about three women escap-
ees who capture Barney and Floyd. That would be a one-liner.
O.K. Now you would take that and write an outline. That outline would come in—Sheldon and Aaron and I would go over it
and make notes on it. The outline would go back to the writer,
and he would write the draft. After we'd reviewed it, our notes
would be given to the writer, and he'd write a second draft.
Then the writer was finished with it—finished with his obliga-
tion. Now sometimes I'd read the draft, sometimes Sheldon
would. Aaron always read it. Then if it needed some tightening,
Aaron would do that. On Thursday that script would be read
around the table by the entire company. When I say entire company, I don't mean guest actors, I mean our regular company:
Aunt Bee, Opie, myself, Don, the schoolteacher, whoever was in
the script. After we'd read it, we'd all get a chance to talk about
it—how we thought it could be improved. Sometimes that script
would not need a lot of changes. Sometimes it would need a
complete rewrite. Sometimes it wouldn't work at all. Sometimes
it worked wonderfully. After we finished with the first script, we
would move on to the script we had reviewed the week before.
Now we had all day to work on that script. Everybody in the
company got a shot at improving it. We'd go over it page by

page and line by line. And in the early days, we would work sometimes till eight or nine o'clock at night. Later, after we knew one another much better, the hours were shorter. Good full day, though. The next day would be Friday. We would come in and reread the script and go over it again and again. Then we would take it to the stage and rehearse it. Then Monday, Tuesday, and Wednesday we'd shoot it.

It should be noted that it was Andy Griffith who insisted upon these very detailed sessions of script analysis. Aaron Ruben, a perfectionist himself, recalls that Griffith would not leave the table until he was completely satisfied with the script. His involvement in the show was both deep and broad, and a large measure of its quality can be attributed to his good theatrical judgment and his insistence that the scripts reflect true human values. According to Don Knotts: "Andy was captain of the ship. He really was. He enjoyed not only being in it, he enjoyed being in charge of it. He was in on everything. We were all involved, but he was more involved in every capacity." Jack Dodson also remarked that "Andy ran the ship," always with a concern for the total performance and not just for himself: "His devotion was first to the pages and/or the characters, and secondly, to his performance. He would ask if the script was funny, not how funny he was or how many lines he got. His concern was always with how good the story was, and how believable it was."

II Stages One and Two

The Andy Griffith Show was filmed at the Desilu Studios. During the 1950s and 1960s almost all of the successful comedy was filmed there: *The Danny Thomas Show*, *The Dick Van Dyke Show*, *Hogan's Heroes*, *My Three Sons*, *I Spy*, *Gomer Pyle, U.S.M.C.*, and *Mayberry, R.F.D.*, to name a few. Griffith recalls the studio with nostalgia:

I was going to tell you a sad thing. Over on the corner of Cahuenga, near Melrose, there was a small studio. It's no longer a studio anymore. Part of it is indoor tennis courts and part of it is a huge warehouse for furniture that these big trucks haul to various points. I was over that way a year or two ago, and I just decided I would stop and see what was going on. So I went and looked onstage—stages one and two—that's where we spent eight years—and they were storing furniture there. This whole studio, I understand, was built during the war, with inferior equipment. They were constantly digging up pipes for leaks. The roofs leaked. Don and I used to do scenes when it rained, and it would often rain in between us. Anyway, there were nine stages on that little lot, and for ten or fifteen years almost all of the comedy that came out of this town came out of that little studio. About 1970 a lot of shows went off the air or were canceled. I had an aborted show that year [*Headmaster*] and we moved to Warner Brothers. *Mayberry* moved to Warner Brothers, too. But when we moved and so many shows were canceled, that little lot died, that little tiny lot died.

The sets for the early shows were few and simple: the courthouse (where most of the interiors were shot); the Taylor living room, kitchen, and porch; the barbershop; the mayor's office; and interiors for Gomer and Goober's filling station. Later a few new sets were constructed, such as Thelma Lou's and Helen Crump's living rooms, the county clerk's office, Howard Sprague's house and bachelor pad, and Emmett's fix-it shop. Unlike the flimsy sets of today's soap operas, the Griffith interiors, though simple, conveyed a sense of reality and substance.

The exteriors were almost all shot in a place called Forty Acres, in Culver City. On this lot was the exterior of the whole town of Mayberry, from Floyd's barbershop to the courthouse. The cast and crew would go out there once a week. Griffith recalls that "it was in very poor repair then, but now I understand it has been leveled. I haven't been out there in a long time. We used to hate to go there. Now I would love to go back one more time."

Almost all of the woods scenes had to be filmed in a special location in order to avoid the local flora of Southern California for a landscape that suggested North Carolina. The area they used can be seen from the top of Cold Water Canyon in Los Angeles. In the ravine below is a reservoir called Franklin Canyon. It was down there that Andy, Helen, Barney, and Thelma Lou had their picnics, that the escaped convict was trapped, and that Floyd and Barney were captured by three female convicts. The establishing shot at the introduction of the show was also filmed there, showing Andy and Opie walking along with fishing poles over their shoulders (while Earle Hagen, the musical director, whistled the jaunty theme song of the series). Griffith has fond memories of Franklin Canyon: "Almost my first day of work ever in California was shot there. We shot the exterior of the house where Will Stockdale was accosted by the draft men in *No Time for Sergeants*. They built a little cabin back in there, and we filmed there."

III One-Camera Comedy

The location scenes were a necessary component of the series. They provided a dimension of believability to the characters and the town. After all, who ever heard of a sheriff who never left his office? It naturally followed that the show had to be filmed the way motion pictures were— with one camera and without a live audience. Television comedy, however, was usually done before three cameras— as it is to this day, even when recorded on video tape.

The distinction between one- and three-camera shows is an important one and generates strong feelings in people such as Griffith and Jack Dodson, who brought a theatrical background to television. A three-camera show is usually filmed before a live audience in one continuous sequence, with occasional editing as it proceeds (for wardrobe changes or shifts in location). The use of three cameras permits movement from one set to another, different angles (close-ups, reaction shots, full shots, etc.), and, above all, an audience to follow the events and to laugh at the jokes. A one-camera show, on the other hand, must be filmed out of sequence. Location shots are all made at one time no matter where they fit into the sequence of the show. Likewise, if there are several sets used, all shots within each set are made separately from the rest of the filming. For instance, if Andy visits Floyd's barbershop on three separate occasions during one episode, all three visits are filmed at one time on the barbershop set (thereby eliminating the need to move the lights, cameras, and other equipment back and forth). And obviously, all exterior shots are filmed separately. The logical sequence of events is reestablished in the editing room. For this reason there can be no audience for the filming of a one-camera show.

Andy Griffith feels strongly that the three-camera operation usually destroys comedy of character. The attention is focused upon jokes, upon getting the audience in the theatre to laugh, and not upon character. Griffith explains:

Three-camera people on a half-hour show have more time to work on their script because they're rehearsing as you rehearse a play every day until the day you shoot. They shoot it as you do a play—two times, a dress rehearsal, and then air. And then if the dress rehearsal doesn't go well, they punch it up with more jokes. I hate that. Again, most of the stuff you see on the air today is three-camera. It's taped but it's three-camera. It's the same thing, except that they can edit as they go with the tape. With that you must have jokes every so often, every few minutes. *Mary Tyler Moore* was able to somehow do that *and* do beautiful character comedy. Most of those three-camera shows don't have character comedy at all. They have joke comedy, as evidenced by the show called *All's Fair*. Terrible show, because they didn't start from character. They started with jokes and there was nothing underneath. The audience is what creates the problem. You must entertain that little handful of people. So you have to have the jokes. When you shoot with one camera you have no audience, so you have character comedy. I prefer that.

Like Griffith, Jack Dodson has given considerable thought to this question:

I detest audience shows. They reduce everything to the lowest possible common denominator, which is all right if you're working in a presentational form like Jackie Gleason and Art Carney in *The Honeymooners* or the *Lucy Show* or even *All in the Family*.

They're broad—they're painted with a broad brush—very presentational. They're also very verbal. It's almost like radio on its feet. Almost nothing is ever done that's visual. Lucy used to do visual stuff. But today television comedy is like sheep—one has to follow the other. Somebody does something successfully; then it all has to be that way. So, *All in the Family* came along and then *Maude*—so that means all comedy to be good in the eyes of these people must be done before a live audience with multiple cameras. In addition, it's cheaper. It is cheap beyond description. They will not spend any money for sets or wardrobe. Do it as cheap as you can. And atmosphere is gone, subtlety is gone, humor is gone.

Dodson goes on to make a significant distinction between one-camera and multiple-camera shows:

In a film you have musical bridges, and I believe the only film comedy show on the air recently has been *M*A*S*H*. When I say film, I mean one-camera—they filmed *Happy Days* and they filmed *Mary Tyler Moore*, but they filmed them before an audience. *M*A*S*H* was made the way we made the *Griffith Show*—one camera, shot like a film, in other words. In a film you have a musical bridge between scenes, or if you're playing a sentimental scene you have a musical background. But in audience shows there's no music, and that means there must always be background laughter. To get that you must have a pattern—line, line, line, laugh—line, line, laugh—line, line, laugh—line, line, exit laugh; and it's the same in all shows with live audiences. Let me give you an example. On the *Griffith Show* a scene will open in a barbershop. George Lindsey and I are playing checkers, and somebody, let's say Emmett the fix-it man, is watching. You see the long shot of us sitting at the checkerboard and Emmett watching. Then you come into a close-up of the board and you see my hand reach out and I jump six of Goober's men and take them—and then you get a close-up of Goober—anger, disappointment, jealousy, bitterness—all across his face. Emmett laughs—the door opens, Andy comes in, and the action starts. You can't do a scene like that in these multiple-camera shows. In those shows the scene would be done like this: the three of us would be sitting there, and Emmett would say, "Oh, you guys are playing checkers again. You're always playing checkers." "Yea, I guess we are." Then I'd reach out and jump five of

Goober's men and Goober'd say, "You just jumped five of my men"—everything has to be explained and done with a sledgehammer.

Finally, Dodson argues that it is a mistake to build a comedy show upon the response of a live audience. He does not, in fact, think that the people watching the show being filmed or taped are a reliable index of the comedy. He explains:

The makers of multiple-camera comedy insist in believing that the people who come to a show are an audience, but they're not an audience in the sense of a theatre audience, where you sit in the theatre and you look at the stage and look at the actors and you listen to what is being said and you respond. These people come in and they're experiencing watching the *making* of the television show, which is different from being an audience. They're warmed up and they're told, "We need your laughter, folks." All these people are wonderfully cooperative—too much so—and every time you open your mouth, they'll either laugh uproariously, or you'll be late in starting due to some technical hang-up, everybody gets madder than hell, and they won't respond at all. So you either get over-response or under-response. At the same time they're watching—"Oh, look a camera is moving"—"Oh, she's shorter and fatter than I thought she was," or "He looks older than I thought he did"—"Oh, is that the way they do that?" Their attention is distracted. So you come to a sure-fire joke—a joke you know is really funny, or a moment you know is really good—the camera man is adjusting his camera, and the boom man is adjusting his equipment for the next shot—the people watch that, miss the punch line, and don't laugh. The writers go into a panic and rewrite it between the first tape and the second tape. We did that constantly [in *All's Fair*]. Drove me crazy. I'd say, "My God, I've been doing this for twenty years. I know it's funny. You guys wrote it. I'm doing it right, and it's funny." The audience didn't laugh for whatever damn reason, but they're not important. It's the guy sitting at home—it's what *he* sees. We never worried about whether anybody would laugh or not with the *Griffith Show*. We worked scenes out around the table. And since we had the combined expertise of all these people, if something was distasteful to one person he'd say so and the rest of us would either agree or disagree. There was a consensus of opinion over practically every moment of the script. And we did it with the assurance that it was as good as we could make it within the time we were allotted. Shows today are done in panic. They are rewritten every day. You go to work, you rehearse all day, five days a week, to the point of exhaustion. If you happen to have a page and a half scene and you've worked on it for five days, on the fifth day you go out and do it in front of the audience, and if they don't laugh, the whole damn thing is rewritten. And you have to learn it in twenty minutes and go out and do it again. Part of the success of the *Griffith Show* was the fact that the pressures of television weren't as great then as they are now.

Don Knotts, who has had much experience in both multiple and one-camera shows, offers an observation similar to Dodson's:

Today practically all the situation comedies are performed in front of live audiences. It's a good idea, except that now if the producer doesn't hear the belly laughs, he worries. In my opinion one should separate the audience in the studio from the audience at home. That always confuses me whenever I do a variety show. You have an audience here and one in the camera. You're trying to please both and you can't. You really can't. When you're doing theatre you play to the audience. When you're doing film or television you play to the camera—that's where it counts. I think doing a television show before a live audience diffuses the focus of an actor and even the people in charge because they're always listening for what gets a laugh and they're punching up the lines with jokes. On the *Griffith Show* we never used jokes. Well, sometimes we would but they were very well disguised. As Andy would say, "If it sounds like a joke, throw it out." That's what we did.

Sheldon Leonard, on the other hand, reacts to the use of cameras from the perspective of a producer who has to adjust the medium to many different performers. He says that one camera was perfect for Griffith, but "for other performers, like Dick Van Dyke and Danny Thomas, multiple cameras allow greater latitude for improvisation and a greater feeling of spontaneity, also a much more highly

developed rapport with the audience, which was there."
Recalling Griffith's theatrical and motion picture background, Leonard continues:

Andy's work was more precise and more carefully worked
out, and therefore he didn't place the same premium on spontaneity and on audience presence that the others did. Dick Van
Dyke, for example, had a background as an entertainer in
nightclubs, and obviously Danny's background as a nightclub
entertainer was extensive. Lucy and Desi were at home only in
the presence of an audience. The other shows that were done
with audiences and with multiple cameras were done to fit the
needs of the performers in the show. And Andy's needs were
best fitted by the single-camera show.

Aaron Ruben disagrees with Griffith, Knotts, and Dodson that the multiple-camera show distorts humor of character. He feels that *The Andy Griffith Show* obviously had to
be a one-camera operation *simply* because there had to be
so much shooting outdoors. Ruben's experience as producer of *The Phil Silvers* (Sergeant Bilko) *Show*, several variety shows starring Eddie Cantor, Milton Berle, and Sid
Caesar, *Sanford and Son*, and *C.P.O. Sharkey* leads him to
favor the three-camera format for comedy. His *Gomer Pyle,
U.S.M.C.*, again because of the need for much exterior
shooting, was filmed with one camera. In any event, he
argues that the three-camera show has "much more spontaneity and much more reality. You're moving all the time
in front of that audience: it's theatre. Whereas in a one-
camera show, if a take doesn't work, you do it again and
again, perhaps up to twelve or fifteen takes, until you get
that spontaneity."
    Despite his general distrust of multiple cameras for his
sort of comedy, Griffith speculates that his show might
have worked even with several cameras:

I think if our group of people had done the show with three
cameras, much of it would have been the same. I believe that,
because later, after Don had left our show, I did a special called
"Looking Back," and Dick Linke hired a couple of writers to

write and produce it. Well, my idea, I know, still was a good one. I don't want to blame the writers for it. It's just that somehow our chemistry didn't work. We got up a bunch of scenes, a bunch of sketches, from my memory of what impressed me when I was young. And Don and Ernie Ford were on that show. I was doing some sketches and was very nervous. Don called me aside—the panic was rampant in me then—and he said, "Andy, this stuff is not going to work. What we have to do is get with some planners." So, one night I called Aaron Ruben, and I said, "Aaron, I'm in a lot of deep trouble. I've got some stuff that's not working, and all I'm doing is spinning my wheels and I'm living in panic and I don't know what to do." He said, "I'll meet you at eight o'clock tonight." And I met Aaron that night and he and I wrote a sketch—based on Aaron's idea—about what it was like when he was young in Chicago, during the Depression. It dealt with two guys who had a double date and about 88¢ between them. I don't remember the jokes, but they were reading (remember Chinese restaurants used to put their menus in the window)—standing reading the menu trying to figure out what they were going to eat, how they were going to take out these two girls who, on top of it all, were cheerleaders. The next night Don and I and Jim Fritzell and Everett Greenbaum sat down and wrote another sketch about two guys sitting on their front porch listening to the radio—it tied everybody together. Ernie Ford was in a radio studio singing with a group of girls, and the scene dissolved through to these two guys, our own ages, in our forties at that time, sitting there, playing checkers, listening to the radio, talking about the wonders of this man's voice coming through the air all the way from Hollywood, California, into this box right here. We talked about many things, and then I said, "I'm told it won't be long before a picture will come through the air." Don's character, who was called Barney, got madder and madder at me about the impossibility of all this. The point I'm making is that he and I did those two sketches, and they were the same kind of sketches we had for the *Griffith Show*, written by the same guys, and they got laughs, big laughs. We shot with multiple cameras, but we didn't have an audience. We could write it any way we wanted to. We didn't have to have jokes because we didn't have an audience.

The fact remains, nevertheless, that one camera was settled upon for the *Griffith Show*, the major considerations

being Griffith's own character and background, the need
to establish an exterior rural atmosphere (the woods, lake,
and streets of Mayberry all contributed greatly to the atmosphere of the series), and the desire to emphasize character over mere situation and jokes.

IV Backstage Comedy

There was a great deal of affection among the crew and
cast of the *Griffith Show*. And for the most part, they
worked as a harmonious team. Griffith remarked that

> everybody in that company had knowledge and instinct, and we
> also had a deep respect for one another and a care for one an-
> other, as people and as actors. And we also had a great care for
> our characters. We were all very happy with our work and with
> the time we were there. What Mary Tyler Moore said about her
> company (namely, that it was like a family that enjoyed working
> together) was very true of our company.

The one person on the set who probably knew the most
about the goings and comings of everybody on the show
was the make-up man, Lee Greenway. Everyone had to sit
in his chair three mornings a week. He knew all the gossip and functioned as the peacemaker. Occasionally, when
Frances Bavier, who was a very sensitive woman, would get
her feelings hurt, she would call in to say she was not feeling well and would arrive late. Everyone knew this meant
she was angry or disturbed about something. Greenway
would soon have things patched up. He was unofficially
the make-up man in that sense. But most of the cast remember him for his practical jokes. The very fact that he
could play them so successfully attests to the healthy atmosphere of the crew. Jack Dodson recounts one of
Greenway's practical jokes:

> We were filming three days. First day, Monday, this actor came
> into make-up, which is the first thing you do in the morning,
> and Lee said, "Would you sit down right here, please, in the
> chair." The guy sat down, and Lee said, "Would you take your
> left shoe off please?" He said, "Yea," and took his left shoe off.

Lee put the makeup on the guy. He said, "Fine, you look real nice. Put your shoe back on. Thank you very much." Next morning the guy came in for the second day of work, sat down in the chair, and Lee said, "Forgot to take your shoe off." "Oh!" The fellow took his shoe off, and put it down, and Lee made him up and then said, "Now you can put your shoe back on" and thanked him. Wednesday morning the guy came in, sat down in the chair, took his shoe off, put it down, and Lee said, "No, no, this is Wednesday. We don't take our shoe off on Wednesday."

Even the minor frictions on the set had a humorous cast. One of Don Knotts' few complaints was that his job on the show physically wore him out, and he relates this bizarre story of how he acquired a chair on the set:

Andy had a definite feeling of protecting me in the show and he moved that over into real life. He would always speak up for others, but there was something in Andy's nature that kept him from treating himself like a star. It was almost as if he wanted to deny that fact, and so even the things that he was entitled to he wouldn't ask for. Well, in most company series or movies the principals have little canvas chairs with their names on them so that when they come out of a scene, they have some place to sit; otherwise the extras just sit in all of the chairs and the principals have to stand around. The camera man had a chair, because he brought his own in with his name on it, and of course the camera man is really the king of any set. Nobody ever argues with the camera man, not even the director. So nobody bothered him about it, and when he had a chance he sat down, slept too. We used to kid him [Sid Hickcox] about it because he would be sitting there sleeping during the lighting and he didn't want anybody to know he ever slept. He was an old man. Then someone would say, "Sid, what do you think?" and he'd say, "Shoot it," without even looking.

Anyway, my only complaint about the whole show was that I would get fatigued from the physical workouts. I would get irritable by the end of the day, even though I was having a hell of a good time. One time everybody was sitting down and I didn't have a place to sit, so I (Sid Hickcox wasn't around) started to climb into his chair, and Reggie [Reggie Smith, the propmaster] said, "Oops, that's Sid's chair." And something turned over in my head. "Hey, Reggie," I said, "Come here. I want a chair with my name on it." This subject had never come up before, and we were in our third year. I'm thinking, "I'm out of line here, because the star hasn't asked for this and I have." Reggie said almost the same thing that Ron [Jacobs] said: "We don't do that in this company." I said, "We're going to do it now." "You're serious, aren't you?" "Yea, I am deadly serious. I'd like to have a chair by tomorrow, with my name on it. That's where I'm going to sit from now on." And he couldn't quite believe that anybody in this company could have made that request. Unknown to me, Andy happened to be standing there listening, and it really delighted him. He said, "Reg, I want one, too," and Reggie said, "Well, I'll be damned—are you guys serious?" Then we both said, "Yeah, we want the chairs." The word got to Frances Bavier that we were getting our own chairs, and she said she wanted one, too. The next day we came onto the set, under two spotlights they had Andy's chair and my chair with our names on them. Then all principals got their chairs. Dick Linke had one, and he was only on the set about five minutes a day. I used to kid him about that. He'd come in and I would say, "I guess you're pretty tired when you get over here, Dick? You sit down a lot." He never sat in it, by the way.

Despite the control and polish in the completed filming, the actors frequently lacked that control during the early takes. Don Knotts, for example, could not watch Howard McNear work because he would begin to laugh uncontrollably. On one episode Barney had to look closely into Floyd's face, and here is Knotts' account of that moment:

I had sworn in Gomer and Floyd as deputies. Floyd was just standing there and he'd ask a question. I'd snap back, "Did you get permission to speak?" He'd reply, "No, Sir!" I'd walk over close and look at him—he would look at me as if with fear of this almighty deputy. Every time I looked at the man I cracked up. We must have shot that scene twenty times before I could do it without laughing. The more I laughed the more everybody else would, and then Andy would fall, and it was pandemonium for about two hours. We finally got a shot. Howard was a funny man.

Sometimes Knotts would have the same effect on Griffith:

Andy was my best audience when it came to comedy. I could just look at him in a certain way and he'd break up. Usually when he had to do a close-up, I'd look at him funny and he'd just go. Finally he'd say, "Stop it, you son of a bitch." We were always mean to each other in funny ways.

CHAPTER 4

Developing a Cast

I Andy and Barney

Don Knotts came into the show via a circuitous path with an interestingly varied background. He was born in Morgantown, West Virginia, where his father and relatives were farmers. He majored in speech at West Virginia University, hoping to become a teacher. Military service interrupted college and he spent more than two years in the army, a good part of it touring the South Pacific doing a comedy act in a service show. He later completed his college education and began to look for an acting job. He acquired a regular part on *Search for Tomorrow*, which gave him employment off and on for three years. He was cast as a catatonic fellow who could relate only to his sister. He was to be speechless in the presence of anyone else. This situation led to a humorous incident: "My part was easy, of course, but this guy who was on with me froze and I couldn't help him. He kept looking at me as if to ask, 'Are you going to help me here?' I couldn't, so finally right on camera, because the show was live, he turned around to his floor manager and yelled, 'What's the line?' The prompter didn't whisper it loud enough and he yelled back to him, 'What?' Then I said, 'Are we in rehearsal?' Finally the guy heard his line and the show continued."

It was Knotts' creation of the little nervous character, however, that made him a national comic favorite:

I had seen a guy actually speak at a banquet back in West Virginia who was very nervous, shaking, and spilling water all over himself. I thought it was a very funny scene because we have all been in that position, but it didn't occur to me at the time to make a character out of it. Then one night I dreamed about it, even dreamed about half the routine. I proceeded to write out the monologue and did it first in *The Gary Moore Show*.

He then went to audition for Steve Allen's *Tonight Show*:

I walked in and a friend of mine, Bill Dana, was in charge of the audition. I was surprised because Bill was strictly a writer, but apparently was also a sort of talent scout. He said, "What have you got that I haven't seen you do?" I did the monologue and he fell down laughing. "Do you want to go on tonight?" I said, "Sure," and it was either that night or the next that I first went on.

Knotts soon became one of the "Men on the Street" and stayed with the show as a regular for four years.

While doing the *Tonight Show* Knotts also got a part in the Broadway play *No Time for Sergeants*, where he first met Andy Griffith. Knotts stayed with the play a year longer than Griffith, and they temporarily were out of touch with each other. But then Steve Allen moved his show to the West coast, where it ran for another year. When it was canceled, Knotts began looking around for work: "I saw Andy's pilot on *The Danny Thomas Show* and noticed he didn't have a deputy. I learned Andy was on vacation in North Carolina, so I called him and said, 'It would be neat if you had a deputy.' He said, 'Yeah, that's a good idea. Why don't you talk to Sheldon Leonard?'" Knotts, out of work, walked into Leonard's office with some old scripts he had tucked under his arm to give the impression that he was bristling with offers. Leonard quizzed him on his concept of the role of deputy, auditioned him, and signed him on the show with a five-year contract. Little did Knotts know at the time that his role as Deputy Barney Fife would assure him super stardom, five Emmies, and a believability that, to this day, causes people to yell at him, "Hey, Barn!"

As Don Knotts developed the character of Barney Fife,

the acting style of Andy Griffith began to change. There was a period during the early years of the show when Griffith was still performing in the style of his recorded monologues, such as "What It Was Was Football." He spoke in a frantic, sometimes halting manner, grinned every few minutes, and, in general, played a heavy-handed rural clown. He gradually abandoned that overpowering comic role and became more serious and thoughtful, as noted by Aaron Ruben:

> He was being that marvelously funny character from *No Time for Sergeants*, Will Stockdale—not quite that broad because he was still sheriff, but in that direction. One day he said, "My God, I just realized that I'm the straight man. I'm playing straight to all these kooks around me." And he told me once, "You know, I find it hard to look at the first year's show on reruns." He didn't like himself—and he was right, and in the next season he changed, becoming this Lincolnesque character.

When Griffith first attempted the role of Andy Taylor, he had, as he said, "only a feeling and an instinct." The evolution of the character was one of the most significant factors in the popular and artistic success of the show. Griffith explains how the introduction of new characters helped to define his own role:

> Now in the ninth show we put in a barber, and the old gentleman was just scared to death—he couldn't remember his lines and he wasn't funny—so we reshot all of his scenes later with another man named Howard McNear, who played Floyd the barber. He was the second character we added. Over the years we added various other characters as we needed them, and our show became what it was—what it didn't start out to be, but became what it was.

As Andy's character developed, he took on the role of protector. Not only did he shield Barney Fife from harm, he inevitably solved the problems created by many of the other characters. Sheldon Leonard describes how this development affected the structure of the series:

People with a valuable function were those who created complications for Andy. Andy was different in this respect from the central characters of many other comedy shows. Lucy created her own complications by the nature of her temperament. In *All in the Family* Archie Bunker created his own complications by his attitude and his philosophy. In Andy's case, what we needed were characters who continually created problems for him because Andy himself was established as a man of solid, rocklike common sense, and could not, therefore, by definition, make problems and troubles—so we had to have people who did. Otherwise you got no comedy.

Barney Fife obviously caused Andy more problems than anyone else. Knotts did not model this character after any particular person, as he did with the nervous character. As he explains it,

the composition of the character unfolded from the interaction between myself, the writers, and Aaron. I guess the best way to put it is that I thought of Barney as a childlike man who was funny mainly because he was never able to hide anything in his face. If he was sad, he really looked sad. If he was angry, he acted angry. Children do that—pout, get overjoyed, or whatever. Barney never hid anything. He wasn't able to. In my mind that was really the key to Barney's character.

When told that Ruben felt there was a great deal of Don Knotts in Barney Fife, Knotts' eyes grew round and he exclaimed, "Gee, I hope not *too* much!"

The interaction between Andy and Barney is clearly the most memorable aspect of the show. Griffith comments on their relationship:

The relationship between Andy and Barney seems to be a simple one, easily understood and recognized. It is easy to watch. But it is not easily understood unless you examine it very closely. Garry Marshall, a very successful man with two of the top comedy shows on the air [*Laverne and Shirley* and *Happy Days*] approached me one day about writing a show for me. And as he talked to me, it became obvious that the other character he had in mind was Don. I said, "Why don't you see if he is interested, and if he is, I would be very interested." Well, he came up with a script, but he didn't understand our characters. The two guys [Andy and Barney] had the same faces but he missed their relationship altogether; he didn't understand it at all. They were throwing barbs at one another, yelling at one another, and making jokes. My character was making jokes at the expense of Don's character, and it didn't work at all. I turned the script down altogether. Don kept calling me. "We can fix it, we can fix it," he said. I said, "I know we can fix it, but why get in bed with somebody who doesn't understand?" That's where Aaron's genius comes in. Aaron understood. The characters were very fond of each other. Whenever there was any little joke between them, it was always based on that fondness—that was always in the background. And Andy was always very protective of Barney. He might laugh, have a lot of fun, and know Barney would get madder than hell, but you knew that in a little while it would be worked out. He was always by his side, just in case. Barney was often hit with things—he had to be hit with things—but Andy Taylor was always in the wings, always there.

Griffith believes that Aaron Ruben, who was producer, story consultant, and writer, was primarily responsible for acquiring or creating material that was perfectly suited to Barney's and Andy's characters:

Aaron knew these guys. And when he came up with something for them, it was just them. One time we did a show where we were at Barney's house looking through a box full of stuff from our old high school annuals. (Fritzell and Greenbaum wrote this.) And Barney came up with a rock, and he looked at it a long time in silence, and he said, "You know what this is?" And I said, "What?" "My dad's rock." And we both looked at this stupid rock—and then he explained that his dad used to strike matches on it when he was a little boy, and he would watch him.

The detailed accuracy and affection with which Griffith recalls such moments from the show attest to its human dimension. A spot of nostalgia, skillfully underplayed, brings the two characters together for a brief moment. The episode Griffith cites epitomizes the subtle affection that underlies the relationship between Barney and Andy.

As Griffith has noted, Aaron Ruben had a deep and sensitive knowledge of the relationship between Andy and Barney, and as producer and story consultant it was his job to develop and protect the believability of the characters. He explains his role on the show: "The guy who really knows the show, knows the characters, knows the philosophy and direction of it, and knows all the elements that make it work is the man who should be the producer." Griffith once said to Ruben, "You set the style for this show." One day a script was submitted to Ruben that had Barney faint after his gun went off. Ruben said, "I don't think he'd better faint because if he faints—paraphrasing an old maxim from George Burns which I never forgot— if he faints this week, next week he will have to faint funny, then the following week he will have to faint funnier, and soon the credibility of the character is gone."

Ruben felt that the relationship between Andy and Barney was a very subtle and challenging one to achieve and maintain. He explains the problem:

Here was Andy, who was the father figure in town—wise, very perceptive, and possessed of a marvelous instinct insofar as other human beings were concerned. He had a wonderful approach to knowing how to deal with an old-maid aunt, with a motherless child, and with the various kooks in the town. Here he was with this wonderful wisdom—how would he tolerate a guy like Barney Fife? It was always a borderline case, and we always had to make sure that Barney presented enough humanness—and not kookiness and not burlesque—to make him acceptable to Andy. The audience would have loved it if he had fainted, I'm sure. They would have loved it if he had done the nervous character that he had done on variety shows, but he'd be out the window for us and for Andy because the character would have lost its believability. What kind of a sheriff can it be who would accept a nut? So we had to keep Barney's character within the confines of reason. And I must say it is a credit to Don that he was able to achieve that. He was the only tilted character in a responsible position. A barber could be a nut, Andy's aunt could be kooky, anybody in town could be—Goober, Gomer—but not a guy who carries a gun and is a lawman. That took attending to.

Even in his other productions Ruben always insisted on meaningful relationships between characters:

People come to me and say, "I've got an idea for a series," and it's usually a gimmick idea. I ask what are the relationships? If it is a father-son show, how do they respond to each other? What do they mean to each other? That's what we have to explore from week to week so the show can continue for a number of years. And the ones with the best relationships are the ones that do continue.

Besides the *Griffith Show* one need only recall the first three years of *Sanford and Son* (which Ruben not only produced but made black, the original *Steptoe and Son* being white) to see a demonstration of his skill. A modest man, Ruben said, "I really think if I were to ask for any kind of credit, it would be that I saw to the relationships, that they were believable, human, and, of course, funny; and that they were good, strong relationships."

II Aunt Bee and Opie

The character of Aunt Bee, played by Frances Bavier, provided a stable domestic center for Andy and Opie. Like Griffith, Knotts, and Dodson, she had a strong theatrical background. Born in New York City, she attended Columbia University and the American Academy of Dramatic Arts. After graduating from the Academy in 1925, she was cast in the stage hit *The Poor Nut*, directed by Howard Lindsey. From there she joined a series of stock company plays and toured the Middle West. A succession of plays followed, including *On Borrowed Time*, *Kiss and Tell*, and *Point of No Return*. During the second world war she toured the European and Pacific areas with USO shows. Following the war she appeared in several Hollywood shows, such as *The Lady Says No* and *Rawhide*. *The Andy Griffith Show* provided her with her longest and most successful run—from 1960 to 1971. Unlike Griffith, she continued in the series when it became *Mayberry, R.F.D.* As the fussing and matronly Aunt Bee, Bavier's acting was always precise. Kindly, sympathetic, domestic, and somewhat naive, Aunt Bee was at her best when housekeeping for the Taylors or becoming "tiddly" after purchasing some tonic from an itinerant medicine man. Although she sometimes provided complications for Andy—as when she appeared to be dating the married butter-and-egg man, or when she went off on a visit, leaving Andy to maintain order in the house—she ostensibly served as a sort of mother-aunt-wife to Andy, one who looked after his home, son, and stomach. They cared for each other, respected each other, but there was not a strong emotional tie between them. Both characters, but especially Aunt Bee, kept a tight rein on their feelings in favor of domestic and social propriety.

Sheldon Leonard remembers Frances Bavier as "a rather remote lady. Highly professional and a fine comedienne, fine actress with very individual character. She was rather self-contained," he continued, "and was not part of the general high jinks that centered upon Andy on the set." Richard Linke says that she was "very touchy and moody due to her age, and you had to be very careful how you treated her and what you said around her. I think Andy offended her a few times, but they became very close friends." Jack Dodson's reaction to her is similar:

> I think Frances thought I was a gentleman. I'm not, really, not any more so than anybody else. Since I had fewer scenes to do with her, I had fewer opportunities to swear in front of her, which is why we never had any difficulties. Frances was temperamental and moody but she kept 99% of that to herself. Once in a while she would get mad at someone. She was the only person in the whole company whose feelings you had to be careful not to hurt.

The youngest member of the cast, of course, was Ronny Howard. Ronny was born in Duncan, Oklahoma. His father, Rance, was in the Air Force attached to Special Services as a director of entertainment programs. Ronny and his brother Clint (who appears in the *Griffith Show* as the silent Leon, always offering his half-eaten sandwich to Barney) were thus early exposed to show business. Before joining the *Griffith Show* Ronny appeared (at age two) in the play *The Seven-Year Itch*, and later on in such television programs as *The Red Skelton Show* and *Playhouse 90*. He was only six years old when he joined the Griffith series, where the whole nation could watch him grow into his teens. He quickly adapted to the rest of the company, and the other actors all enjoyed working with him. His father was always with Ronny on the set, helping him with his lines. Sheldon Leonard, who had worked with child actors before, took care to make the surroundings as comfortable for Ronny as possible:

We allowed him to bring his skates on the set. We saw that the refrigerator was stocked with ice cream and other things for him, so that it was a pleasant environment. I don't remember having trouble with any of my child actors, but of them all, probably Ronny Howard was the most adaptable to what we needed to do and the most promising in terms of a permanent acting career.

Don Knotts was very impressed with Ronny both as a person and as an actor:

Ron was always such a down-to-earth boy. He was not like most of the movie kids that I know, most of whom are precocious and have become insensitive. I think this is mainly due to their parents, who don't handle them right and who allow them to get everything out of perspective. But Ronny's father and mother (his father in particular) were right there to keep Ronny's perspective where it should be, so he never got out of line. When you meet Ron today you'll see about as nice a young man as there is on this planet.

Knotts thinks that Ron's acting ability was largely instinctive:

The director would say to him, "This is the scene where your father and you are having this little problem and I want you to think about that because it is very sad." And, God, they would turn the camera on and that boy would come out just perfect. I'd say, "Jesus, I've been doing this for twenty years now, and he just walks up and does it." That has to be instinct. What else would you call it?

III Supporting Characters

Even as Andy's and Barney's characters were developing and becoming more clearly defined and as Aunt Bee continued serving up good down-home dinners, the town of Mayberry began filling out around them. At first it was not located in any particular section of the country, but Griffith felt that not to be specific was to limit the show's believability. So he and the other members of the show began naming places. Griffith's home state of North Carolina served as the central focus. Real and slightly disguised names soon flourished: Mt. Pilot (after Pilot Mountain), Siler City, and Raleigh became the favorites. Raleigh represented the big city and Mt. Pilot a neighboring town. Mayberry, a fictional name, was slightly modeled after Mt. Airy, the birthplace of Andy Griffith. Soon a host of minor characters populated the town: Mayors Stoner and Pike, Floyd the barber, Clara Edwards (Aunt Bee's friend), a group of typical, small-town church women and gossips, a druggist, itinerant workers and swindlers, visiting state officials from Raleigh, old men sitting outside the courthouse, Otis the town drunk, Gomer and Goober, who work at Wally's service station, Helen Crump (Andy's girlfriend), Thelma Lou (Barney's girlfriend), a crude mountain family, and the town band. Most actors for these background characters were hired for particular episodes and then dropped. A few of them, however, became part of the permanent cast, and these included Howard McNear as Floyd, Hal Smith as Otis, Jim Nabors as Gomer, George Lindsey as Goober, Aneta Corsaut as Helen Crump, and Betty Lynn as Thelma Lou.

Howard McNear was brought into the show during its first year and stayed with it until his death in 1967. His portrayal of Floyd the barber was unquestionably one of the finest comic characterizations in television. McNear was born in Los Angeles and studied at the Oatman School of the Theater. After working with a San Diego stock company for several years and as a radio actor, he came to Hollywood to play the role of "Doc" in the radio version of *Gunsmoke* from 1952 to 1961. His first motion picture was *Fort Bravo*, followed by *Irma La Douce* and *The Fortune Cookie*. He was considered primarily a dramatic actor until his flair for comedy was demonstrated on *The George Gobel Show*. From there he went on to refine his comedy on *The Jack Benny Show* and *Private Secretary*. Griffith fills in other details of this amazing character actor's life:

Howard, first of all, was a leading man in the San Diego theatre years ago. He never was in New York in his life. He developed this comic character, I believe, on *The Jack Benny Show*. Howard was a nervous man and he became that man, Floyd. Then Howard had a stroke and was bad off for a long time. He was out of our show for about a year and three-quarters. We did a lot of soft shows, that is, those that were not hard on comedy—stories about the boy or the aunt. But we needed comedy scenes to break up things. We were working on a script one day, and Aaron said, "Boy, do I wish we had Howard." And one of us said, "Why don't we see if we can get him." So right then we called up Howard's house and we got his wife, Helen. "Oh," she said, "it would be a godsend." Well, we wrote him a little scene. He was paralyzed all down his left side and so we couldn't show him walking. We had him sitting or we built a stand that supported him. He could then stand behind the barber chair and use one hand. Most of the time, however, we had him sitting. His mind was not affected at all. He was with us about two years after that before he died. Finally poor Howard died. I'm sorry because there was never anyone like him. Kind, kind man.

Hal Smith, who played Otis, the town drunk, first showed up in the Mayberry jail for throwing a pie in his wife's face. But on the next show he was locked up for drunkenness, and for the rest of the series he continued to reappear as the town drunk. The jailhouse became his home away from home. He would lock himself up after a night of drinking and remain in jail until he recuperated. He also enjoyed Aunt Bee's home cooking during his stay. The character of Otis was made to interact with Barney more than with Andy. Andy assumed a sympathetic and protective attitude towards him, while Barney either berated him or applied "scientific" police methods or pseudo-psychological techniques upon Otis to rehabilitate him. Smith became so typecast—acted his role so well—that he later appeared twice on the police drama *Adam 12* as a drunk driver. Seeing him stumble out of his car on a Los Angeles street makes one wonder how Otis ever got that far away from Mayberry. Officers Reed and Malloy were hardly as sympathetic towards him as his former jailers.

The addition to the series of Jim Nabors as Gomer Pyle provided Mayberry another actual southerner. Born and raised in Alabama, Nabors joined the cast during the third year of the show in an episode featuring Barney investing his life savings in a used car. He remained in the show a little more than a year, playing the role of an addlebrained service station mechanic who inevitably disrupted the lives of Andy and Barney. His character was broad and presentational and consequently had to be used judiciously so as not to overwhelm the other characters. In the show's fourth year Aaron Ruben wrote, directed, and produced an episode entitled "Gomer Pyle, U.S.M.C." This was the pilot that shows Pyle joining the Marines and that introduces Sergeant Carter, played by the late Frank Sutton. The next year Ruben left the *Griffith Show* to produce *Gomer Pyle, U.S.M.C.*, of which he owned a large share.

George Lindsey, who replaced Gomer and played the role of Goober, had earlier auditioned for the role of Gomer and almost had it until Nabors arrived on the scene. Lindsey became a regular on the show during its fifth year, and after Knotts left at the end of that year he began to get a larger part in the scripts. Like Nabors, he played the role of a child in the body of a man. He wore a beanie, read comics, was frightened of women, and, in general, played a good-natured country boy. Unlike Gomer, however, Goober was more animated, and he seemed more naive than stupid. Lindsey also came from Alabama and attended Florence State College, where he divided his time between football and campus theatricals. After three years in the Air Force he taught American history at Hazel Green High School in Huntsville, where he was also head coach. He soon left teaching to attend the American Theater Wing at Hunter College in New York. After studying dramatics for two years he developed a comedy routine, which he introduced at the Duplex in Greenwich Village. He later appeared at the Number One Fifth Avenue and the Living Room. His first television appearance was on *The Jack Paar Show* in 1961. Joshua Logan directed his appearance in *All American* on the stage and *Ensign Pulver* in the movies. With a background as a stand-up comic, Lindsey brought to the *Griffith Show* a much broader and less subtle character than did Griffith, Knotts, and Bavier. Despite the stereotype of the dumb southerner conveyed by Goober's character, his boyish naiveté managed to make him fit more harmoniously into the town of Mayberry than did Gomer.

Some of the minor characters who made frequent appearances during the early years include Denver Pyle* and the Dillards as the Darling Family, Howard Morris as Ernest T. Bass, and Parley Baer as Mayor Stoner. Griffith, who frequently played the guitar on the show and who enjoys bluegrass music, arranged to have the Dillards on the show to provide an atmosphere of genuine country music. The Darling Family represented a weird set of mountain folk who occasionally descended upon peaceful

*Now of *The Dukes of Hazzard*.

Mayberry with their superstitions, jugs of moonshine, and bluegrass. Their essential function in the show was to provide a comic menace to the town, usually by attempting to force a marriage between one of their family and someone in the town. Ernest T. Bass, another mountain man, always shattered the tranquility of Mayberry, whether through demanding an "ejacation" or through raucously seeking out a woman to take back to the hills with him. Invariably the problems created by the Darlings and by Ernest T. were solved by Andy.

When I said to Sheldon Leonard that the boys in the Darling Family reminded me of the sodomists in *Deliverance* (they never spoke—only stared out of crude, expressionless faces) and that they were more threatening than funny, he replied:

> Well, we tried to make use of them as funny. But you lose perspective if you have been in on a show from the concept to the final delivery of the film. Taken out of context, I suppose those characters could be considered threatening—they did threaten—they held rifles up to Andy and others. But our feeling was that it was comedy menace rather than legitimate menace.

Ernest T. Bass also presented a menace with his rock-throwing and general riotous behavior. His single-minded needs—a woman or an education or a desire to join the Army—brooked no interference. Because his character was so primitive and strongly single-minded, he could not appear in too many episodes lest he completely dominate the show. Leonard refers to Ernest T. as "a mad kind of hillbilly character who was very funny but who had to be used very sparingly because of his exotic, eccentric nature. Like too much garlic, he could become a liability rather than an asset."

Mayberry had two mayors during its early development, Pike and Stoner. Mayor Pike, played by Dick Elliot, was a short, plump man with a nervous lisp who insisted on having things done his way to the detriment of the town and its citizens. In "Mayberry Goes Hollywood," for instance, he demanded that Mayberry's oldest tree be cut down because it was an eyesore that might keep a Hollywood producer from filming the town's main street. The mayor added injury to insult by having his tone-deaf daughter sing at the tree-cutting ceremony. Fortunately, Andy managed to save the tree and also to save the townspeople from having to hear a second chorus from the mayor's warbling daughter. Mayor Stoner, played by Parley Baer, was a much more intimidating figure than Pike, whom he replaced in the show's third season. Extremely nervous, compulsive, and bureaucratic, he laid down rigid orders that Andy had always to temper with humanity, common sense, and guile. When Mayor Stoner made his apoplectic refusal to allow the Mayberry band to attend the state band festival in Raleigh, Andy sneaked some professional musicians into the local band at rehearsal before the mayor and convinced him the group was good enough to attend. One would have thought that the dyspeptic mayor could have been a continuing source of comic trouble for Andy, but Sheldon Leonard felt otherwise:

They (Pike and Stoner) weren't enough to us to be put on a continuing contract basis, and so sometimes they were available and sometimes not. If they weren't available, we got somebody else. They had no valuable function on the show. People with a valuable function were those who created complications for Andy.

The characters of the mayors, however, did create problems for Andy, and their function did appear valuable. On the other hand, there are just so many actors a producer can put on a continuing contract, and in comparison with Hal Smith (Otis) or Jack Dodson (Howard Sprague), Parley Baer was dispensable. Artistically, the mayor is an important ingredient for the town of Mayberry (and in a motion picture he would be there, always), but in terms of a long-term television production, sometimes art must bend to economic realities.

IV The Trouble with Women

The role of women in Mayberry presented a problem from the beginning of the series. The writers made Andy Taylor a widower and Barney Fife and Howard Sprague bachelors so as to increase their flexibility in future episodes. Jack Dodson explains that "unless the series is going to be about marriage, it is a tremendous hindrance to the writer to have married characters because it deprives the writer of the freedom to create circumstances. A character needs to move from one environment to another, and he would not always be believable if he were married." Even more to the point is Dodson's observation that the best and worst marriages have a sameness to them, "a pattern and a sameness that is not conducive to a story line."

Various women were brought into the show during the early years in an attempt to give Andy Taylor a romantic dimension. As Sheldon Leonard explained it, "There had to be women in his life or else we'd have been suspected of homosexual inclinations. There had to be a feminine aspect in his social life. We had different girls on the show, and sometimes the chemistry worked and sometimes it didn't."

Actually none of the women used during the first three years worked successfully with Griffith, including Elinor Donahue (as Ellie, the druggist) and Sue Ane Langdon (as Mary, the county nurse). There were others brought in as well, but they lasted an even shorter time. Andy Griffith offers an interesting and honest analysis of the problem:

We never knew how to write for women. We never did know, and because of my peculiar nature, and my personal relationship with women, and the difficulty that I've always had with them—it became even more difficult for us to write for women. Elinor Donahue was a regular in the company before we ever started, and we were so lucky to get her, we thought. Well, she didn't work out at all. It wasn't her fault. It was our fault. And it starts with me. She asked to be relieved from duty after that first season. It became evident that we couldn't write for her, so we had her in just a few token shows. We had her, but not really. She asked to be relieved, and we were glad to oblige her because we didn't know what else to do. But we knew that there was a whole area in which we *needed* something. So we tried this one and that one and tried the other one, and finally realized that it wasn't any of their faults. It was our fault. We decided to hell with it. Then, we had a show once where Opie was talking about history and how he was having trouble with it, and I told him not to worry about it, that I never was worth a dime at it myself. So he thought he didn't need to bother, and he told his teacher what I'd said, and his teacher came over madder than hell. And her name was Helen Crump. (I remember we made a lot of fun at that name.) Well, we used her in that episode. Each time there was something to do with the school, we used her again. Then we started to develop a natural relationship between Andy and Helen so that they never did seem to have to court—which was a hump that we bypassed. They were close, they were in love with one another, they were friends, and it was a nice relationship. But in those days, in television, we had a tough time talking about anything unless we talked about what we were going to take on a picnic. That was always a problem; we couldn't talk about anything that we really might like to, as they can today.

Richard Linke elaborated on Griffith's inability to handle romantic parts:

Andy, you have to realize, is not really a lady's man. He doesn't know how to go chasing the ladies. If you'll notice, he rarely kissed anybody in the series, and only rarely did he hold Helen Crump. He never did a real kiss. He is that way in real life. Even in some scenes with Sherri North in *Winterkill* he didn't know how to do it—to hug and kiss on screen romantically.

Don Knotts was also very much aware of Griffith's difficulty in relating to women, though he did not think much about it at the time: "Each year Andy would say, 'I got to get another girl on this show.' I think he related to Aneta Corsaut (Helen Crump) the best. He's very shy with women."

In any event, Helen Crump solved the show's problem

with women. She was attractive, intelligent, warm-hearted, sensitive, and always very proper. Unlike Ellie, she was never aggressive and threatening to Andy Taylor's masculine superiority. And unlike Joanna Moore, she was not a sexual creature who needed to be dealt with in romantic terms. She was Andy's "girl," but she could have been his sister. There was some talk among the staff that perhaps Andy Taylor ought to get married to Helen, but each time the subject came up Knotts would remind Griffith of what happened to Mr. Peepers, and Griffith would stand fast against marriage. Knotts remarked:

I used to love Wally Cox as Mr. Peepers. I really just loved him. He was a nebbish schoolteacher, sort of helpless, whom Tony Randall kicked around. Then suddenly he got married, and the whole show changed. You didn't feel sorry for him anymore because he had a partner, someone to lean on.

The real "marriage," of course, on the *Griffith Show* was between Andy and Barney, who in many respects were the original odd couple.

CHAPTER 5

Changes In the Cast

I Barney Leaves

After five extraordinarily successful years of *The Andy Griffith Show*, two significant events took place: Aaron Ruben left the show to begin his new series, *Gomer Pyle, U.S.M.C.*, and Don Knotts left to make a motion picture with Universal, *The Ghost and Mr. Chicken*. When word leaked out that Knotts was leaving the show, Aaron Ruben received a call from *The New York Times* asking, "What's going to happen to the show now that you and Don Knotts are leaving?" Ruben's response was

I hope nothing happens to the show, because if anything does happen to it, then everything we've built for five years is going to mean nothing. If our leaving is going to harm the show, then all the time that we've taken to build up a town, a spirit, an atmosphere, a star, and a relationship is going to mean nothing. As Sheldon Leonard said, "the show is already on track" and could be taken over because after five years one knew the kind of stories that were needed.

Ruben went on to note, "It turned out that Knotts' leaving did not hurt the show. The ratings stayed right up there, because we had developed an atmosphere, a community, and a series of relationships that people wanted to see, whether Don was in it or not."

Sheldon Leonard seemed less concerned than Ruben with Knotts' decision to leave the show:

I have lots of people leave my shows at one time or another. A show has to be built on the premise that everybody is replaceable, nobody is indispensable, with the exception of the star. Look at the *Lucy Show*, how over the many, many years she had her husband disappear, her occupation change. That didn't make any difference.

The different emphasis in Ruben's and Leonard's remarks may be determined by the fact that Ruben was working exclusively with the *Griffith Show*, whereas Leonard was producing several shows at one time, including the popular *I Spy* and *The Dick Van Dyke Show*. While it is true that the series remained in the top ten, it is also true that one of the most delicately tuned relationships in television comedy was lost forever. Perhaps that can best be realized in viewing the reruns.

The reason that Knotts left the show has not been told before. His leaving actually came about through a misunderstanding, as Don explains:

Andy had originally signed to do the show for five years, and I had a five-year contract. He said, "I'm only going to do this for five years and then move on." Even in the beginning of the fifth year he was still saying that. So I started self-protecting immediately and began searching out what I was going to do next. I interviewed with all the networks. I was very hot with that show, so I could have had almost anything I wanted. Finally I wound up getting a very nice feature deal with Universal to make *The Ghost and Mr. Chicken*. Anyway, it came down to this: I hadn't actually signed with Universal yet but had made of lot of deals and had negotiated for a long time. Then all of a sudden Andy turned around and changed his mind. He came to me and said, "I've decided to stay on. What do you think? We've got a new deal to offer you. Do you want to stay?" But by then I had already really committed myself to Universal, where I had an opportunity to make features. Although I didn't have a production company, they gave me an office, my own writers, and a five-year contract. It was a nice deal, and by then I thought it was time for me to move on—so I did. I came back and did a few shows with Andy. I used to kid them when I came back. I'd say, "Are you still working with that little screen?" Then they'd yell, "Here comes the movie actor!"

Thus, Barney's departure from the show conjures up a memorable and prophetic line he spoke when, in one episode, he thought he would be fired as deputy for not passing the physical: "Into the dust bin of history: exit Barney Fife."

After five years Knotts had created for millions of fans a wonderfully believable and comic character that could never be replaced. Sheldon Leonard and Griffith began to give more comedy to Goober and Floyd in an attempt to fill the void. Still, they felt that Andy needed someone in particular to relate to as he had with Barney. So Griffith and Bob Ross (who replaced Ruben, having been his story consultant for a time) began looking for Barney's replacement. Griffith tells the sad story of hiring Jack Burns to play Warren, the deputy:

> We went to San Francisco and met this very funny stand-up comedian. We thought his performance was fine and decided to make him Floyd's nephew on the show. So we put him on—and we said we were not replacing Don—but we *were* replacing Don and we were giving him Don Knotts material—and it didn't work. I can't begin to explain how uncomfortable we were. I get strung out pretty easily, and if I'm uncomfortable I'm hell to be around, and I was *very* uncomfortable. Just before Christmas we decided we had to let him go and pay him off for the rest of the year. I didn't want the William Morris people to tell him then, but they told him before Christmas. I saw Jack some years later and he said he was bitter for a while, but he got over it. It wasn't Jack's fault, it was our fault.

Jack Burns was best as a stand-up comedian. His humor depended on jokes and very broad comedy. His frantic ineptitude as Deputy Warren was a parody of Knotts' carefully developed and subtle comedy of character. Ruben's fear that Knotts' leaving would hurt the show was being realized.

The 1965-66 season opened without Knotts with an episode entitled "Opie's Job," soon followed by "Aunt Bee, the Swinger." Producer Bob Ross was following Ruben's lead in opening the season with shows that featured those two characters. A study of the ratings had revealed that stories dealing with Aunt Bee and Opie were the most acceptable for the opening shows. But then, in the fifth episode of that year, came Warren instead of Barney in "The Bazaar." The story line sounded familiar—Andy's eager-beaver deputy jails Aunt Bee and her friends for gambling at their charity bazaar—but oh how different was the show! Barney could have pulled off that madcap adventure, but Warren, who had established no relationship with Aunt Bee, seemed like a foolish automaton in rigidly carrying out the letter of the law. He continued in a dozen more shows, and his role made not only Griffith but the whole audience very uncomfortable. After Burns left, Griffith recalls, "We just left that space open. Goober and the others hung around the courthouse and wanted to take over as deputy. We got a lot of mileage out of that vacancy." Once Griffith, Leonard, and Ross realized that Knotts was irreplaceable, the show went on successfully as always.

Nevertheless, the seventeenth show of the season, "The Return of Barney Fife," was an exceptional success. Barney comes back to Mayberry to attend his high school reunion and discovers that his old girlfriend, Thelma Lou, has gotten married. The next show, "The Legend of Barney Fife," also featured Barney, this time displaying his legendary courage to Deputy Warren. Over the years Knotts returned to make three more guest appearances: "A Visit to Barney Fife" (in which Andy makes a hero of Barney, who had been a failure in his job with the Raleigh police department), "Barney Comes to Mayberry" (in which Barney plays up to his old friends his importance as Detective Fife), and "Barney Hosts a Summit Meeting" (in which Barney arranges an East-West summit conference in the Taylor home). Knotts received five Emmies for best supporting actor, most of them for his performances in these later episodes. The last show in which he appeared, "Barney Hosts a Summit Meeting," on January 29, 1968, has been listed as one of twenty television comedy shows drawing the largest audience in the history of television.

II Howard Arrives

The most important new character that the series acquired after Knotts left was Jack Dodson, who played Howard Sprague, the county clerk. Dodson studied at Carnegie Tech from 1949 to 1953, joined the Army, and then got involved with José Quintero's playhouse in New York, the Circle in the Square. He worked very closely with Quintero for several years, acting in such plays as *Under Milkwood* and several of Thornton Wilder's one-act plays. Then in 1964 he and Jason Robards acted in Quintero's production of the American premiere of Eugene O'Neill's *Huey*. In the spring of 1965 they took the play to San Francisco and Los Angeles. After one of the sell-out performances in San Francisco, Andy Griffith went backstage and introduced himself to Dodson: "He came into the dressing room after the show and he raved about how wonderful he thought I was. He thought it was the best acting he'd seen in years. I didn't think much about it after that." Dodson returned to New York with no immediate prospects for work and thought, "If you're ever going to try to crack television and film, now's the time to do it, for I had very good reviews there." Dodson explains how through a series of comic twists he finally broke into television as a regular on the top-rated *Griffith Show*:

It was about October that I had an interview down at the old Desilu Cahuenga studio to meet the head of casting, a woman named Ruth Birch. (I wanted to concentrate on comedy because I knew I could make a mark more quickly in that field than any other.) It was like walking into a brick wall. She was not interested in talking to me. I was in the office with her a flat forty-five seconds and out the door. So I said to my agent—"Listen, Andy Griffith came backstage and was very complimentary about my performance in *Huey*. Maybe there's some pursuit there. I would like to crack that lot." I figured if I worked there, I could go from one show to the other. So, my agent went to Ruth Birch's assistant, Mike Fenton, and said, "Well, Andy was very complimentary about this man's work—very impressed with it. Maybe something will crop up that Andy will think right

for this guy and we'll have a crack at it." So Mike Fenton went to
Andy to get his reaction to this actor named Jack Dodson, and
Andy said, "I never heard of him. I don't know who in the hell
you're talking about." My agent explained this to me, and I said,
"All I know is that he came backstage and he raved. Rarely have
I ever come upon anybody that complimentary. If it had been
somebody just saying, 'Gee, I enjoyed your performance,' that
would be one thing, but the man raved on and on." My agent
said, "I'll ask again. He went back to Fenton, and Mike said he'd
ask Andy again. Andy said, "I don't know who the hell you're
talking about." Well, Mike got mad at my agent for believing the
"bullshit" that I was handing to him—and my agent got mad at
me. So in order to straighten this out I specified more details of
the meeting, what was said, and what night it was. Mike Fenton
brought it up again, and Andy said, "God damn it, I told you
before I never heard of the son of a bitch. Now don't mention
his name anymore." And that night Andy went to see—now understand, I hear all this much later—went to see a picture called
Darling, which had gotten rave reviews. And on the way home
he said to his wife, "That's just god-damned junk. I don't know
what the hell everyone likes that for, but I know that's the worst
picture I've seen and it was boring." He went on to say, "The
best acting I've seen in years was those two guys in that play. Oh,
damn, *that's* who that guy is!" So, he got hold of Mike Fenton
and they sent for me. Now I was embarrassed. My agent said,
"Andy Griffith wants to see you onstage tomorrow." I said,
"What the hell for?" He said, "He just wants to talk to you." So
I went down to the old Cahuenga lot where he was shooting,
and Andy said, "How-do-you-do, I'm so sorry, I just didn't remember." And so I said, "Oh, that's all right." I did not want to
meet the man. I had nothing to say to him. I saw the director,
Alan Rafkin, who was directing this segment, and Don, who was
back making a guest appearance. Meanwhile, I was getting
more and more embarrassed because I didn't have anything to
say to them and we'd run out of idle chit-chat. At that time a
tremendous thunder shower broke loose with lightning and
thunder, which never happens in Los Angeles. So we all ran out
on the stage, looked up, and the sky was boiling black like I've
never seen it before. I said, "Oh—I've got to go. I left all the
windows open in my car." I got out of there as quickly as I could.
I was terribly embarrassed by the whole experience. I don't like

to impose on people in that way. The next day they called my agent and asked if I would come back down to read a two-page scene for a part as an insurance salesman. Aunt Bee has lost a piece of jewelry and she calls the agent to make a claim on her insurance. The agent, of course, misunderstands, thinking they want to increase their insurance. Very funny scene, very short scene, but one that was particularly well-suited for me. It was an opportunity to do a little mugging, and it went very well. During the course of filming it, Andy mentioned a character that they had in mind—a guy who lived with his mother and who always had a cold or the sniffles—complained a lot and was like a county clerk and sort of a busybody. He asked me if I thought I could do a role like that. I never had, but I thought I could. It was a stage in my life when I thought I could play anything. I even did a western, where I played a heavy. I learned not to do that again. Several weeks later I got a call to come in and do this character. Howard Sprague was introduced in the spring of 1966. Then we did one segment where I was applying for membership in the lodge. After that they called to ask if I wanted to sign on to the series. I signed on, and the show ran another year before it became *Mayberry, R.F.D.* So actually it was five years of steady work.

The timing was fortuitous for Dodson. He did not know that at the time the character of Warren was not working out and that the Griffith crew had an urgent need to add this new character. Dodson found the role to be a challenge:

I had never played a character like that before, so it was a truly creative situation. I figured Howard Sprague to be about thirty-five. This was a private thought of mine. I had to remember myself at the age of about fourteen. I always figured that Howard, at the age of thirty-five, wasn't through puberty yet. He was going to get there but he hadn't quite made it yet. And that's how I played his relationship with women. I had to be careful not to make Howard a sissy. He was a character who always wanted to be one of the guys and always wanted to play basketball and baseball but just wasn't any damned good at it. His heart was in the right place.

Dodson attributes a large share of the creation of Howard Sprague to Andy Griffith:

Andy had a lot to do with the creation of the character. Part of Howard's character was shaped by his mother, who never allowed him to do anything—that's what Andy's childhood was like. His mother would say, "Oh, don't go swimming, Andy. What would happen if you drowned? You're my only son and I love you so much." Or, "Oh, don't play that game. You're liable to fall down and split your head open." There was a lot of that in Howard, and it came from Andy.

The character of Howard Sprague changed over the years from the initial concept. Dodson felt that "if the character had remained living with a mother that dominant, then the character in time would become more pathetic than amusing. So we eliminated the mother, although there would be occasional references to her." The episode entitled "The Wedding" is the one in which Howard acquires his freedom. In it Howard's mother remarries and moves away. Howard then remodels their home into a "swinging" bachelor pad. Although a necessary show, it is a painfully embarrassing one to watch. Dodson, who is himself a remarkably comfortable and genial host, managed to portray in that episode an awkwardness with his guests, Andy and Helen, that was *too* convincing to be funny.

A few of Dodson's own characteristics were worked into the scripts. He talks through his nose and has numerous allergies. Those traits were given to Howard. In one episode Howard tries his hand at fishing, and his ineptitude practically destroys the outing (though ironically he catches the legendary bass from Myers' Lake). Dodson recalls the first time he went fishing:

I went to Hatteras with Andy. We were on the beach and, by God, if you wanted to see Howard Sprague in action, you should have seen me out there in all sincerity trying to cast from the beach. I got all tangled in the damned line and at one point hooked myself by the seat of the pants. Had that been filmed, people would have said it's too ridiculous, too exaggerated.

Despite his allergies, his mother, his adolescence, and his physical ineptitude, the character of Howard Sprague survived for five years and helped to keep both *The Andy Griffith Show* and *Mayberry, R.F.D.* in the top ten.

During his association with the series Jack Dodson grew very fond of Howard McNear. He admired his comic style, liked him as a human being, and worked with him in dozens of episodes, including "Floyd's Barbershop," the 211th in the series and the last one in which McNear was to appear. Having survived his first stroke years earlier, he died quickly after the second one in 1967. Dodson recounts the details of his last encounter with this talented comic actor:

Unfortunately, I didn't know Howard before his stroke. Even after his stroke he was just a wonderful human being and a splendid actor. Sadly, it was during the playing of a scene with Howard that we realized he couldn't go on anymore. It was the segment where I wanted to raise the rent on the barbershop. The characters had a great falling out and then, at the end of the show, they were brought back together in the courthouse. Howard had a little difficulty with that segment. We had to change our shooting schedules a little so that his days were not quite so long as they had been. And then, finally, we had a very simple scene of reconciliation. He couldn't remember it. He went over and over it, frustrated with himself. Seeing his despair and anxiety was the most painful experience that I've ever had. Ever. And then he didn't come back after that.

Many members of the cast and crew of the show attended McNear's funeral. Richard Linke was among them:

We went to the funeral, and I have to say that it was the only funeral I've ever been to where the laughs exceeded the tears. There were a couple of people who knew him well. They spoke in the form of a eulogy—I guess you could call it that. Oh, but it was funny. They related Howard McNear stories from the pulpit. It was something else. Really, it made a nice thing. I think

Hal Smith, who played Otis, got up there. It was something else, those stories. And yet, it was all done with dignity. Oh, he was a nice man.

CHAPTER 6

Going Out
A Winner

Toward the end of the eight years of the series, as Andy Griffith planned his exit, Ken Berry was hired to play the gentleman farmer Sam Jones. He was introduced in the episode entitled "Sam for Town Council," in which his character is established to be that of a leading citizen of Mayberry, a role similar to that of Andy Taylor. The next two shows, "Opie and Mike" and "A Girl for Goober," reverted to tried and true story lines, this time involving Sam. Berry appeared again in the last show, entitled "Mayberry, R.F.D.," which was the pilot for the series of the same name, designed to replace *The Andy Griffith Show.*

Richard Linke recalls the week after shooting the final show:

After we shot our last episode we had a big, big party. The Nielsens came out and we were number one. Now how could we go out? At that point we could have gone on. Mike Dann was the head of programming at CBS then, and Dann and I were very close, and I was close to the sponsor. I could have said, "Mike, look, let's not fool around. We've got the number one show. I'll make you a deal for four years, noncancelable, at one million dollars a year for Andy." I could have done that. But Andy had gotten to the point where he was physically and mentally tired and felt he couldn't add any more to the character. Well, I looked at it from another point of view—who gives a damn, as long as it works and your public wants it?

After eight remarkable years that brought together some of the most talented producers, directors, and actors in the business, *The Andy Griffith Show* quietly expired. But because of the show's enormous success, the sponsor, General Foods, did not want to relinquish the series altogether. In those days powerful sponsors like Procter and Gamble and General Foods had control of certain time slots on television, a control now exercised exclusively by the networks. So the compromise was to continue the general character of the show with Ken Berry in Griffith's place. Sheldon Leonard at this time relinquished his executive function, while continuing, like Griffith, to share in the ownership of the property. *Mayberry, R.F.D.*, which essentially was Griffith's concept, continued to affirm the basic values of small-town life. It remained in the top ten rankings for its three-year run and, remarkably, was number seven when it was canceled by the network.

After Griffith left his show in 1968, he and his manager, Richard Linke, faced some hard times. After eight years of outstanding success, they experienced the pain of multiple failures. The tastes of the people were beginning to change, but more importantly, the power behind the network was beginning to shift in sinister ways for the Griffith people. James Aubrey, who was made president of CBS in 1959, got *The Andy Griffith Show* on the air in 1960, and it was his first great success. He followed it up with *The Beverly Hillbillies*, *Petticoat Junction*, *Mister Ed*, and *The Jim Nabors Variety Hour*. By 1971 the new network executives had lumped all these shows, including *Mayberry, R.F.D.*, together in their minds as "rural shows," and because they felt they were disgracing CBS with their mindless, down-home humor, they canceled them all with one devastating blow. Andy Griffith, meanwhile, had developed two new shows, *The New Andy Griffith Show* and *Headmaster*. They, together with *Mayberry, R.F.D.*, were among the victims of the "rural massacre" that came toward the end of the 1971 season. It was a strange, confused time. CBS must have spent two million dollars in promoting *The New Andy Griffith Show*, and *Mayberry, R.F.D.* was beating the competition in the ratings—and still the ax fell.

The new executives at CBS, such as Bob Wood and Fred

Silverman, were responsible for eliminating the so-called rural shows in favor of more "sophisticated" urban programs. *Mayberry*, for example, was replaced by *Arnie*, starring Herschel Bernardi, who played a plant foreman turned executive. The urban format was beginning. Griffith and Linke were especially bitter about the cancelation of *Mayberry*. Linke recalls the day of the massacre:

> '71 was a tough year for us. CBS canceled all three of our shows on the same day: *The New Andy Griffith Show, The Jim Nabors Variety Hour*, and *Mayberry, R.F.D.* Fred Silverman and Bob Wood issued this automatic blanket order: no more rural shows. Today they'd kiss our asses to have a show in seventh place. *Mayberry* was number seven. It broke our hearts. I thought that show would go five to eight years with Ken and establish him as a star. There's no permanence in this business, and the word "gratitude" doesn't exist in it either.

Griffith and Ruben resented the fact that *The Andy Griffith Show* and *Mayberry* were put under the same dismal umbrella as *Petticoat Junction, Green Acres*, and *The Beverly Hillbillies*. Griffith declares that "we were not a rural show in the sense of *Green Acres* or *Petticoat Junction*. None of those shows were true to their characters." Ruben felt that the critics and network people

> never saw through to the sophistication underlying the show. If the men aren't wearing Brooks Brothers clothes and the women aren't wearing the latest hairstyles and fashions and they're not discussing something terribly chic at cocktails, then it isn't sophisticated. Andy felt very strongly about that attitude, really resented it, and he's not a bitter person, as you know. Those other shows were fine for what they attempted, but ours was a different type of show entirely.

Sheldon Leonard, perhaps better than anyone, attests to the craftsmanship and artistry that sustained the *Griffith Show* for its eight years:

> I think *The Andy Griffith Show* maintained a higher level of quality than almost any other show I can think of. I think it

received less recognition for that level of quality than almost any show I can think of, because its rural nature tended to downgrade it when it came time for handing out awards of recognition. But an inspection of the show will prove to any discriminating operator in our area of entertainment that the story construction, the performance, the direction, the editing, and the scoring were of a quality that has seldom been equaled.

The Andy Griffith Show had an interesting impact on some of its people. The producers, directors, and writers, as has been previously noted, all went on to achieve great successes with other shows and remain powerful influences in the industry. Not all of the actors, however, who were seen and remembered by millions of viewers, were so fortunate. Andy Griffith had two shows collapse under him and has had to work hard at restoring his status. He has made a number of very successful films including a made-for-television movie entitled *Savages*, in which he played a sadistic motorcycling hunter who stalked a human prey. From that he went on to play such roles as an unscrupulous hack writer for westerns in the feature picture *Hearts of the West*, the Father in a brilliant television version of Pirandello's *Six Characters in Search of an Author*, the L.B.J. character in the popular television mini-series *Washington: Behind Closed Doors*, and the professor who researches the history of the town in the television drama *Centennial*. Despite all of these commanding roles, whenever Griffith appears on a talk show, the host inevitably questions him first about his role as Sheriff Andy Taylor.

Don Knotts, too, has suffered a little from his identification with the character he played on the *Griffith Show*. It is ironic that an actor should have to pay a price for having the genius to establish a believable character. His creation returns to haunt him. Knotts has gone on to make a great deal of money in a large variety of parts in feature films, but his having been Barney Fife for eight years has left its mark in the minds of audiences. Knotts commented on this identity problem:

I was careful to do a lot of guest appearances on variety shows during the hiatus periods because I didn't want to get stuck with the name Barney, although some people continue to call me that. I wanted to be sure that people knew *my* name. I wanted my own identification. The only trouble I had, and still do, was that people would say, "Let's get him to do that Barney Fife thing or that nervous guy." I like to do a wide variety of things. That's why I did this play *A Good Look at Boney Kern*, written for me by Jonathan Daley. I love Barney, but I don't want to keep doing him.

Knotts now watches the reruns occasionally and laughs at Barney Fife as if he were a complete stranger: "I've seen some of them over and over again, but I really watch them now like I'm an audience, watching them and cracking up. I'm saying, 'Wonder what they're doing,' or 'Look at that guy.' It's a strange reaction. I guess I don't feel like it's me at all when I see Barney."

His first motion picture, *The Ghost and Mr. Chicken*, of course, did exploit the character of Barney and the Man on the Street for Knotts' role as Luther. The script, after all, was written by two writers from the *Griffith Show*. In fact, the picture is very reminiscent of the episode entitled "The Haunted House," in which Barney and Gomer attempt to retrieve Opie's ball that landed in a spooky mansion. In any event, Knotts' subsequent family entertainment films moved him years away from the original character of Barney.

Jack Dodson discovered that his successful association with *Mayberry, R.F.D.* turned out, ironically, to hurt his professional career:

In order to justify the cancelation of our show, the executives said they were ashamed to have a program so lacking in merit, and along with that we were blacklisted. Every time my name was brought up for anything at CBS, they'd say, "No, we don't want him!" And some of those people working for CBS who got used to scratching my name off the job list moved over to ABC. It took me five years to get off the ground again. I still haven't really broken through all the barriers that were erected when they sent out the barrage of publicity about what garbage all those rural shows were and how ashamed they were for having relied upon them so heavily all those years. We weren't a rube hillbilly show at all.

Dodson's experiences after *Mayberry* have left him cynical:

I have respect for very damned few people in television, and I don't have much respect for myself for doing as much of it as I do. I try to be careful about what I do, but even still I take roles that I prefer not to play but have to for the money. I look back on my association with the *Griffith Show* with an enormous sense of pride.

The relationship that developed between Griffith and Knotts on the show is still very much alive in their personal friendship. In the backs of their minds there is always an urge to try to get back together professionally. For a long time Knotts thought they could work together again: "I think the reason we both felt that way was that those years were probably the best in our professional lives. Still, we have to feel lucky that we had them because they were really great years. Naturally, we felt that we'd love to keep doing shows together." Nevertheless, Griffith and Knotts cannot return to Mayberry, no matter how attractive the prospect. They have changed, and so has the time. When Garry Marshall offered Griffith and Knotts a chance to team up again, Richard Linke gave Griffith this perceptive and realistic analysis:

I thought about this a lot. I'd like another hit, too. But I'm against a team. Someday you'll work with Don in a picture or a special. "Don't forget," I said, "you're over fifty years old and Don is fifty. You can't recapture the past. You can't go on blind dates or chasing women and all that—that would seem really silly now. You had your eight precious years and did them well. It's like breaking up with a girl or a wife—you can date again but it's never going to be the same. It's never going to be the same, and you'd better realize it."

Opie and Aunt Bee make friends in "The New Housekeeper," the first
episode in the series.

Sheldon Leonard, Executive Producer of *The Andy Griffith Show*.

Top: Goober joins the Taylors at home to watch television.
Bottom: Howard Morris in "The Education of Ernest T. Bass."

Barney leads the search for Helen and Andy in "The Cave Rescue."

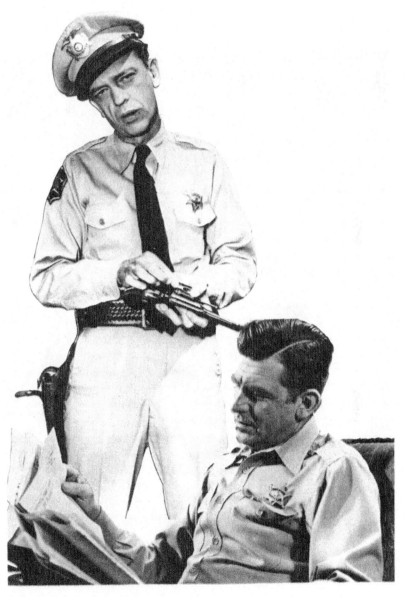

Left: Deputy Fife prepares for action with his single bullet.
Right: Sheriff Taylor relaxes with the *Mayberry Gazette*.

Opie raises orphaned birds in "Opie the Birdman."

Jack Dodson as Howard Sprague, 1967.

PART
2

(Preceding page)
Harvey Bullock and Andy on the set, January 1965.

CHAPTER 7

The Comedy of Nostalgia

A television series, like any creative enterprise, has a form or structure, a principle of organization to make it meaningful to the viewer. Most television series have a formula, or established pattern, that determines each of its episodes. Different types of shows, such as situation and domestic comedies, westerns, mysteries, and soap operas, have their own particular patterns. *The Andy Griffith Show* is an ingenious blend of two forms, that of the situation comedy and that of the domestic comedy, and in order to appreciate the structure and inventiveness of the *Griffith Show*, these two forms will be examined first.

The world of the situation comedy is usually limited to a one-room set, with the scene sometimes fading into another one-room set. Originally affected by budgetary considerations and the availability of studios in Southern California, the set for situation comedy almost always excludes the outer world of trees, houses, and streets. In the *Lucy Show*, for example, most of the action takes place in Lucy's apartment or the office where she works. There is little attempt to make these rooms appear realistic or lived in, since the emphasis in this type of show is always upon what happens to the principal characters. The set is simply an artificial backdrop or enclosure that keeps the focus clearly upon the characters and does not detract from or affect their actions.

Given a simple and interior setting, this form of comedy sets forth a series of events that creates something funny. A character, such as Lucy, is put into a humorous "situa-

tion," one that complicates her day and forces her to unen-
tangle herself from a web of circumstances. In getting out
of her situation, she generates a great deal of comic confusion. This pattern is clearly illustrated in one of the Griffith episodes. An order comes down from the state that
says all police officers must be five feet eight and weigh at
least 145 pounds. Barney is thus faced with losing his job
unless he grows an inch and gains ten pounds. This is the
"complication," for it puts Barney into a situation that
leads to a series of comic events as Andy and Aunt Bee try
to fatten him up and stretch him out so that he can pass
the physical. Although they succeed in stretching Barney
by an inch, they manage to add only eight pounds to him.
On the day of the physical, Andy discovers that the officers
are allowed to wear their police whistles for the weigh-in.
Nothing is said, however, about the chain that carries the
whistle, so Andy puts a two-pound chain around Barney's
neck and he passes the examination.

The formula here is simple: a complication generates a
series of comic events, and the complication is finally resolved. The resolution, as this episode illustrates, usually
does not evolve out of the comic events that preceded it,
but comes seemingly out of nowhere, in this case, out of
Andy's brainstorm to hang a chain around Barney's neck.
Although the comedy is the essence of the show, the resolution is an important convention. Despite its unbelievabil-
ity, it provides a definitive solution to the problem and
links the sitcom with dreams and fantasy literature, where
solutions are magical and satisfying and anxieties are dramatically relieved. Comedy is basically a very conservative
force, one that demands that things be returned to nor-
mality and order.

Finally, the stars of situation comedies are notable for
their childlike innocence and inability to cope with the
way things are. Such characters as Lucy and Laverne and
Shirley share these traits as they good-humoredly fumble
through life, doing their best, only to complicate things
for themselves and those around them. They are clearly

two-dimensional characters who resemble human beings in their comic antics, but they are lacking in depth and emotional range.

Whereas the situation comedy stresses comic dilemmas and events, the domestic comedy emphasizes setting. *Father Knows Best* and *My Three Sons* are classic examples of this form of comedy. The opening scenes of these shows focus upon the exteriors of upper-middle-class houses. These establishing shots convey a strong sense of place upon which all the episodes heavily depend. The interiors reinforce the sense of reality created by the opening scenes, for unlike the rooms in the sitcom, which are settings for things to happen in, the interiors of the domestic comedy reflect the lives and personalities of the characters. They are places that are lived in, rather than acted in. In *Father Knows Best* the mother scrubs the kitchen, her special domain, and the father, domestic lion that he is, commands the den.

In *The Mary Tyler Moore Show* there are special rooms for particular people, each exhibiting its unique personality. Ted's office walls are lined with photographs of himself, thereby reflecting his blinding narcissism. Mary's apartment, like Mary herself, is neat and tidy and a trifle formal. Rhoda's is more casual, tending towards the sloppy. The newsroom is a functional place where many characters interact and plots are hatched. Lou Grant's office, on the other hand, reflects his no-nonsense approach to life. No one enters his space without his permission, and when one is in there he or she is surrounded and dominated by his presence. In the domestic comedy one is always aware of what room he is in and acts accordingly.

*M*A*S*H* successfully carries on the tradition of the domestic comedy. Its opening shot, depicting a team of helicopters rushing the wounded towards the medical unit, emphasizes the importance of the Korean War setting. The interior scenes are also special. The operating room is the place of dedicated professionals. Appropriately, there is no laugh track used in these scenes, even though the characters sometimes crack jokes during the operations. The various tents mirror the personalities of their occupants. Radar O'Reilly, for example, has a teddy bear tucked under the covers of his bed. Colonel Potter's office, on the other hand, suggests more serious military business. Nevertheless, the Colonel, like Lou Grant, keeps a bottle of liquor in his desk drawer to help him handle emotional crises among his personnel.

In *The Mary Tyler Moore Show* and *M*A*S*H* character is more important than situation. Furthermore, the characters of those shows exhibit a respect and love for one another. There is either a literal family or a closely-knit group that strongly resembles a family. Lou Grant is like Mary's father, Mary is like Rhoda's sister, and Ted Baxter is like their sophomoric brother. Ted may be the most "disliked" member of the family, but he is also the most naive and vulnerable, and therefore the other characters go to great lengths to protect him from harm and embarrassment. In *M*A*S*H* Colonel Potter is the father figure, and Hawkeye and B. J. are like older boys who look after their kid brother, Radar.

The characters in a domestic comedy have well-rounded and carefully defined personalities. Any one of them can be featured in a given episode, whereas in the sitcom the star must always be the center of attention. This flexibility is clearly seen in *The Mary Tyler Moore Show*, where Lou, Ted, Rhoda, Phyllis, and Murray all have had episodes built around them. Similarly, in *M*A*S*H* there have been shows that focussed upon Radar, B. J., Corporal Klinger, Colonel Potter, and Margaret Houlihan. These characters do not depend upon jokes or rely upon slapstick for laughs. The humor flows from their unique personalities.

A notable example from *The Andy Griffith Show* of a supporting character being featured is "Floyd, the Gay Deceiver." This episode focuses upon Floyd Lawson, the barber, who has joined a lonely hearts correspondence club. Representing himself as a wealthy businessman, he had written to a lonely widow up north, who suddenly decides to visit Mayberry. The news throws Floyd into a panic, and his first instinct is to run away to Nashville. He later comes up with a plan to deceive her by pretending to be wealthy, and the following dialogue between him and Andy exhibits a fine portrait of this comic barber:

Floyd: I can't face her. You've got to help me.
Andy: How can I help you?
Floyd: Help me pose as the man I wrote I was. She's only going to be here a day.
Andy: Well, that would be lie on top of lie. Floyd, I can't . . .
Floyd: Then I'm going to Nashville.
Andy: You're not going anywhere. Quit flying all over the room and give me that haircut.
Floyd: Hah! haircut! I can't give you a haircut. I just haven't got it this morning, that's all! Give me a haircut, he says! [*Looks into mirror*]: Floyd Lawson, you're a miserable, deceitful wretch!

The next day Floyd visits Andy to say that he can't face the prospect of meeting the widow and that he is therefore going to leave town: "I'll get over it. What was that saying—let's see: *Tempus edax rerum.* Time heals everything. You know who said that? My Latin teacher in barber college. And so I'll go to Nashville, stay a few days. Maybe I'll come back, maybe I won't. Maybe I'll go into a monastery." Andy finally agrees to help Floyd, and it turns out that the widow is also a deceiver, out to get Floyd's money. In order to keep this spotlight on Howard McNear, Don Knotts was not in this episode and Andy Griffith assumed a minor, supporting role. Over the years many of the other characters in the series were also featured.

As television critic Horace Newcomb points out, "Peace, love, and laughter are the central virtues of the world of the domestic comedy. In the situation comedy there is much laughter, there is a form of love, and there is very little peace of the sort indicated here. The domestic comedy is filled with such peace. It grows out of the love, and in the context of these two we discover a gentler form of laughter."* Behind these virtues is the family's or group's sense of shared values articulated by and embodied in the father. Colonel Potter and Lou Grant have solid, good sense and possess a clear moral code of an earlier time that usually guides them in solving their families' problems.

The Andy Griffith Show combines the best of both worlds, the sitcom and the domestic comedy, with the emphasis upon the latter. Many of its episodes have a story line conducive to the humor of a situation comedy: Barney buys a used car from a crooked old lady; Barney rescues Andy and Helen from a cave; Barney investigates noises in the town's haunted house. The comic line is straightforward and the humor is often physical as well as verbal. The situation is central to the episode, and the sets merely complement the action. These episodes, viewed in isolation from the rest of the series, would correctly be labeled situation comedies, sharing the basic pattern of such programs as *The Lucy Show* or *Laverne and Shirley*. Such a view, however, ignores the essential feature of the *Griffith Show*, namely, that it is a series that consistently focuses upon the establishment and development of character, not situation. The situation merely provides a framework in which Andy, Barney, and the others work out their characters and relationships to each other.

One of the major differences between this show and earlier sitcoms is the dependence of the star upon other characters, one in particular. It is a difference that at first created a problem. In the pilot film on *The Danny Thomas Show*, there was no deputy and no firm, believable relationship between Andy and another character. Essentially, Andy had to work alone, responding to Danny Thomas' outrage in being given a speeding ticket and dealing with the various problems brought before him by the people of the town. The show was farcical, a true sitcom, with Griffith playing the funny man with a cracker-barrel wit. It

TV, The Most Popular Art (New York: Anchor Books, 1974), p. 55.

focused upon jokes more than it did upon character, and consequently fitted neatly into the format of the series of *The Danny Thomas Show*.

But in the opening episode of *The Andy Griffith Show*, Don Knotts was added, and a new chemistry began slowly to develop, one that would turn the series into something very different from the traditional sitcom that gave it birth. At first Andy and Don did not know how to play to each other, and the writers and producers did not know how to deal with the two characters. And so, they were presented as two funny fellows who got involved in ridiculous situations that always managed to get worked out. As the star, Andy usually had to resolve the problems himself, even while he continued to grin and laugh at Barney. He eventually became a new kind of straight man, very different from the familiar Bud Abbott type. Abbott was a very wooden figure, with no depth to his character. He would scold, nag, and harrass his absurd partner, but he was an empty person. Andy brought a warmth and human dimension to his role: he had a young boy whom he dearly loved, an aunt whom he respected, a girlfriend whom he enjoyed. He showed concern for others, expressed joy and sadness, and was, in short, a totally believable human being. Such creatures did not exist in sitcoms. Along with Griffith, the writers and producers began to realize that they had created a comedy of true character, that the audience welcomed it, and that Don Knotts was the main comic force.

Now the character of Barney Fife had to change. He remained childlike, naive, and wonderfully inept, but he became more human; he had genuine feelings that had to be protected. His uncontrolled enthusiasm, his bravado and vanity frequently made him ridiculous, but his essential good nature and self-respect prevailed. He exhibited a wide range of feelings—from a poignant sense of his own inadequacy to genuine courage—that marked him, like Andy, as something new in television comedy.

Given believable characters, care had to be taken that

the sets reflected their personalities. The main setting for the *Griffith Show* was the courthouse, ruled by Sheriff Andy Taylor and his deputy. It is the one place in town to which every character, at one time or another, is drawn. Aunt Bee delivers Andy and Barney their lunch. Otis sleeps off his previous night's drinking in one of the two "maximum security" cells. Opie visits his father there after school. And so on. It is a very homely place. The back room contains a bed where Barney frequently naps, a mirror (in which he transforms himself into Rock Hudson and Frank Sinatra), and a coffee-maker. The cells are decorated much like the rooms of a boarding house, and the prisoners are treated to home-cooked meals, courtesy of Aunt Bee.

The set for Andy's house is also very comfortable and reflects Aunt Bee's careful housekeeping. More often than not, the Taylors' kitchen is the primary set, for here the family is brought together by the fine cooking of Aunt Bee. Frequently, too, we watch Andy, Opie, Helen Crump, or Barney enjoy Aunt Bee's scrumptious meals at the dinner table. Food is very important in this household. It reminds us that the characters have bodies and appetites to satisfy, and the daily ritual of eating brings them together in a pleasant and natural way.

Another important set is Floyd's barbershop. Here is the center of Mayberry's male population, where gossip and small talk abound and where the various characters express their anxieties, anger, and concern. The barbershop is the forum for many communal projects: here the townspeople hatch their campaign plans to re-elect Andy sheriff; the local anglers discuss the strategies to be employed at the annual fishing contest at Myers' Lake; and, in general, when Andy or Barney wants to know what's going on, he visits Floyd, who embodies the gossip of the entire town.

The backdrop for all these sets, of course, is Mayberry, North Carolina. The establishing shot in the *Griffith Show*, that of Andy and Opie walking with their fishing poles down a country road to the lake, roots the program in a real rural atmosphere. The many location scenes—the exterior of the town, the Taylors' front porch, Rafe Hollister's farm—are reminders of the geography of a series in which the sense of place is of considerable importance. Human characters require a believable setting. Furthermore, the rural background fosters a sense of peace and closeness to nature. The people here not only get along well with each other but they also work in harmony with the natural world. Andy, for example, allows a fellow townsman being held prisoner to return to his farm during the day so that he can harvest his crop.

Life in Mayberry mirrors the best qualities of any small town. Despite the constant reminders that the setting is North Carolina, Mayberry is really Small Town USA. Andy and Gomer are the only two characters who have a pronounced southern accent. The speech of the other characters does not suggest any particular region. In a few of the early shows Knotts attempted to give his speech a southern flavor by occasionally saying "right cheer" for "right here," but he soon dropped that because it sounded fake. Andy, too, abandoned his exaggerated southern accent for his natural speech pattern by the end of the second year of the series. Mayberry thus became a paradoxical town: localized in North Carolina and universal at the same time.

More important than the sets and the situation are the characters themselves. They are comprised of a well-defined number of individuals, many of them stereotypes, who interact as a family. There is not only the actual family of Andy, Aunt Bee, and Opie, but the "family" of the town itself. Andy is the central authority in Mayberry and acts as a father figure. The childlike antics of the town's comic innocents—Gomer, Goober, and Floyd—are carefully monitored by his watchful eye. He keeps the town (and the show) within the boundaries of reason, checking the raucous behavior of such characters as Ernest T. Bass and the two zany girls from Mt. Pilot, Skippy and Daphne.

Peace, love, and laughter abound in Mayberry. The humor flows naturally from the characters of the townspeople. Floyd's comedy, for example, does not depend upon a contrived situation or another character's jokes about him. He is funny because he sees things in an eccentric way and because he delivers his staccato lines with a mastery of timing. He also looks funny, always startled by the ordinary events going on around him. His opinions and feelings seem to change from moment to moment as he accommodates himself to the most outrageous conditions. In the episode in which he and Barney are captured by three female escaped convicts, we find Floyd making himself at home in the midst of a dangerous situation. As one of the convicts forces Barney to dance with her, Floyd watches them admiringly as he peels and eats a banana while tapping his foot to keep time with the music. Like a child, he is caught up in the music, in the moment, and loses sight of the entire situation. Later, when he and one of the convicts return from a trip to town to get some food, they enter the abandoned cabin where Barney is being held by the other two women, and Floyd, coming through the door announces, "We're home!" Those two brilliantly chosen words carry the comic essence of this lovable barber.

Although the plot of each episode of the *Griffith Show* is carefully constructed, it does not manipulate the characters in an obvious manner, as in a typical sitcom. In the show entitled "Dogs, Dogs, Dogs," for instance, Barney's character is expressed through this straightforward plot: Opie picks up a stray dog that he brings to the courthouse. More dogs keep ariving until the place is overrun by them. Meanwhile Barney and Andy are expecting the state inspector and desperately try to get rid of the dogs before he arrives. After several futile attempts at dispersing the animals, Barney takes them in the squad car and leaves them out in the country. A storm comes up, Opie worries about the safety of the dogs, and warm-hearted Barney retrieves them. The inspector arrives, and Andy and Barney see their hopes of acquiring new supplies for the courthouse expire. It turns out, however, that the inspector loves dogs, and he congratulates Barney and Andy for their fine collection of them and grants all of their requests for supplies. A simple and pleasant story, but the real strength of the episode resides not in the plot but in what the plot brings out in Barney's character.

The following scene from this episode illustrates the importance of character over plot.

Opie: I'm worried about them.

Barney: Opie, you don't have to worry about them. What can happen?

Opie: Well, that lightning. What about that?

Barney: A dog can't get struck by lightning. You know why? Cause he's too close to the ground. See, lightning strikes tall things. Now if they were giraffes out there in that field, now then we'd be in trouble. But you sure don't have to worry about dogs.

(*Crash of thunder*)

Opie: I'm worried about them, Pa.

Andy: Well.

Barney: Ah, look Opie. What were dogs a million years ago? Wild animals, right? Wolves, coyotes—they know how to hunt and fish and look for shelter. Take them two big airedales. Why, they looked healthy as horses to me. And the little spotted one? He was in fine shape.

Opie: But the little one I first came in with, he was a trembler, wasn't he?

Barney: Him? Well, the big ones will look after him. See, they take care of their own.

(*Another crash of thunder*)

Barney (*less convincing*): And you know dogs have a way of keeping dry. You know that. They're insulated, you see. They've got this fur and that keeps them cool in the summer and warm and dry in the winter. They're really set up a lot better than human beings as far as that goes.

(*Another crash of thunder*)

Barney: As far as the little one goes, the bigs ones, they'll take care of him. The little, trembly one . . . (*crash of thunder*). And they're short, you see, close to the ground, and that way they can't get struck by lightning. Now if they were giraffes, they'd

have been hit by now. But dogs are short. They take care of
their own. Giraffes don't. No, giraffes don't at all. (*A meditative
pause.*) Boy, giraffes are selfish, just running around, looking
after number one, getting hit by lightning. But dogs (*thunder*).
(*To Andy*) Are you just going to sit there, or are you coming
with me . . . ?
Andy: What?
Barney: To get those dogs!

This is a clever piece of dramatic writing that explores
Barney's character as he attempts to console Opie. Under
the influences of the crashing thunder and the boy's pathetic face, however, his tone becomes less assured, until
finally he abandons his entire magnificent rationalization
and goes after the dogs. One of the finest touches in Barney's speech comes after he has constructed the elaborate
comparison between dogs and giraffes. He gets so caught
up in his own analogy that he becomes disgusted with giraffes. In his crazy analogy *he* made them selfish, and now,
as their creator, he bemoans their behavior. Besides, he
almost makes it sound as if they enjoyed running around
and getting hit by lightning.

In terms of the plot, it is necessary to get all of the dogs
back to the courthouse, but before that action is set in motion, the audience is treated to a full draught of Barney's
comic, human character. His bravado, twisted science, self-
doubt, concern for Opie, and good will are all exhibited in
a satisfying, comic self-portrait. The long speech about the
giraffes does not expedite the action but enhances and reveals the character and mind of Barney Fife.

According to Maurice Charney, "Repetition may be the
single most important mechanism in comedy. . . . The
world of comedy is simple, perhaps even simplified, and
complex motivation and subtle psychology are reduced to
a working model that everyone can understand. Difficulties are smoothed over, or at least redefined into practical
formulas that may not apply to real life, but are admirably
suited to the oppositions and balances of comedy."* Over

*Comedy High and Low (New York: Oxford University Press, 1978), p. 82.

the years various visual and verbal comic formulas were developed that functioned as running "jokes" in the *Griffith Show*. Whenever Barney entered the jail cell, for instance, one could feel sure that he would inadvertently pull the door behind him and lock himself in. It was a very funny scene, one that worked time and again. Another recurrent action was Barney's demonstration of gun safety or his dexterity in handling his pistol, an exhibition that always climaxed in his accidentally discharging his revolver as he returned it to its holster. Those occurrences led to still another running joke, namely, Andy's restriction that Barney carry only one bullet, in his shirt pocket. Whenever a crisis arose, Barney would anxiously fumble for that bullet to load his gun.

Sometimes, the repetition on the *Griffith Show* was verbal, a tag line or a catch phrase that kept cropping up regardless of the context. A well-known example has already been quoted, in which Barney plans his evening: "Know what I'm gonna do? Go home, take a nap, go over to Thelma Lou's," etc. In a subsequent episode a nervous businessman, forced to linger in Mayberry because of car trouble, listens to Barney go through that line several times until he grows so impatient he screams out: "Well, *go* home, *take* a nap, *go* to Thelma Lou's!"

"Nip it" became another popular phrase as Barney pontificated once upon the necessity of "nipping in the bud" the rowdy behavior of Mayberry's children before they became hardened criminals. The following exchange between Andy and Barney from "One-Punch Opie" is a classic:

Barney: I don't like it. I don't like it one bit. I tell you, this is just the beginning. Going around breaking street lamps! City property, mind you. Next thing you know they'll be on motorcycles and wearing them leather jackets and zooming around. They'll take over the whole town! A reign of terror!

Andy: Barney, these are just boys you're talking about. They're only about eight years old.

Barney: Yeah, well today's eight-year-olds are tomorrow's teenagers. I say this calls for action and now! Nip it in the bud!

First sign of youngsters going wrong, you've got to nip it in the bud.

Andy: I'm going to have a talk with them. What else do you want me to do?

Barney: Well, just don't mollycoddle them.

Andy: I won't.

Barney: Nip it! You go read any book you want on the subject of child discipline and you'll find every one of them is in favor of bud nipping.

Andy: I'll take care of it.

Barney: There's only one way to take care of it.

Andy: Nip it . . .

Barney: In the bud!

Barney's impetuous nature is behind much of this repetition, as in the episode where he demands the speeding laws be more strictly enforced: "If you let them take thirty, they'll take thirty-five. If you let them take thirty-five, they'll take forty. If you let them take forty, they'll take forty-five. . . ." Andy finally interrupts him, lest he go on forever. Later in the show, however, Barney gets to repeat his lecture.

By featuring certain stereotyped characters, the show provided repetition of another sort. Otis, the town drunk, stumbles into the courthouse and locks himself in one of the cells to sleep off his stupor, an action that is repeated countless times over the years the show ran. Ernest T. Bass, the mountain man, hurls rocks through the town's windows practically every time he arrives on the scene. The recurrent humor of these two characters depends largely upon their mechanical predictability.

It is precisely because the characters of Otis and Ernest T. seemed so fixed and their habits so intractable that Andy and Barney sought to reform them, and these attempts led to new comedy. "My Fair Ernest T. Bass" is a classic episode, in which G. B. Shaw's story is updated for Mayberry. Andy and Barney attempt to civilize Ernest T. in order to pass him off as a gentleman at a swank party being held by the pompous Mrs. Wiley. The education proves about as difficult as it would be to put britches on a wild boar. Ernest T. nevertheless is fitted out in store-bought clothes and manages to remember a civilized sentence, "How do you do, Mrs. Wiley," which he mechanically grinds out at all the wrong times. But his true nature reasserts itself by the end of the episode when he cracks a vase over the head of a man dancing with his sweetheart, thereby reducing the elegant party to a riot and asserting the basic principle of Mayberry that what is natural and good must not change.

The comic conventions of the *Griffith Show* impose reassuring patterns of order and stability upon the series. Contained within this ordered structure is the dream world that gives the program its essential imaginative life. Supporting and strengthening the characterization, plots, settings, and comic formulae is our remembrance of childhood. The fundamental appeal of the show is that it produces out of the confusing world we have to live in a vision of a simple world we would like to live in, namely, Mayberry. In our middle-class, technological society, we may understandably feel separated and cut off from the people and places around us, but our memories of childhood seem to testify that we were once really a part of the world, a world that was small, understandable, and secure. We knew where we fitted into it and we knew who we were. Our self-assurance was bolstered by our sense that everyone around us had clearly defined roles and worked together in purposeful harmony.

Everyone's sense of identity on the *Griffith Show* is crystal clear: Andy Taylor is the sheriff, and he maintains law and order; Aunt Bee's job is to feed and look after Andy and Opie. Their personalities and distinct roles merge smoothly together. They like who they are and have no reason to want to change themselves. Their stability and self-assuredness is reflected in the town at large. Mayberry is totally conservative, and its people revel in its traditions: Founders' Day, the weekly church services, and the annual picnic and band concert. The town's identity, like that of its members, is unambiguous. It is guided by its traditions and rituals and resists change of all sorts. Floyd may dream of owning a three-chair barbershop in Mt. Pilot, but he never leaves Mayberry. Otis tries out life in a Mt. Pilot jail but returns happily to the more elegant cells in Mayberry, where he is truly cared for. Andy and Barney both have job offers in other towns and turn them down. The mayor attempts to keep the town band from its annual appearance at Raleigh and fails.

One episode in particular, "Big Fish in a Small Town," is especially well constructed to illustrate the value of tradition and legends in Mayberry. Old Sam is a bass that has been living in Myers' Lake for many years. Many people claim to have caught a glimpse of this huge creature, and some, of course, claim to have hooked him, only to lose him at the last minute. The always elusive Old Sam becomes a legend and his capture the dream of every angler in Mayberry. As the fishing season rolls around, Andy, Goober, Floyd, and Opie decide to try their skill at snagging Old Sam and reluctantly allow the county clerk, Howard Sprague, to join them. This is Howard's first fishing trip, and with beginner's luck he captures Old Sam and donates the fish to an aquarium in Raleigh. Howard thus unwittingly destroys one of the town's legends. Old Sam's real value lay in his elusiveness, in his ability to stimulate the angler's imagination. What would there possibly be to look forward to next year? The dream is gone, and the myth is now just a biological specimen in an aquarium. The townspeople become so upset with this situation and with Howard that Howard finally retrieves the fish from Raleigh and returns it to the lake. The bass regains its legendary qualities, and the townspeople regain their composure.

Mayberry also resisted outsiders who, more often than not, consisted of con men, gangsters, or bank robbers. There are no genuinely evil people in all of Mayberry. But evil characters do try to penetrate with serpentine guile the heart of this good town. A woman speeder corrupts the testimony of Opie and Floyd to avoid a citation. Bank robbers pretending to be film-makers trick Barney into letting them into the bank. A pickpocket passing through town is chosen as the visitor of the year. But none of these invaders succeeds in doing any permanent harm. They are found out and summarily arrested. The innocence of the town may be exploited temporarily, but Andy's wisdom is there always to keep that innocence intact. Mayberry remains a sort of Garden of Eden *before* the fall. The serpent doesn't have much of a chance there.

An important variation on this theme appears in a very early episode entitled "Stranger in Town." The conservative theme here is that change, if it must come, must come slowly. A stranger arrives in Mayberry who seems to know everybody in the town, even small details about their lives. The entire community is upset by this man's uncommon knowledge, and their suspicions as to his identity grow by leaps and bounds. One old lady thinks he may be from the supernatural world. Barney thinks he may be a foreign spy and wants to run him out of town.

Ed Sawyer, the stranger, finally tells Andy how he came to know so much about Mayberry and its citizens. Ed was an army buddy of someone from Mayberry: "I used to envy Joe Larson because he was from *here* and I was from no place. Living alone, hotel, no family—that's like being no place." Ed read Joe's hometown paper, talked to Joe, and continued to subscribe to the paper after he left the service: "I learned everything there was to learn about Mayberry. Pretty soon I started telling people I came from here. All of a sudden I started believing it myself." And when he read that George Sepley's gas station was for sale, he decided it was time to make his move to Mayberry, "my home town."

Andy cautions him: "You're a little bit over-anxious. You like the town, you like that little girl, but you've got to give them time, you see, to like you back. Folks like to take things *sloow*."

The town meanwhile gathers outside the courthouse

and tries to run Ed Sawyer out of town. Andy goes out and lectures them: "His only crime was he tried to fit in a little too fast, made some of you feel suspicious, made some of you feel foolish, scared some of you." After Andy's righteous appeal to their sense of justice, one by one the citizens offer to help Ed settle into Mayberry.

This episode is important not only for establishing early in the series the theme of permanence and stability, but also for capturing an essential truth about small-town America: it *is* conservative, and because it treasures its past, it is suspicious of outsiders who threaten the community's shared values. At the same time, the show demonstrates that the town, when no longer threatened by too sudden a change, is willing to take in an outsider and allow him to grow gradually into full family membership.

Another episode reveals what happens when an outsider inadvertently leads the town momentarily to betray its own conservative principles. A Hollywood film-maker by the name of Harmon wants to make a picture in Mayberry and is given a tour through the town to see its basic features. The Mayberry theme song plays in the background during the tour, a theme song that echoes the harmony and pleasantness of the town itself. Harmon meets many of the citizens, including the mayor, Floyd, Mr. Monroe, the TV repairman and mortician, Aunt Bee, and Opie. The presence of the Hollywood producer, however, causes the townspeople to change their life-style. The businessmen, for example, begin to dress up their shops. Floyd's barbershop becomes a "Tonsorial Parlor," featuring Cary Grant–styled haircuts. Barney puts on a state-trooper uniform sent down by the mayor and tries to get Andy to join him in the more stylish outfit.

Meanwhile, the town council is gathered at the mayor's office to consider a special program to honor Mr. Harmon. Besides the changes already effected, the mayor wants the town's old oak tree cut down since he sees it as an eyesore and not acceptable for the movie. Andy becomes exasperated and speaks out: "What in the world are you all doing?

You've changed yourselves, your stores, your clothes. You've given Barney and me ridiculous-looking uniforms to put on, and now you're going to cut down the oldest oak tree in the entire town!" But the mayor and the council prevail. Andy goes home and announces: "It's a pleasure to be back in my own home where nothing's changed," only to discover that both Aunt Bee and Opie have dressed themselves up in new clothes.

When Mr. Harmon arrives on the scene, he sees how the whole town has changed and intervenes just as the old oak tree is about to be felled. He lectures the townspeople: "What have you done to the town, to yourselves? This isn't the Mayberry I wanted to photograph. I could have built a set like this in Hollywood. I wanted you the way you were when I first met you. . . . The way you were when you were natural, genuine, real. That's what I wanted in my picture." The town learns its lesson: its traditions and simple life-style are the real treasures and not the Hollywood illusions of glamor and fame.

In the epilogue, Barney accidentally locks himself in one of the cells, and Andy exclaims to Opie, "Yes, everything's back to normal in Mayberry." At the end of practically every episode this important fact is established. Life in Mayberry may have been jarred, upset, or tilted, but eventually everything gets back to normal.

One reason that innocence and stability prevail in Mayberry is the absence of sexuality. There are no Eves. Ellie from the drugstore, Peggy, the county nurse, and Helen Crump are all innocent as children in their relationships with Andy. They may hold hands, occasionally kiss each other on the cheek, and go on countless picnics, but they remain totally wholesome and chaste. The subject of sex had to be played down, not only because of the television ethics of the 1960s, but more importantly because it would destroy the illusion of innocence that lies at the very heart of Mayberry.

Once the character of Helen Crump was introduced, Andy became her faithful beau until the end of the series.

Although Barney also had a steady girlfriend in Thelma Lou, he had the potential to be a bit wild at times. We are led to believe that he occasionally dates Juanita, the waitress from the diner. And it is Barney who arranges the disastrous dates with Skippy and Daphne from Mt. Pilot. These three women all lack the sophistication and wholesomeness of Thelma Lou and Helen, and their presence comes close to expressing a sort of illicit sexuality. But Juanita's invisibility and Skippy's and Daphne's comic coarseness keep the suggestion of Andy's and Barney's "infidelity" from ever amounting to anything. Besides, the story lines always manage to preserve the two men from these humorous sirens and return them safely to the arms of Thelma Lou and Helen.

The Andy Griffith Show may not have been sexual, but it certainly was sexist. The male population of Mayberry rules the town, and the women, for the most part, joyfully accept their positions as homemakers whose function is to keep their men happy. Whenever Aunt Bee steps out of her domestic role she proves to be a failure. In one episode she takes a job at the town printshop and is too naive to realize that the proprietors are counterfeiters. Her job consists of mindless busy-work as she unknowingly becomes the front for this crooked operation. In another show she and Howard Sprague both decide to run for the office of town councilman. It turns out that she is simply too ignorant of the issues to win the confidence of the town; whereas Howard, who has been records clerk for several years, is extremely well informed and wins the town's vote. Aunt Bee recognizes her limitations and happily returns to her mundane duties in the Taylor household.

Despite the fairly consistent theme of male domination throughout the series, there was a surprising exception to this early in the show's history. "Ellie Runs for Council," the tenth episode in 1960, presents a feminist thesis that was very advanced for its time. The very fact that Ellie Walker is a pharmacist suggests her unusual status in Mayberry. There were not many women pharmacists in the United States in 1960. She is presented as a strong, independent-minded woman who retains a distinct, traditional feminine charm. In this episode she happens to read in the newspaper that all of the people running for the office of city council are men. She thinks that is horrible and asks Andy (who convincingly plays the role of the male chauvinist) why there are no women candidates. His answer: "Because one of them might win." At that, she walks off in anger and vows to run herself. Andy, of course, grows concerned: "This has never happened in Mayberry before. It could stir up a good-sized hornets' nest." He tries to reason with her but only succeeds in making things worse:

Andy: Oh, Ellie, you don't want to concern yourself with government business. You want to let the men worry about that. All you want to worry your pretty little head about is women's stuff. You know, going shopping, looking in windows, trying on hats, making little bitty sandwiches for having at parties, and gossiping. You see what I mean?

Ellie: I see. A woman should keep her place and stay where she belongs. A woman shouldn't try to think on the same level as a man, because we're simple-minded little fools!

Ellie reasserts her determination to run and to encourage other women to run as well. Before long the town is split between the men and the women. Even Aunt Bee sides with Ellie and exclaims, "Isn't it exciting? The first time in Mayberry a woman ever ran for office! Why, we're growing up, like the big city!" After much argument and many hurt feelings, Ellie says that all the ill will she has stirred up is not worth it, that she is withdrawing from the race. Upon hearing this, Opie asks, "Does that mean we've beat 'em, Pa? We beat them females! We kept them in their place!" These remarks convince Andy that he has been a bad example to his son, and he undergoes a change of heart and makes this conciliatory speech before a gathering of the town:

Now we're against Ellie because she's a woman, but when you try to think of any other reason, you kind of draw a blank. I heard my little boy, Opie, just a while ago say something against women. And I want to tell you the truth, I was ashamed. He was just parroting what he had heard me say. I've made him anti-women. And by and by one of these times, when he's grown up and wants to get married, why, if you've ruled out women, that cuts down the field a good bit. What I'm getting at is—I hate to admit it—if Ellie wants to run for council, I reckon she's got a right to.

It may have required Andy's intercession, but the fact remains that Ellie wins the election and the women triumph in the end. The feminist theme is raised a few more times in subsequent episodes, but after the character of Ellie disappears from the show, so does the theme. Helen Crump, her permanent replacement, helped to stabilize the series in favor of traditional male domination through her quiet and reserved manner and her unassuming role as schoolteacher.

Having created a world of wonderful stability, innocence, joy, peace, and love, the actors, writers, and producers all faced a crisis when Don Knotts decided to leave the show. If the townspeople of Mayberry were up in arms when a fish was taken from their lake, imagine how millions of fans of the show must have felt when Barney Fife was taken from Mayberry. Sheldon Leonard, as has been pointed out, was not upset by Don's departure, since he saw Andy as the key ingredient of the show. From the point of view of the producer of sitcoms, this is a reasonable reaction, but the show had evolved into something very different, with a delicate human dimension and symbolic value that even its executive producer failed to recognize. Knotts' absence would not only remove Griffith's necessary comic foil and the sheriff's dearest friend, but would threaten the carefully established sense of permanence in the fictional world of Mayberry.

The idea of death is unacceptable in a comedy series. When McLean Stevenson wanted to leave *M*A*S*H*, the

writers contrived a story in which his character dies in a
plane crash, but this was an uncomfortable and unfunny
way out of a casting problem. In the case of the *Griffith
Show*, we are told that Barney has gone to work in the Raleigh police department. Andy, Floyd, and Aunt Bee speak
of him occasionally, sometimes they receive a letter from
him, and they remember him fondly. But the fact remains,
Barney Fife is gone. Mayberry, which has successfully resisted even small changes in the past, has let us down.
Change reminds us of time, time of age, and age of death.
Corruption has finally touched the town, not in the form
of a woman or a bank robber, but through a series of real
life circumstances (the Disney offer, etc.) that carried Don
Knotts and Barney off the show. The seamless dream
world of Mayberry ironically received its first crack from
the real world, that of Hollywood deals and contracts.

With the best of intentions, the caretakers of the series
subsequently invited Don to make a number of guest appearances on the show. But from the perspective of one
who can view the entire series as a completed work—and
not, as the producers and actors had to, as an on-going
process—the idea of bringing Barney back to revisit Mayberry proved to widen even further that crack in the delicate dream world that took years to create and polish; and
in one episode, it came perilously close to destroying the
illusion altogether.

When Barney revisited his home town, he quickly got
into the swing of things. He reestablished his old rapport
with Andy, and it seemed as if he had never left. Happy
days were here again—Mayberry had reasserted her stability; and people, places, and relationships were immortal
after all, it seemed. But then came that fatal episode which
shook the dream.

Barney returns to Mayberry to attend a grand high
school reunion. As he and Andy visit the courthouse, it is
made clear that things in town haven't changed during the
years he has been in Raleigh. "Same old courthouse," Barney remarks comfortably. They go inside, and Barney con-

tinues to enjoy finding things the way they were: "Same old desk. Same chair." And then Barney brings up the question foremost in his mind:

Barney: Thelma Lou's not coming, eh?
Andy: I guess not.
Barney: That's too bad. She'd get a kick out of seeing how I've come up in the world.
Andy: Are you still sweet on her?
Barney: Ah, no, no, no. What's gone, Ange, is gone. Can't go back. Of course, sometimes a man wonders.

Then a telegram arrives from Jacksonville announcing that Thelma Lou is coming. Barney immediately drops his pose of philosophical resignation and shouts aloud: "Hear that, Ange, ole Thel's coming! I bet anything she heard I was going to be here!"

Barney gets dressed up in his old pepper-and-salt suit, the one with a tuck in it so that he can do the dip, which was his civilian "hallmark" in the early episodes. Thelma Lou, after all, was the only love of his life, and now is his chance to shine, to rekindle a flame that was nourished during several years on the show.

At the reunion Andy, like Barney, is excited at the prospect of once again enjoying the good old days. He says to Helen: "It'll be like old times, won't it? You and me and Thelma Lou and Barney." When she finally arrives, Barney's eyes light up as he begins to assume all his old poses to conceal his strong and sincere feelings. He dances with her, makes some small talk, and then she matter-of-factly introduces her husband to Andy and Barney. He is appropriately the foreman of a wrecking crew. Barney swallows his joy, pride, and, one would guess, a sense of profound betrayal not only by Thelma Lou but by the writers of the script. Barney has received blows before, but never one this devastating, one that can not easily be remedied. He pretends to take the revelation in stride: "That's the way life is, Ange. It's a rough life. You can't cry about it." But then, a second later, he confesses his true feelings: "She's the only girl I've ever loved and the only girl I will love."

The illusion of a timeless Mayberry is broken—things *do* change, love and affection are *not* constant, time is both real and cruel. Barney was right—"Can't go back." We all know those things and accept them as commonplace in life and in realistic literature and films, but these notions violate the essence of the mythical town of Mayberry and the innocent character of Barney Fife. In the past Andy could always restore Barney's hurt pride with a good word or a clever contrivance—they were both playing according to the rules then. But here, Andy gets Barney interested in another girl who had secretly admired him in high school, and Barney accepts her ready-made compliments as sufficient recompense for the loss of the girl he had loved for years. He has been turned into an absurd puppet, manipulated by a lethal script. The failure of this episode is in direct proportion to the success of all the previous ones in establishing the myth of permanence.

It is a remarkable testimony to the power of the innocent fiction of Mayberry that it survived Barney's departure and Warren's brief tenure as deputy. The main reason that the show survived may well be the powerful illusion embodied in Mayberry itself. Over the years the mythical town actually became more important than any one of its inhabitants. Mayberry survived the loss of Ellie, Peggy, Mayors Stoner and Pike, Gomer, Barney Fife, Warren, and Floyd. Andy, Helen, Aunt Bee, Opie, Howard Sprague, Goober, and Emmett continued to represent the solid core of the community and its values and its traditions.

Horace Newcomb has pointed out that in most television series there is only an illusion of continuity: "The series may continue over a period of years, revolving around the actions of a set of regular characters. . . . However, there is no sense of continuous involvement with these characters. They have no memory. They cannot change in response to events that occur within a weekly installment, and consequently they have no history."* The Griffith se-

---

*TV, The Most Popular Art, p. 253.

ries, on the other hand, presents characters who do have memories and histories. While each episode is self-contained, the characters frequently refer to the past in general and to past episodes in particular. When the girls from Mt. Pilot or Ernest T. Bass descend upon Mayberry, Andy and Barney, not to mention the viewing audience, are all too familiar with their past riotous antics. In one episode Andy and Barney rush into the courthouse to hear their favorite singer, Leonard Blush. In a later episode, Barney's singing teacher impresses him by announcing that she once gave lessons to Leonard Blush. Perhaps the best example of the characters playing with their memories of the past can be seen in the following dialogue between Andy and Barney, who are looking through their old high school annual, *The Cutlass*:

Barney: (*reading*): "Andrew Jackson Taylor. Second Vice-President 4-H. Secretary, Philomethian Literary Society." What was that Philomethian, Ange?
Andy: It was a group that got together and cut out current events and pasted them in a book.
Barney: Sorry I didn't get in on that. Sounds like fun.
Andy: Well, you were up for it. Well, we won't get into that. (*looking at photograph*) Will you look at that head of hair! There must be ten pounds of it.
Barney: Did somebody blackball me, or something?
Andy: Jack Egbert didn't like you. Don't you remember? I told you about it and you cried.
Barney: Oh yeah, Jack Egbert.
Andy: Hey, look at you, Barn.
Barney: I was painfully thin then.
Andy: And you were mighty slow in filling out.
Barney: Well, I got my mother's family's frame. When I was seventeen I could reach into a milk bottle and take out an egg.
Andy: You can't do *that* anymore.
Barney: Nooo.
Andy: That proves you filled out some.
Barney: You want to know something? Jack Egbert was no prize.
Andy: (*reading*): "Bernard Milton Fife. Hall Monitor; Volleyball

Court Maintenance Crew; Spanish Club." I didn't know you
were in Spanish Club.
Barney: Si.

They then come upon the picture of Ramona Wiley, and
Andy reads what she had written on Barney's copy of the
annual:

Andy: "Always Ramona"—that sounds pretty serious.
Barney: Don't you remember how crazy she was about me?
Andy: It was a big thing, huh?
Barney: Well, it was all one-sided. I wasn't interested but she
really had a case on me. I'll never forget one note she wrote:
"Barney beloved—The tears on my pillow bespeak the pain
that is in my heart."

The series is full of such references to the past, and they
provide essential threads that help to weave the episodes
together and to bring the characters into a closer, believable relationship.

Perhaps the most fundamental appeal of the mythical
town of Mayberry comes from its morality, which is the life
force of the community and the force that guarantees the
town its everlasting innocence. The moral complexity of
real life has been reduced here to simple and clear examples of right and wrong. Andy, the embodiment of
common sense and wisdom, is the judge. He possesses a
firm sense of justice that is tempered with sympathy and
understanding. This aspect of his character is clearly
brought out in the following speech by Barney Fife, while
testifying at a hearing in which Andy's competence to continue as sheriff is at issue:

Andy's the best friend I have in the whole world. As far as I'm
concerned, he's the best sheriff, too. His using the squad car for
personal reasons—sure, he was delivering groceries to Emma
Watson because she was too sick to get down to the market. And
that's just one example of the things Andy's done for the folks
in this town. You've got to understand, this is a small town. The

sheriff is more than just a sheriff. He's a friend. And the people of this town don't have a better friend than Andy Taylor. As far as Andy doing his job—there hasn't been a major crime committed in this town, thanks to Sheriff Taylor. The only ruckus you'd have in Mayberry is if you tried to remove him from office. Then you'd have a riot. You ask me if Andy runs a taut ship. No, he doesn't, but that's because of something he's been trying to teach me ever since I started working for him. And that is, when you're a lawman and dealing with people, you do a whole lot better if you go not so much by the book, but by the heart.

Basic to the morality of Mayberry is the idea of a strong family unity. This was established at the outset of the series in the relationship between Andy and Opie, and the family soon extended to include the whole town. The strong father-son relationship depicted in the series is a model of tasteful and unobtrusive moralizing. The moral lessons that Andy imparts to Opie are always based upon substantial actions in the story and are never empty platitudes. Sometimes Andy gets his britches caught on his own pitchfork, as he says, and learns some home truths from Opie.

One of the most movingly dramatic moments between them came in an episode when Opie, after being warned by his father to be careful how he used his new slingshot, carelessly killed a mother bird, leaving her babies helpless. Andy goes up to Opie's room, and outside the window can be heard the cries of the little birds. Andy says, "I'm not going to give you a whipping." He turns and opens the window and says, "Do you hear that? That's them young birds chirping for their mama that's never coming back. And you just listen to that for awhile."

Opie not only learns respect for life, but he takes on the responsibility of motherhood in raising the fledglings. This is especially poignant since Opie has no mother himself. Also, like a mother, he learns that he cannot possess his charges and must finally let them go free. After weeks of patient care he screws up enough courage to return the birds to the wild and remarks how empty their cage now looks. Andy, looking up, simply remarks, "But don't the trees sound nice and full?"

Mayberry reassures us that human problems can be solved and that moral codes of behavior are important in shaping the lives of the young and the life of the entire community. Ethical conduct is not, it seems, ambiguous after all, at least in Mayberry. Opie, we feel sure, will grow up to be as wise and moral as his father, thereby preserving a life-style that is firmly rooted in basic Christian values.

There are precious few television programs today that embody the high moral and artistic standards of the *Griffith Show*. Lust, anger, betrayal, greed, and violence seem to be the order of the day. Soaps such as *All My Children*, *The Young and the Restless*, and *As the World Turns* and popular evening melodramas such as *Dallas* all show people to be fundamentally immoral and the family to be a focus of strife and anxiety. Is it any wonder, then, that the reruns of the *Griffith Show* have enjoyed such success? The series offers a needed parable for our times. Like the solid old westerns that create a dream vision of the American past, with its clear moral code, the *Griffith Show* captures a romantic myth that continues to entice and satisfy our yearnings for a simpler world, one filled with hope, purpose, respect, love, laughter, understanding, and a sense of belonging and permanence.

CHAPTER 8

Two Writers

The Andy Griffith Show was blessed with an unusual number of talented writers, but two of the very best were Harvey Bullock and Everett Greenbaum. These two men, with their partners, wrote over sixty scripts during the first six years of the show, nearly one-fourth of all the scripts in the series. Unseen and unheralded (except by the inner circle of the television industry), these writers nevertheless provided the lifeblood of the show. The familiar words "nip it in the bud," Barney carrying his one bullet in his shirt pocket, and the loaded goat all appeared first in the writers' inventive minds. The actors adhered closely to the scripts, and all of the feelings, dreams, and humor of the characters they portrayed evolved directly from the thirty-odd pages of material they collectively memorized each week. Although there is ample visual comedy in the series, the writers' creation of colorful characters and quietly comic and poignant dialogue is the hallmark of *The Andy Griffith Show*.

I Harvey Bullock

Harvey Bullock was born in Oxford, North Carolina, a small town about fifty miles to the north of Raleigh and within a career's striking distance of Mayberry. Although his family moved from Oxford to upstate New York when he was only three years old, Bullock later returned to the Tarheel state in order to attend Duke University, where he

majored in English. He began his writing career in New
York City in 1947 on audience participation shows. His
first comedy assignment was as a staff writer for *The Abe
Burrows Show* on CBS radio in 1949. He then worked for
Dave Garroway on the pioneering *Today Show*. In 1950 he
began collaborating with Ray Saffian Allen, an association
which continued until Allen's death in 1981, one of the
longest running writing/producing partnerships in the
medium.

Their first assignment was a sketch starring Gertrude
Berg on NBC TV's special *Salute to Baseball*, which won
them the Random House Award. They next went to Lon-
don in 1958 to write all twenty-six episodes of *Dick and the
Duchess*, starring Patrick O'Neal and Hazel Court. Returning to New York, Bullock wrote for Johnny Carson's *Who
Do You Trust?* and *The Charley Weaver Show* while maintain-
ing a trans-Atlantic liaison with Allen, who was producing
shows on British television. The two writers were rejoined
in California in 1961 when NBC bought their original pilot and series *McKeever and the Colonel.*

During the next ten years Bullock and Allen wrote over
three hundred episodes for the top comedy shows in television, including *Hogan's Heroes*; *Gomer Pyle, U.S.M.C.*; *The
Real McCoys*; *The Danny Thomas Show*; *I Spy*; *The Dick Van
Dyke Show*; *My World and Welcome to It*; *The Doris Day Show*;
and of course, *The Andy Griffith Show*. Their incredible success as writers earned them the position of executive producers for *Love American Style* at Paramount. From there
they joined Hanna-Barbera as executives in charge of program development, where they created and produced the
acclaimed animated series *Wait Til Your Father Gets Home.*

In 1975 they formed their own production company
which, during the next three years, provided seven network series of children's programming, such as *Monster
Squad*, *The Red Hand Gang*, and *Poppa and Me*, an hour special that won them an Emmy nomination. They also served
as executive producers at Warner Brothers for the pre-

miere year of *Alice*, for which they also wrote several episodes. After their production company dissolved, they joined Aaron Spelling Productions in 1978 as writers-producers for *The Love Boat*, positions they held for the next three years. After Allen's death, Bullock continued with *The Love Boat* as creative consultant. His most recent assignment is an animated theatrical feature called *Asterix the Legionery* for French television.

Despite their busy schedule in television, Bullock and Allen managed to write six feature films: *Honeymoon Hotel* in 1964, starring Robert Goulet, Robert Morse, and Nancy Kwan; *Girl Happy* in 1965, starring Elvis Presley; *Who's Minding the Mint* in 1967, starring Jim Hutton and Walter Brennan; *With Six You Get Eggroll* in 1968, starring Doris Day and Brian Keith; *Don't Drink the Water* in 1969, starring Jackie Gleason and Estelle Parsons; and *Goin' Cocoanuts* in 1978, starring Marie and Donny Osmond.

Out of his rich, varied, and long career in television and motion pictures Bullock has acquired the wisdom of an elder statesman. The following discussion of his involvement with *The Andy Griffith Show* is based upon an extensive commentary that he provided me both in a personal interview and, later, in writing. He begins: "It's a standard reaction whenever writers are asked which show they enjoyed most working for that they never name the show they are currently doing. If I were asked today, without hesitation I would name *The Andy Griffith Show* as my all-time favorite. Moreover, going against custom, I'm sure that if I had been asked even at the time I was working on it, it still would have been my favorite. In the past twenty-five years I have written episodes for over forty different comedy series. What made that one so special? The answer is elusive, complex, and subjective."

The early 1960s were halcyon days for comedy writers, and with dozens of series shooting over thirty episodes a season, work was plentiful. Despite this, however, almost every television writer hungered for an assignment on *The Andy Griffith Show*. The "soft" comedy of that series, combined with its highly respected production team and supremely talented cast, marked it as a show of unique quality. So, a writing credit on Andy's show was impressive not only to fellow writers but also to producers of other shows. "I benefitted by this coat-tail effect," Bullock notes, "for after just one completed script for the *Griffith Show*, my agent was able to get me assignments on many other programs, such as *The Danny Thomas Show* and *The Dick Van Dyke Show*. The *Griffith Show* was truly an open sesamè."

The Andy Griffith Show, however, meant much more to Bullock than simply an entree to other shows:

> In itself, it was such a very special entity that it made you feel good as a writer to be a part of it. Credit goes to Sheldon Leonard and Aaron Ruben. They had a deep understanding of the free-lance writer's psyche. They knew the toll of the long, lonely hours at the typewriter, which distorted and amplified our insecurities. We were easily replaceable transients, supplicants on a never-ending treadmill going from show to show, homeless and second-class citizens. They countered by making us feel important; they nurtured our fragile egos in even the most minute ways. When we had appointments to pitch stories, they never kept us waiting in an outer room. And when with them, they did not take routine phone calls. They gave every stray notion respectful consideration. The coffee pot was on, the cigar humidor open. We were all, quite obviously, their most favored nephew for whom they had been waiting all day to talk to.

Another remarkable aspect of *The Andy Griffith Show* was that despite its being continuously bombarded by appeals from agents and writers seeking assignments, it remained accessible to aspirants. Leonard and Ruben placed the discovery and encouragement of writers high on their priority list. Bullock recalls the excitement of his first connection with the show:

> I got a chance on the basis of just *one* script, which Sheldon had seen, a pilot my partner Ray Allen and I had done in New York. I was in Los Angeles alone in a super-economy motel seeking work. My wife and three small children were in New York

hoping for the good word. My agent called—Aaron would see me. It was a wonderful meeting. I was greeted as if I were Shakespeare reincarnate and totally cosseted. Best of all, I sold Aaron my story, "Opie's Hobo Friend." I called my wife to pack. California was going to be good to us. And it certainly was.

Bullock's speech and background were essentially northern, but when he started writing scripts for *The Andy Griffith Show* something strange happened:

Somewhere in the genes, some other force was tapping the typewriter keys. I found myself having Andy "carry" Helen to the dance; fat folks became "heavyset"; the gas station became the "fillin'" station; ladies didn't perspire, they "felt the heat"; people had "half a mind" to do things or were "just fixing to." No big earthshaking things, and nothing that Andy wouldn't have amended "hisself" . . . but I was fascinated watching my own typewriter with a mind and a patois seemingly of its own. Perhaps it was a déjà vu from watching other episodes. But I like to think it was a little hereditary nudge from my Old North State forebears.

The Andy Griffith Show was also unique in that it brought its free-lance writers together in seminars. At the end of the filming season, a half dozen writers and/or writing teams would be invited to a three-day session with Sheldon Leonard and Aaron Ruben. At these seminars everyone would toss stray story notions back and forth. Bullock describes the scene:

The story would start to snowball a bit, gathering substance from all. As it bounced about, jokes would fly, outlandish suggestions would convulse all us simple-minded ones, new details would bring mock moans and groans, and even appreciative cheers. The flood of ideas would come in torrents—or trickle to numb silence. But throughout, Sheldon was the masterful conductor, keeping the wildly dissimilar minds in harness, prodding, provoking, always staying optimistic about every idea until it became obvious that it was without hope. But good workable ideas were forged, and as soon as they were in shape enough to be recognized as a potential story, they were quickly titled and set aside, and the flow went on to another story.

At the end of these remarkably cooperative seminars, Sheldon Leonard would dole out the approved story ideas, balancing his idea of which writer would be best suited for each story against the appeals that some writers would make toward getting a particularly enticing story line. At the close of one seminar, writer Fred Fox was anxiously hoping that Leonard would give him "The Pickle Story." "When Sheldon mentioned the coveted story," Bullock recalls, "Fred, a stutterer, looked in anguished appeal to his partner, Izzie Ellinson, wanting desperately for Izzie to claim it. But Izzie's attention was on some notes he was making and he didn't respond. Sheldon's eyes went around the room, unaware of Fred's gasping for air, and Sheldon finally gave me the story. Fred now found his voice and jumped up, indignantly screaming, 'For G-g-g-g-g-g-god's sake, Izzie, you just b-b-b-b-b-blew "The Pickle Story"!'"

These sessions would produce numerous good story ideas, and the writers would work on them during the period when the set was closed down so that Ruben could begin the next season with a dozen scripts piled on his desk. This was important, as Bullock notes, because "the never-ending maw of the camera heartlessly devoured a script every week. It was a ceaseless struggle of the producer to keep ahead of it with good material."

One major problem for free-lance writers was that they had to seek work constantly. The standard payment for half-hour scripts in the 1960s was $3500. Most writers worked in teams so that a completed script, after agent's and manager's fees, would net each writer a little over a thousand dollars. One script a month was not enough, and so, in the middle of writing for *The Andy Griffith Show*, Bullock had to stop, drive to another studio, meet with the producer of the show there, work on some ideas, and perhaps get an assignment, perhaps not. Then he had to return to writing the script for the *Griffith Show* until the next

interruption the following day. Writing scripts for several
shows, then, the bedraggled author waited to receive the
words of blessing from the producer: "It's in mimeo."
"Those were the most wondrous words," says Bullock, for
they indicated that the writer had successfully completed
his assignment.

As happy as all the writers were with the seminars for
The Andy Griffith Show, they grew extremely apprehensive
when Andy Griffith showed up one morning. As Bullock
says, "For writers to listen to other writers is a near miracle; for them to listen to an actor is totally beyond belief."
So, when Andy strolled into the seminar, "none of us actually threw any furniture at him. We writers are basically
sensitive and caring people who would never do bodily
harm to an interloping actor . . . not in front of witnesses.
We appreciate what they do, but we are ardent separatists.
Our creed is: we'll stay out of the acting, you stay out of
the writing.

"Writing is like wrestling crocodiles," Bullock observes.
"The better you do it, the easier it looks." So the actor on
a well-written show is deceived. He thinks writing is a snap
and forgets entirely that "first you need years of practice
against lots of crocodiles." Furthermore, Bullock says,
"The actor has done his lines so well that he begins to believe that he actually originated them, and he begins to feel
qualified to contribute to and improve the scripts, especially with regard to his own role." All of these feelings
surfaced when Andy made his first dramatic appearance
in the seminar room. Bullock recounts the actual moment:

When the story meeting began, Andy did something wonderful—nothing. Not a word the first morning, just some nodding
and laughing, "enjoying hisself." He surpassed himself that
afternoon. He referred to some of the past shows written by
those in the room as "real outstanding." As for new shows, he
didn't "have an idea one in the world." We were ready to bronze
him. Then, wonder of wonders, he became helpful. He
dropped little hometown tidbits: "This one fellow put shoes on
his cow." That became the idea for the episode entitled "The

Cow Thief." Not one word about making his part stronger, longer, wider, or deeper. We never wanted to start a meeting without him.

In developing stories for the show, the most difficult to devise, according to Bullock, were those which featured Andy. "Stories tend to develop around problems when someone goofs. But Sheriff Taylor seldom goofed. He had virtually no frailties. He didn't cheat on his taxes, wasn't in deadly fear of donating blood, never was a love-struck loon, wouldn't try to hide a traffic ticket or pretend to qualities he didn't have. He was sensible, and that wondrous quality is deadly in sitcoms, at least in the sitcoms we all had worked on." So Andy's involvement with stories had to be "by osmosis." Barney Fife or Opie would have problems and Andy's role was to help them. "This takes some doing," Bullock says, since "when you're not directly involved, you mustn't become a lecturer or meddler. Andy understood the subtlety."

All of the writers wanted to write Barney Fife stories, but Aaron Ruben knew the show had to be balanced and made sure that Aunt Bee and Opie and others had their moments center stage as well. Bullock believes that Frances Bavier was the most underrated performer in the series: "Andy was strong as the father figure, Opie was an open winning delight, and Barney Fife was a comedic treasure. Yet Frances, with none of these obvious strengths to work with, turned in a consistent solid background that enabled the other characters to work as well as they did. Her artistry lay in the fact that her contribution was so natural you never thought to examine it. That is talent."

Between 1961 and 1966 Bullock wrote over thirty scripts for *The Andy Griffith Show*, a few of which were in collaboration with Ray Saffian Allen. Included among the titles, with episode numbers in parentheses, are the following: "Opie's Hobo Friend" (40); "The Pickle Story" (43); "Jailbreak" (50); "Andy and Barney in the Big City" (57); "Wedding Bells for Aunt Bee" (58); "The Bookie Barber" [with Allen] (60); "Mr. McBeevee" [with Allen] (66); "Andy and the New Mayor" [with Allen] (69); "The Bed Jacket" [with Allen] (75); "The Loaded Goat" (81); "Rafe Hollister Sings" (83); "The Great Filling Station Robbery" (85); "Andy's English Valet" (89); "The Rivals" (91); "The Big House" (95); "The Haunted House" (98); "Opie the Birdman" (101); "Barney and the Cave Rescue" (109); "Andy and Opie's Pal" (110); "Prisoner of Love" (114); "Hot Rod Otis" (115); "Andy Saves Gomer" (119); "The Return of Malcolm Merriweather" (124); "Back to Nature" (127); "Aunt Bee's Romance" (130); "The Pageant" (138); "Opie's Newspaper" (153); "Opie Flunks Arithmetic" (157); "Malcolm at the Crossroads" (164); and "The Legend of Barney Fife" (177).

Although Bullock wrote some of the classic episodes featuring Andy and Barney, his scripts ranged broadly over the cast of characters, giving focus to Aunt Bee, Opie, Floyd, and Otis. He possessed an uncanny skill for relating Aunt Bee and Opie to the other characters. In "The Pickle Story," for example, all the fun derives from Andy's and Barney's efforts to avoid hurting Aunt Bee's feelings over her "kerosene cucumbers." Watching Andy and Barney eat jar after jar of Aunt Bee's horrible tasting pickles is enough to make anyone's mouth pucker shut. The firm but loving relationship between Andy and Opie in "Opie the Birdman," Andy's willingness to sacrifice his favorite fishing pole in order to get Aunt Bee a present in "The Bed Jacket," and the outrage of the town over Opie's devastatingly honest gossip in "Opie's Newspaper" all attest to Bullock's keen sense of both the Taylor and Mayberry families. He was, of course, equally adept at portraying the more ludicrous aspects of Mayberry, including the dynamite-eating goat, Floyd's encounter with bookies, and Barney getting lost on a camping trip. Essentially, however, Bullock's comic genius lies in his perception of the small weaknesses we all recognize in ourselves and in his ability to render those frailties in gentle, comic terms. The broad vision of Mayberry conveyed through his many scripts is one filled with joy, compassion, and understanding.

Bullock summed up his career for me: "What show did I most enjoy working for? I repeat, *The Andy Griffith Show.* A new question—what did I think of the star? Well, our only son was born in 1962. A heck of a kid. We named him Andy."

II Everett Greenbaum

Raised in Buffalo, New York, Everett Greenbaum came to Hollywood by a circuitous route. He attended MIT for three years, only to discover that he was not very good at math. So, he dropped out of college and joined the Navy. He spent three joyous years as a flying instructor at the Naval Air Station in Peru, Indiana. From there he came to New York in an attempt to break into show business, but failing at that, he used his G.I. Bill to study for a year at the Sorbonne in Paris. Returning to the United States, he acquired his own radio program (for no pay, at first) at WKBW in Buffalo. His live broadcast of "Greenbaum's Gallery" was aired each Sunday evening with the opening announcement: "Good evening, friends of radio in the greater Buffalo area, welcome again to 'Greenbaum's Gallery,' thirty minutes of good music and distinguished commentary on contemporary American living." Influenced by Bob and Ray, Henry Morgan, Vic and Sade, Benchley, Thurber, and Perelman, Greenbaum began to develop a unique style of humorous writing that would later flourish into some of the finest comedy of character ever heard on television.

He was soon offered a two-week writing assignment, collaborating on a new situation comedy for NBC with Jim Fritzell, who was to become his life-long writing partner until his death twenty-seven years later. The series, *Mr. Peepers*, delineated the life of a small-town high school science teacher, played by the bespectacled and tweedy Wally

Cox. The rest of the cast included such talented actors as Marion Lorne, Pat Benoit, Tony Randall, Ruth McDevitt, Georgann Johnson, Jack Warden, and Reta Shaw. The show quickly became a hit, and Fritzell and Greenbaum wrote its scripts for the next three years. At the end of the first year *Mr. Peepers* was presented with a Peabody Award, and Fritzell and Greenbaum received an Emmy nomination for their writing. The show was performed live and, unfortunately, no quality film of those wonderful three years has been preserved, other than some kinescopes. Nevertheless, other kinescopes such as *The Honeymooners* and *Playhouse 90* have been shown in syndication. Owned now by David Swift, the creator of the format for *Mr. Peepers*, the films were discovered in a warehouse on Long Island after the death of Fred Coe, the NBC producer of the show. As one who grew up watching *Mr. Peepers*, I can attest that after *The Andy Griffith Show* it is the best character comedy I have ever seen on television. The characters were warm, gentle, funny, and human. There were no jokes in the show; rather, the humor flowed from the various characters' personalities, their unique ways of looking at and saying things.

Mr. Peepers ran from 1952 through 1954, and shortly after it went off the air Greenbaum left New York and headed to Hollywood, where he began writing for *The George Gobel Show*. Later, when Fritzell arrived in California, they collaborated for five years on writing for *The Real McCoys*. All three of these shows, with their emphasis upon character and small-town life, were excellent preparation for the next assignment given to these two talented writers.

Hired to write for *The Andy Griffith Show* in 1961, Fritzell and Greenbaum found themselves in perfect harmony with executive producer Sheldon Leonard, producer Aaron Ruben, and Andy. Greenbaum describes Andy's unique role in the show as follows:

It was the first time we had worked with a star who participated in script meetings. At these, he was not only an asset in the creative process, but his presence made them joyful events. Basically Andy is a small-town southerner, happiest on the marshes with his rifle and hunting dogs. Like my wife, Deane, he brims with that southern rural humor, which in its knowledge of the human condition is very sophisticated.

Greenbaum remembers Andy as "a large man of large appetites and emotions." In the late sixties, in a little bungalow at Universal Studios where he and Fritzell were writing the script for the movie *Angel in My Pocket*, Greenbaum did his impersonation of Claude Rains for Andy, and Andy "laughed so hard he punched his fist right through the wall."

One of the characters from the show that Fritzell and Greenbaum helped to create was Gomer Pyle. Here is Greenbaum's recollection of the birth of the rustic oddball:

I had recently driven into a gas station with motor trouble. The attendant could think of no cure except to add more gas to the tank. We decided to write such an incompetent into the script. We called him Gomer after a writer, Gomer Cool. The last name we took from an actor on the show, Denver Pyle. We had no idea who was going to play the role, but it was necessary to give him a speech pattern. I had always enjoyed the style of character actor Percy Kilbride, and we used it as we wrote.

Andy saw a young singer-comedian named Jim Nabors at the Horn, a nightclub in Santa Monica, hired him, and the rest is history. After Nabors became a big star and began hobnobbing with motion picture celebrities, families of presidents, and famous athletes, he left his Mayberry family behind him. As Greenbaum puts it, "He left all of us behind and, to this day, has never looked back."

Between 1961 and 1964 Fritzell and Greenbaum wrote twenty-nine scripts for *The Andy Griffith Show*. Here are the titles, with episode numbers in parentheses: "Quiet Sam" (29); "Andy and Opie—Bachelors" (65); "Andy's Rich Girlfriend" (67); "Barney Mends a Broken Heart" (68); "The Mayberry Band" (72); "Convicts at Large" (74);

"Man in a Hurry" (77); "The Bank Job" (78); "High Noon in Mayberry" (80); "Class Reunion" (82); "Opie and the Spoiled Kid" (84); "The Darlings Are Coming" (88); "Barney's First Car" (90); "Dogs, Dogs, Dogs" (93); "Mountain Wedding" (94); "Briscoe Declares for Aunt Bee" (96); "Gomer the House Guest" (97); "Ernest T. Bass Joins the Army" (99); "Up in Barney's Room" (104); "A Date for Gomer" (105); "Citizen's Arrest" (106); "Barney's Sidecar" (112); "My Fair Ernest T. Bass" (113); "The Song Festers" (116); "Andy's Vacation" (118); "Divorce, Mountain Style" (121); "The Rumor" (125); "The Education of Ernest T. Bass" (133); and "The Darling Baby" (139).

The members of *The Andy Griffith Show* Rerun Watchers Club owe a singular debt of gratitude to Fritzell and Greenbaum, for seven of their scripts rank among the top ten in the club's recent poll, "Barney's Sidecar" and "My Fair Ernest T. Bass" being numbers one and two respectively. The bizarre mind and language of Ernest T. and Gomer are the creations of these two writers, whose flair for dialect and zany thought is unequaled among the various writers for the series. They also wrote some of the funniest dialogue Barney ever spoke in such episodes as "Barney's Sidecar," "Man in a Hurry," and "Up in Barney's Room." "Convicts at Large," which is one of my personal favorites, is a masterpiece of plot, characterization, visual humor, and dialogue. Who can forget Floyd's continual reference to Barney as "Al" (Barney reminds one of the female convicts of her old boyfriend named Al), the tango that Barney dances with Big Maud, or Floyd's blasé attitude as he munches on a banana during his and Barney's stressful captivity? The characters in all of these shows are so funny and believable, it is only upon reflection that one realizes that their language and feelings are the product of two men, sitting at their typewriters, who quietly and consistently conjured up the situations and words for the waiting actors.

In writing these and other shows, Greenbaum had a perfect partner in Jim Fritzell. In many ways they were two very different men. A first-generation American of Scandinavian parentage, Fritzell was raised in San Francisco. Greenbaum, on the other hand, describes himself as "a third-generation Jewish mongrel, raised in Buffalo." "Yet we'd been marinated in the same American juices," Greenbaum goes on, "had shared the same Judeo-Christian ethics and the same storehouse of cliches." Over ninety percent of the time they agreed on what was funny and were in complete rapport as writers. "We were like a team of acrobats communicating telepathically. One began a sentence; the other finished it," Greenbaum recalls.

Each man had distinctly different interests in life. Fritzell enjoyed sports news, poker games, drinking, and smoking. He showed little interest in higher forms of culture, such as theater, science, travel, literature, or music. Addicted to television, he enjoyed watching quiz shows and old cowboy pictures for hours on end. Greenbaum recalls that his partner had "great kinship with the average American—the hardhat, the serviceman, the minor-league baseball player—he had a finely tuned ear for their dialogue." Greenbaum, on the other hand, delighted in flying, drama, novels, music—in short, all those things eschewed by Fritzell. Between the two of them, their interests covered the broad spectrum of American life. They were the perfect odd couple, and the creative tension that developed between their two perspectives lead to startling and original comedy. One assumes, for example, that the structure of "My Fair Ernest T. Bass," modeled after the broadway play, *My Fair Lady*, was the brainchild of Greenbaum, but the rich common touch that brings the script down to earth through the character of Ernest T. owed something to Fritzell.

Shortly after a writer by the name of Larry Gelbart created a television version of the motion picture *M*A*S*H*, he invited Fritzell and Greenbaum to write for the series. For the next five years they produced brilliant scripts for this unique show. In many ways *M*A*S*H* resembles *The Andy Griffith Show*: both were shot with one camera with no audience; both stressed character comedy over jokes or slapstick; both possessed a sense of family unity; both employed a restrained laugh track—not used at all, incidentally, in the operating room scenes of *M*A*S*H*; and both dared to be serious at times.

Perhaps the most publicized script from *M*A*S*H* was the one that removed McLean Stevenson from the series. Stevenson's desire to act in Las Vegas, find motion picture roles, and appear in plays gradually lead to problems on the *M*A*S*H* set. Scripts had to be rewritten so that he could accept some of the offers he sought, and soon his demands increased beyond a point acceptable to the producers. Thus, it was mutually agreed that he would leave. The task of writing him off the show fell to Fritzell and Greenbaum. The last page of their final script was kept a secret even to the other actors on the set. The story line has Colonel Blake (McLean Stevenson) leave the surgical unit by helicopter to catch a plane back to the United States. That is all the story that the actors knew. Then, during the last scene, in which the doctors are hard at work in the operating room after Colonel Blake's departure, Radar enters with an announcement: "Colonel Blake's plane went down in the Sea of Japan. No survivors." The doctors and nurses continue operating but with tears in their eyes. The actors were as startled as the audience at the news of Colonel Blake's death, and the tears were, in part, genuine.

Fritzell and Greenbaum received thousands of letters, half damning and half praising them for the unusual episode. Greenbaum wrote to his detractors that although *M*A*S*H* was entertainment, it was also an anti-war show and that "the essence of war is the quick and final departure of a loved one." For the first time in television history, one of the principal characters of a comedy had been killed off. When Don Knotts wanted to leave *The Andy Griffith Show* it would have violated the theme of that show to have him killed in a car crash on his way to Raleigh. Because of the war and bloodshed that constantly loomed in the background, the death of Colonel Blake did not violate the theme of *M*A*S*H*; rather, it daringly introduced a tragic element into television comedy, a bittersweet mix long familiar to dramatists and screenwriters.

Besides their work in television, Fritzell and Greenbaum wrote a number of motion picture scripts during the late 1960s as a result of their work on *The Andy Griffith Show*. These include *The Ghost and Mr. Chicken*, *The Reluctant Astronaut*, and *The Shakiest Gun in the West*, all made at Universal Studios and all starring Don Knotts. They also wrote the script for *Angel in My Pocket*, starring Andy Griffith. Then, in 1972, Greenbaum collaborated with Wally Cox (whose personal life at this time began to disintegrate, leading to his untimely death four years later) on writing a children's book, *The Tenth Life of Osiris Oakes*, published by Simon and Schuster.

Without a writing partner now for several years, Greenbaum is still working in television, but his great hope is to get a play on Broadway. This is a long-standing hope. Years ago he wrote that "I would have given up ten years of TV success to have a play open in New York." His idol is the great comedy playwright, George S. Kaufman, a man he came briefly to know and who has inspired him ever since.

Greenbaum now resides with his wife in Encino, California. Within striking distance of the old Desilu Studios where *The Andy Griffith Show* was born, Greenbaum still keeps in touch with Andy Griffith, Don Knotts, Bob Sweeney, and Aaron Ruben. But time has weakened some of the strong ties in the old Mayberry cast. Greenbaum wrote me that "Ron Howard is now a grown movie director and I pass him often at Fox Studios without mentioning who I am (or was)." And so it goes.

Barney is startled by the advances of Daphne, one of the "fun girls" from Mt. Pilot, played by Jean Carson.

Viacom

Gomer joins the Marine Corps in "Gomer Pyle, U.S.M.C." and Sergeant
Carter (Frank Sutton) lays down the rules.

Left: Barney goes undercover to test the Mayberry bank's security in "The Bank Job."
Right: George Lindsey as Goober.

Andy, Barney, and Gomer discover "spirits" in "The Haunted House."

Ronny Howard in "Opie Finds a Baby."

Andy and Barney handle an explosive case in "The Loaded Goat."

Disguised as a store dummy, Barney watches for suspects in "The Shop-lifters."

"Mmmm, good!" Andy and Opie enjoy Aunt Bee's cooking.

Barney gets caught on the wrong side of the bars in "The Big House."

Jim Clark

Howard raises the rent on Floyd's barbershop in "Floyd's Barbershop."

Doug Dillard

The Darling Family and Andy. Top row (l. to r.): Mitch Jayne, Rodney Dillard, and Dean Webb. Bottom row (l. to r.): Douglas Dillard, Margaret Ann Peterson, Andy Griffith, and Denver Pyle.

Everett Greenbaum

Bob Sweeney, Andy, and Everett Greenbaum pick and sing on the set.

Andy and Opie head to the lake.

PART

3

(Preceding page)
Frances Bavier and Ronny Howard in "The New Housekeeper."

CHAPTER 9

Don't Look Back

Actors, like sharks, must continue to move, always with their eyes open, seeking new scripts and fresh opportunities to devour in order to stay alive. Andy Griffith, Don Knotts, Ron Howard, Howard Morris, Jack Dodson, Jim Nabors, George Lindsey, Aneta Corsaut, Hal Smith, and Denver Pyle are among those from the cast of *The Andy Griffith Show* who continue to extend their professional lives along lines that lead further and further away from the Mayberry that once brought all these talented people together. Unlike the fans of the show, who devote their best leisure hours to revisiting Mayberry time and again, the actors have left town, once and for all, and seldom look back. In terms of their professional careers, this is a wise decision. Even the Bible and classical mythology teach this lesson. When Lot's wife turned to view Sodom she was turned into a pillar of salt, and when Orpheus glanced over his shoulder at his beloved Eurydice, whom he was leading out of Hades, he lost her forever.

Having shaken off the dust of Mayberry, Andy has undertaken a variety of new television roles in recent years. It is interesting to note that while there were no murders in Mayberry, Andy Griffith has gone on to appear in a number of television productions where homicide is the central theme. In 1981 he won an Emmy nomination for his role in the television movie *Murder in Texas*. Starring Katherine Ross, Sam Elliott, and Farrah Fawcett, the film is a dramatization of the murder case centering upon Houston plastic surgeon Dr. John Hill, who was accused of killing his socially prominent first wife. The script is based on the book *Prescription: Murder*, written by Hill's second wife, Ann Kurth (played by Katherine Ross). Andy's role is that of Hill's father-in-law, the wealthy oilman Ash Robinson. Convinced that Hill had murdered his daughter, Robinson patiently and doggedly seeks to expose his sinister son-in-law.

In 1983 Andy undertook the starring role in the television film *Murder in Coweta County*, based upon the book of the same title. This picture presents the true story of an infamous killing that took place in southern Georgia in 1948. Johnny Cash plays the role of the righteous sheriff dedicated to justice, and Andy portrays a corrupt southern land baron who murders a poor black man and who arrogantly assumes that his actions are above the law. In the last scene we see him with his head shaved (he is actually wearing a rubber cap to make him appear bald) as he is strapped into the electric chair. He is executed and justice triumphs, though we sense that this reckless man never understood what all the fuss was about. Not since *Savages* have we seen Andy play the role of a ruthless murderer, something which he does very convincingly.

Perhaps the most important recent event in Andy Griffith's life was his marriage to Cindi Knight. They were married in a private ceremony at Andy's home in Manteo in April 1983. A charming, intelligent woman, Cindi is a schoolteacher in southern California. Here is a case of life imitating art. Andy Taylor also married the schoolteacher. Cindi, incidentally, had a small role in *Murder in Coweta County* as a mother, holding a small child, who serves as a witness during the trial scene.

Andy's career was seriously curtailed for over six months during 1983 when he fell victim to Guillain-Barre Syndrome, a viral nerve infection that affects the sensory response of the extremities and impairs locomotion. This illness caused him to drop out of his scheduled role in the CBS miniseries *Chiefs*. Charleton Heston replaced Andy, and the show was aired during the summer of 1984.

Now totally recovered from the disease, Andy signed a year's contract with the American Telephone and Telegraph Company to appear in their television and newspaper commercials. Given Andy's years of experience with Mayberry's solitary telephone operator, Sarah, and given his image as a conservative, relaxed, honest, no-nonsense country boy, he was the perfect choice for AT&T to represent them in its battle with MCI, Sprint, and other telephone companies that are expanding their markets now that the government has dissolved AT&T's long-standing monopoly.

Maybe Andy does not seek a return to Mayberry, but AT&T certainly exploits his down-home personality in its first television commercial. It shows Andy sitting comfortably in his easy chair. He is wearing a checkered shirt and casual slacks and appears as satisfied as if he had just finished eating the special at the Bluebird Diner. Looking the audience straight in the eye, he handles the phone at his side and says, "You know what I'm going to do during the biggest revolution in telephone history? Relax." It is a very effective commercial, designed to quiet the anxieties of millions of people who face a complex series of choices to make about their telephone service. One is reminded of Dr. Harrison Everett Breen in "The Sermon for Today," who preaches to the folk in Mayberry: "Relax, slow down, take it easy. What's your hurry?" That advice did not work very well in Mayberry, but perhaps Andy's credibility and nostalgia will bring AT&T millions of dollars in revenue if everyone simply relaxes.

AT&T has also taken out full-page advertisements in newspapers with photographs showing Andy, a Trimline in hand, smiling and at ease as he explains the joys of leasing a telephone: "Fresh paint, some new wallpaper. When I redecorated the bedroom, I figured why not change the phones, too. Because I lease my phones from AT&T, I can exchange my old black phone for a fancy Trimline like this. . . . Leasing means I can relax." Not since Andy (again in his checkered shirt) popped the first Ritz cracker into his mouth and let millions of snackers across the country know how "Mmmmmm" good it was has he appeared so prominently on television and in the newspapers.

There are a number of dramatic roles in which Andy may soon be seen. He is scheduled to appear in the popular television show called *Hotel* and in an NBC miniseries called *Fatal Vision*, starring Karl Malden and Eva Marie Saint. Based upon Joe McGinniss' book of the same name, *Fatal Vision* is the true story of Jeffrey MacDonald, the Green Beret physician convicted of murdering his wife and two children while he was stationed in Ft. Bragg, North Carolina. Andy will play the part of the first prosecuting attorney. Beyond that, Andy has no firm plans, though there has been some talk about his starring in a film tentatively called *Rustlers' Rhapsody*, to be set in Spain. Now that he has signed again with the William Morris Agency, Andy is hoping to find a more permanent role in a television comedy or dramatic series.

Meanwhile, many of Andy's old films, such as *A Face in the Crowd* (1957), *No Time for Sergeants* (1958), *Onionhead* (1958), *Angel in My Pocket* (1969), and *Hearts of the West* (1975) continue to show up on late-night television. They have endured remarkably well over the years. In fact, *Hearts of the West*, which was a box-office failure (Andy made only a few hundred dollars from the film because he signed a contract for a percentage of the profits), has grown in recent years to be something of cult film on some college campuses. Steven Scheuer, in his bestselling *Movies on TV*, gives this picture his highest rating. Starring Jeff Bridges, Alan Arkin, Blythe Danner, and Andy Griffith, the film tells the story of a young writer from Iowa (played by Bridges) who winds up in Hollywood. Arkin plays the eccentric director of a western film and Andy takes the role of a likeable stuntman who comes up with a plagiarized script. The film is a very funny and highly unusual examination of the myths of the old west, and it reveals Andy's ability to establish a unique and believable character who bears no resemblance to Will Stockdale or to Andy

Taylor. The film is worth seeing by everyone and especially by historians of Mayberry who want to see Andy's dramatic step out of the fictional southern small-town world that nourished him during the first twenty years of his career.

None of the original cast of *The Andy Griffith Show* has maintained a busier schedule or appeared more regularly on television or in motion pictures than Don Knotts. "All muscle," Barney used to say, pointing to his body. "It's a mark of us Fifes." Over sixty years old now, Don has exercised that muscle in numerous roles demanding enormous energy and stamina. After his successful performance in *The Ghost and Mr. Chicken* in 1966, he starred the following year in *The Reluctant Astronaut*, the story of a bumbling fellow who rises from his job as a maintenance man to become an unwilling astronaut. In *The Shakiest Gun in the West*, a 1968 remake of Bob Hope's *Paleface*, Don plays the role of a Philadelphia dentist who winds up in the wild west facing gunslingers and the seductive Barbara Rhoades. In the next year he played a Hugh Hefner caricature in *The Love God?*, a ludicrous comedy with Anne Francis and Edmond O'Brien. Reverting to the naive character of many of the preceding films, Don played the role of the town patsy, manipulated by crooked politicians, in the 1971 film *How to Frame a Figg*.

The Disney western comedy, *The Apple Dumpling Gang* (1975), brings Don's childlike comedy into play with that of Tim Conway. A trio of orphans, inherited by gambler Bill Bixby, finds a large gold nugget in an abandoned mine during the 1870s, and Knotts and Conway, as the incompetent robbers, plot to steal the gold. The following year Disney used these two comics again in *Gus*, the story of a football-kicking mule whose talent allows a losing team to emerge victorious. Undaunted at having to take a backseat to a mule, Don emerged in still another Disney comedy that year, *No Deposit, No Return*, starring David Niven, Darren McGavin, Herschel Bernardi, and Barbara Feldon. Two wealthy children persuade some incompetent crooks (one of whom is played by Knotts) to offer them for ransom to their grandfather (David Niven) so that they can visit their preoccupied and widowed mother (Barbara Feldon) in Hong Kong.

Disney's third "Love Bug" film, *Herbie Goes to Monte Carlo*, appeared in 1977, starring a Volkswagen Beetle, along with Dean Jones, Julie Sommars, and Don Knotts. Don plays one of the jewel thieves who hides a diamond in Herbie's gas tank while Jones races across Europe. In 1979 Disney brought Tim Conway and Don together again in *The Apple Dumpling Gang Rides Again*, for a second slapstick romp through the wild west. They teamed up in 1980 for still another picture, *The Private Eyes*, in which they play blundering Scotland Yard sleuths seeking a murderer in a dark old mansion. Much of the film was shot on location at the Biltmore House in Asheville, North Carolina, and local residents were delighted to see the return of "Barney" to his "home state." Bernard Fox, who played Malcolm Merriweather in *The Andy Griffith Show*, also appears in the picture. Finally, Don, along with numerous other stars, has a cameo role in Burt Reynolds' new film, *Cannonball Run II*.

During the past several years Don has appeared regularly as the lovable Ralph Furley, the bumbling landlord on the popular television comedy series *Three's Company*. Having stopped production in March of 1984, the producers plan to introduce a new format for the show in the fall. Don, Joyce DeWitt, and Prisilla Barnes have all chosen to leave the series. In January of 1984 the cast of *Three's Company* threw a gala party at Chasen's Restaurant in Los Angeles, to celebrate Don's thirty-five years in show business. Most of the old gang from Mayberry were there—Andy Griffith, Aneta Corsaut, Hal Smith, Betty Lynn, Ron Howard, along with producers, directors, and writers—as well as close friends like Bill Dana and Louie Nye.

Keeping a hand in professional theater, Don has acted in two plays during 1984: *The Mind with a Dirty Man*, written by Jules Tasca and produced at the Celebrity Theater in Phoenix, Arizona, and Neil Simon's *The Prisoner of Sec-*

ond Avenue, produced both in La Mirada and Santa Barbara, California. He has also appeared in television commercials for Kellogg's, and his all-American face has even showed up on some of their cereal boxes.

Despite Don Knotts' enormous box-office success in the Disney films and his great popularity among children—he has become America's clown, a title Red Skelton held in the old days of radio and early television—his more critical adult audience credits his role as Barney Fife as the hallmark of his comic genius. Like Andy, Don cannot afford to look back towards Mayberry, but must continue to establish and polish his unique blend of naive slapstick comedy. There will never be another Barney Fife, and Don knows that as well as do the millions of people who love Barney. Don may have exorcized the demon deputy but the demon will not be stilled: he has possessed the imaginations of countless people around the country, and he is now ours to keep and cherish.

Ron Howard has come a long way since he played Opie Taylor. Once haunted by his childhood fame, Ron acknowledges that his current success derives from his experience working with Andy Griffith: "I used to be afraid that I was going to be Opie for the rest of my life. In fact, there was a time when I pretended *The Andy Griffith Show* didn't exist. The worst thing anyone could ever do would be to call me Opie. *Now* I get the biggest kick out of it; I love it! The show is something I've built on. It's something to be proud of." He recalls fond memories of the series, especially of Andy: "I best remember him sitting around the reading table telling us that it was important for the show to be funny, but it had to be funny because the viewer could identify with the characters and not because we were a bunch of hayseeds and dumb hicks. And, boy, did Andy work to make that show work. It's the hardest I've ever seen anyone work—ever."

Ron's father, Rance Howard, recently recalled that the inspiration for his son's interest in directing began on the set of *The Andy Griffith Show*. For Ronny's eighth birthday

Andy Griffith, Richard Linke, and Aaron Ruben chipped in to buy him an eight-millimeter movie camera, tripod and all. The boy spent the following weeks and months making numerous home movies, and the sheer enjoyment of that experience left him with the lasting impression that filmmaking was fun.

During his many years as Richie Cunningham on *Happy Days*, Ron, like Andy, learned to play the role of the straight man. He says that he never felt passionate about the show as a creative experience but saw it as a way of attaining his ultimate goal as a director. After seven years, he left the series in order to start filming his own motion pictures. He made a two-part return to the show in its eleventh year, appearing as a mustachioed Army man home on leave with his pregnant wife and young son.

Ron has acted in a number of films that prepared him for his work as a director. Included among his acting credits are *Music Man* (1962); *The Courtship of Eddie's Father* (1963); *Smoke* (1970), a Disney production that deals with a young boy (Ron Howard) who distrusts his new stepfather (Earl Holliman) and bestows his love instead upon a stray dog; *The Wild Country*, another Disney film, adapted from Ralph Moody's *Little Britches*, about the joys and pains of a family that moves from Pittsburgh to Wyoming in the 1880s; *American Graffiti* (1973), directed by George Lucas, the man responsible for *Star Wars* and *The Return of the Jedi*; *The Spikes Gang* (1974), starring Lee Marvin as an elderly outlaw who tries to turn three runaway boys (one played by Ron Howard) into bank robbers; *The Shootist* (1976), John Wayne's last film, in which Wayne plays a legendary gunfighter dying of cancer who seeks peace but cannot overcome his reputation for violence; and *More American Graffiti* (1979), an unsuccessful exploitation of the earlier film.

After Ron left *Happy Days* he signed a three-year contract with NBC in 1980, which was to give him valuable experience as a director and producer. In that same year he directed *Skyward*, the sentimental story of a fourteen-year-old paraplegic girl who yearns to fly. Bette Davis plays a former stunt pilot who helps the girl achieve her dream. Ron followed this film with *You Needed Me*, a love story based upon the popular recording by Anne Murray, and *Good Ole Boys*, a comedy western written by his father, Rance Howard. While none of these films is especially distinguished, they provided Ron with the experience necessary to develop character and story lines that would serve him well in his next two undertakings: *Night Shift* and *Splash*.

In directing *Night Shift*, Ron worked with material that would earn the film an "R" rating. The film is a hilarious farce about two enterprising young men, played by Henry Winkler and Michael Keaton, who open a call girl operation in a New York City morgue. The language, nudity, and violence of the film earned it the "R" rating. A large number of young adults are more inclined to see an "R" rated motion picture than one labeled "PG" (more and more the sign of a film for children), and given Ron's experience and desired audience, it naturally follows that his films have inclined toward adult situations.

Splash is undoubtedly Ron Howard's greatest achievement as a director. A romantic comedy about a New York bachelor who unwittingly falls in love with a mermaid, the film stars John Candy, Daryl Hannah, and Eugene Levy. Crediting Jerry Paris and Garry Marshall, director and producer of *Happy Days*, and Andy Griffith for their influence upon his creation of comedy and character, Ron said he came to understand "that there is a rhythm and a sound to comedy." He apparently captured both the rhythm and sound in *Splash* because it turned out to be one of the most successful films of 1984, and it has given Walt Disney Productions its all-time best seller. In promoting the film Disney has taken pains to disguise its ownership of the property because the company feels that its label on a film limits its audience to the youth market. In any event, *Splash* has proven to be a huge financial success and guarantees a new independence for Ron Howard as a director.

Not one to rest on his laurels, Ron has gone to Spain to begin filming a new motion picture entitled *The Rainbow Warrior*. He is also developing a new situation comedy called *Slam* for Home Box Office television.

Because he was so young when he appeared in *The Andy Griffith Show*, Ron Howard turned out to be the one member of the original cast who was least trapped by its success. *American Graffiti* and *Happy Days* provided him with a seemingly natural transition from Mayberry into young adulthood. Young people could identify with that film and that television series even if they had never heard of Opie Taylor. And those people who did remember Opie simply enjoyed watching him grow into manhood, even though he had stepped outside of the city limits of Mayberry. It will be interesting to watch his career develop to see if he takes a further step into serious film and television, as has Andy, or remains in the more comfortable groove of comedy, like Don Knotts.

In addition to his memorable performance as Ernest T. Bass, Howard Morris began to develop a reputation as a talented director on *The Andy Griffith Show*. He directed eight episodes for the series: "Barney's Bloodhound" (episode 128); "Family Visit" (episode 129); "Aunt Bee's Romance" (episode 130); "Barney's Physical" (episode 131); "The Darling Baby" (episode 139); "Andy and Helen Have Their Day" (episode 140); "Otis Sues the County" (episode 141); and "Three Wishes for Opie" (episode 142).

After leaving *The Andy Griffith Show* toward the end of 1964, Morris directed the television spy-spoof series *Get Smart*, starring Don Adams as the redoubtable secret agent Maxwell Smart. Morris then worked on a number of feature films. In 1967 he directed *Who's Minding the Mint*, starring Jim Hutton, Dorothy Provine, Milton Berle, Joey Bishop, Bob Denver, and Walter Brennan. Given small notice at the time of its release, it is nevertheless a hilarious story about a gang of thieves who help Hutton, an employee at the United States Mint, to recover a large sum of money that he accidentally destroyed. The following year Morris directed Doris Day, Brian Keith, Pat Carroll, Barbara Hershey, George Carlin, and Alice Ghostley (Aunt Bee's replacement in *Mayberry, R.F.D.*) in *With Six You Get Eggroll.* Then, in 1969, Morris directed *Don't Drink the Water*, starring Jackie Gleason and Estelle Parsons. An adaptation of Woody Allen's play, the film tells the story of an American family held captive in a totalitarian country called Vulgaria and their ludicrous attempts to escape.

More recently, Morris appeared with some regularity on *The Mary Tyler Moore Show.* Then in 1977 he showed up, along with Harvey Korman and Madeline Kahn, in Mel Brooks' *High Anxiety*, a parody of Alfred Hitchcock's films. Morris' latest film appearance was in another Brooks picture, *History of the World, Part I*, in 1981. He is currently specializing in the direction of television commercials and has been the recipient of both the Clio and Andy Awards for his innovative achievements in the field of advertising. Morris' handiwork can be seen in commercials for Jiff peanut butter, K-Mart, Kellogg's Rice Krispies, and McDonald's hamburgers.

Like Don Knotts, Howard Morris' greatest contribution to comedy seems to lie in his past. The varied and hilarious comic characters he developed for skits on *The Show of Shows* during the 1950s—remember him jumping like a frightened monkey onto the back of Sid Caesar or Carl Reiner?—and his energetic portrayal of the obstreperous Ernest T. Bass represent a unique legacy of comic genius.

Jack Dodson continues to excel as a character actor, having established the enduring image of Howard Sprague as a likeable, though somewhat stuffy, small-town official. It was rather shocking, therefore, to see him in Sam Peckinpah's violent film, *The Getaway* (1972), in which he played the submissive husband of Sally Struthers, a sexually frustrated woman who takes up with a sordid criminal. Openly enjoying an affair with him, she comes home one day to discover that her humiliated husband has hanged himself in the bathroom.

In 1982 Jack appeared in the premiere episode of *Newhart*, Bob Newhart's television comedy series about an innkeeper in New England. Jack played the real estate agent, Mr. Shaver, who sells Dick Loudon (Newhart) an eighteenth-century inn in Norwich, Vermont. Then, in 1983, Jack played the role of Paul Sycamore in the revival of the George S. Kaufman and Moss Hart play *You Can't Take It With You*. Performed at the Plymouth Theater in New York City, the play starred Jason Robards as Grandpa Vanderhof, the patriarch of a bizarre family that has mastered the art of benevolent mayhem. Paul Sycamore, Vanderhof's son-in-law, passes his time making fireworks in the basement, while the rest of the family is engaged in equally ludicrous endeavors. The play closed in December of 1983, but fortunately it was filmed and shown on Showtime in 1984 so that millions of people could see this well-cast and brilliantly acted comedy.

Most recently Jack had a small role in the PBS production of *Concealed Enemies*, a part of the American Playhouse Series that aired during May of 1984. Carefully researched, this compelling film recreates the sensational story of the legal and political contest between Alger Hiss and Whittaker Chambers.

After living in New York City for the past couple of years, Jack recently returned to his home in California. He is a very talented and intelligent actor whose career is no longer circumscribed by Mayberry's city limits. Introspective and possessed of a keen critical mind, Jack is perhaps the most philosophic of the Mayberry crew. He has proven that he can play serious dramatic roles as well as comic ones, and, if he is able to acquire the right parts, he can be expected to continue to flourish as a character actor and one of Mayberry's brightest graduates.

While both Jim Nabors and George Lindsey were incomparable as Gomer and Goober and a vital part of the success of *The Andy Griffith Show*, neither of them has been able to transcend his past. They have been locked into the characters they played so well over the years.

Capitalizing upon his popularity in *Gomer Pyle, U.S.M.C.*, Nabors made guest appearances on *The Carol Burnett Show*, *The Donny and Marie Osmond Show*, and *The Redd Foxx Show*. Since that time his appearances have been largely confined to headlining in nightclubs in Las Vegas and Lake Tahoe. His most recent motion picture appearance was in the Burt Reynolds film *Stroker Ace* in 1983. He also appears in Reynolds' new picture, *Cannonball Run II*.

Nabors has also made a number of record albums featuring popular hymns and love songs. During the early 1980s there were frequent television commercials for Nabors' record album of romantic love ballads. He has a strong, pleasant voice (indeed, it helped him to beat Barney out of his place in the Mayberry choir), but it will take more than Gomer's favorite comic book word, "Shazzam," to turn him into a credible romantic crooner of such songs as "Please Release Me!" Nabors now lives in Hawaii, where he owns a large macadamia nut farm. But he is probably destined to be remembered for his citizen's arrest of Deputy Fife rather than for his macadamias.

George Lindsey has similarly been locked into the role of a country comic ever since leaving *The Andy Griffith Show*. He appeared in several motion pictures that gave him some opportunity to exhibit his broad comedic style: *Ensign Pulver* (1964); *Snowball Express* (1972); *Charlie and the Angel* (1973); *The Cannonball Run* (1981); and *Take This Job and Shove It* (1981). He also had parts in several television shows, including *CHIPS*, *Fantasy Island*, *Profiles in Courage*, and *Twilight Zone*, and he made one appearance on *M*A*S*H* playing a surgeon who graduated from the University of Arkansas medical school. The snobbish, Ivy-league Charles Winchester snubs him as a "boor."

A regular on *Hee Haw* for over fourteen years, Lindsey expressed in a recent interview his frustrations over the difficulty he has had in expanding his talents into new areas and different roles. "There is a lot more to me than Goober," he said, "and it is time to send that boy off to camp!" Unfortunately, his convincing portrayal of Goober, with his beanie pushed back on his head and with his oil rag hanging out of his back pocket, has seemingly cast Lindsey once and for all in the role of country bumpkin. Andy Griffith once explained to Lindsey what the character of Goober was all about. "He's the sort of guy," Andy said, "who goes into a restaurant and says, 'This is great salt!'" George never forgot that description and he proceeded to develop the character into an enduring and important part of Mayberry's simple good humor.

George is rightfully proud of the fact that he has been working steadily on television every week since *The Andy Griffith Show* and *Mayberry, R.F.D.*, despite the fact that he finds most of the doors in Hollywood now closed to him. In the meantime, his exposure on *Hee Haw*, the number one syndicated show in the country, has helped him obtain bookings as a stand-up comic at such major dinner hotels as the Riviera, Frontier, and Sahara in Las Vegas, Reno, and Tahoe. As part of his act, he explains to the audience what it was like playing Goober, and he closes his routine with a piece entitled "What Mayberry Means to Me." In this brief, nostalgic vignette, George says that Mayberry "means going to church on Sunday and then going to the corner drugstore for a cherry coke. . . . It's sitting in your car on Main Street watching the people pass." He concludes his sentimental poem on a realistic note: "When you talk about it you get that very special itch. But the thing I like about Mayberry most of all, it made old Goober rich."

Despite his concern with his stereotyped image, George himself has helped to keep Goober alive and before the public. His record album is entitled "George 'Goober' Lindsey Goes to Town." His public relations company issues a flyer about him as "George Lindsey, 'Goober.'" And besides talking about Goober and Mayberry in his nightclub act, George is currently involved in two commercial enterprises that trade upon his image as Goober. He has recently been named the celebrity spokesman for Getty Oil Company and does all television, radio, and poster work for the company. He appears dressed like a gasoline station attendant, holding a gas hose, wearing a Getty hat, and smiling for all the world like Goober at Wally's old station. He also maintains that down-home country image in his commercials for Liberty overalls.

In 1972 he established the George Lindsey Celebrity Golf Tournament in Montgomery, Alabama. The longest-running tournament of its type in the country, it donates the proceeds to programs that help mentally retarded children. Andy Griffith, Jack Dodson, Jim Nabors, and Ron Howard are among the old Mayberry gang who have played in the tournament, in addition to such notable people as Fred MacMurray, Chet Atkins, and the late Paul "Bear" Bryant. Over the years the event has raised over a million dollars for the Special Olympics and has won Lindsey the respect and admiration of his home state of Alabama.

Looking forward to playing Lester Jetter in a musical based upon *Tobacco Road* at the Town and Gown Theater in Birmingham, Alabama, Lindsey continues to hope for a challenging dramatic role. He has both the ambition and talent to achieve his dream, but the inveterate image of Goober continues to shadow him. Wearing a trench coat, sunglasses, and a mustache that he had temporarily grown, George was recently walking through the Knoxville airport when a little boy pointed at him and yelled, "Mama, there's Goober with a mustache!"

In spite of being somewhat trapped by his past, George looks back upon Mayberry with great fondness. "It was the finest part of my life." His desire to move away from the character of Goober thus remains a paradox: George looks ahead towards new dramatic ventures, but all the while he continues to reflect upon his mythical home town of Mayberry, where Goober can never die.

Before she became Helen Crump, Aneta Corsaut costarred in 1958 with Steve McQueen in *The Blob*, one of McQueen's early films. Her acting career survived that mass of jelly from outer space, however, and her appearance as Opie's teacher in 1963 earned her a continuing role in *The Andy Griffith Show*. After a courtship lasting nearly six years, Andy finally married Helen in the first episode of *Mayberry, R.F.D.* Aneta Corsaut then disappeared from television for several years until she surfaced during the late 1970s playing a nurse in a television series called *House Calls*. Based upon the 1978 motion picture of the same name starring Walter Matthau and Glenda Jackson, the television show continued the hospital satire about a widowed doctor enjoying his sexual freedom in courting a divorcée. Aneta is currently appearing on the soap opera *Days of Our Lives* as the mother of Bo Brady, a character she introduced to the show in 1984.

In a recent interview, when asked how she has changed since the days of Mayberry, she replied laughing: "I've gotten old and tired. Actually, my life is almost perfect. I collect mysteries, do some writing and some acting, have tons of animals, and am still very political." She thinks that the only member of the cast who has changed significantly is Andy Griffith. Andy, she remembered, was very insistent that every member of the cast work hard at the show and was impatient with people complaining about colds or sore throats. Now that he has been ill himself, she believes that Andy has become more understanding and introspective.

While Aneta Corsaut had many opportunities to display her beautiful auburn hair on *The Andy Griffith Show*, Betty Lynn appeared only once in a colored sequence, revealing that she, too, was a redhead. This, of course, was the episode entitled "The Return of Barney Fife," in which Barney discovers that Thelma Lou is married. Betty Lynn hated that episode because she knew that it was her last time on the show, and she did not want it to end. When asked about Barney as a lover, Betty acknowledged that "he kisses well." After attending the anniversary party for Don Knotts, she said that being in the company of the old cast made her "feel secure again for a few minutes." In recent years she has devoted herself to caring for her mother, who is very ill, which leaves her with little time and no immediate plans to return to acting.

Hal Smith (Otis) reports that he began his acting career at the age of six "as a nasty little elf in a play about the mythical Pandora." He subsequently appeared as the next door neighbor in the 1950s television show *I Married Joan*, starring Jim Backus, and he had character parts in such shows as *Smitty the Cop*, *The Great Gildersleeve*, and *Saints and Sinners*. After leaving *The Andy Griffith Show*, Hal did not immediately sober up his act. He appeared as the drunkard, Calver Weems, in *The Ghost and Mr. Chicken*. He then went on to become one of the most famous voices on television. This versatile vocal gymnast does the voices for quite a few animated characters: Winnie the Pooh, Owl, Eeyore, Dr. Doolittle, Cyclops, Dab Dab the Duck, Barney (on *The Flintstones*), and Walt Disney's Goofy and Jiminy Cricket. He is currently doing several of the voices in ABC's *The Little Prince*. Even the former mayor of Mayberry has given his voice to a cartoon character. Parley Baer (Mayor Roy Stoner) is the voice of the Keebler Cookie elf.

No discussion of the whereabouts of Mayberry's unique cast would be complete without some mention of the Darling family. Denver Pyle (Briscoe Darling) has abandoned his four sons in the hills of Mayberry for four nephews and a niece as Uncle Jesse on *The Dukes of Hazzard*. Pyle has made several feature films, including *The Man Who Shot Liberty Valance* (1962); *Shenandoah* (1965); *Bonnie and Clyde* (1967); *Bandolero!* (1968); *Five Card Stud* (1968); *Escape to Witch Mountain* (1975); *Welcome to Los Angeles* (1977); and *Return From Witch Mountain* (1978).

In an article for *The Bullet*, Nashville *Tennessean* reporter Ken Beck tracked down Briscoe's four unflappable boys. The Dillards, as the musical group was called in real life, came to Hollywood from their home in Salem, Missouri. After playing in the Ash Grove, a Los Angeles bluegrass club, and signing a contract with Electra records, the group was hired for *The Andy Griffith Show*. The original Dillards were comprised of brothers Doug and Rodney Dillard and their friends Dean Webb and Mitchell Jayne. Doug now has his own group called the Doug Dillard Band, while Rodney continues to lead the Dillards. Dean Webb still plays with Rodney, but Mitchell Jayne has gone back home to Salem to become a writer.

Doug Dillard also appeared in a few films recently, including *The Rose* (1979), starring Bette Midler, and Robert Altman's superb real-life cartoon *Popeye* (1980), starring Robin Williams and Shelly Duvall. Doug plays the banjo in *Popeye*, even as he played most of the banjo music in *Bonnie and Clyde*. Doug told Beck that his appearance on *The Andy Griffith Show* was "the highlight of my career." He also recalled a wonderful piece of trivia, namely, that the Darling brothers spoke only one line on the show, and that was "Great beans, Aunt Bee," after Bee once fed the boys at the jail.

Many people have asked if there will ever be a reunion of the cast of *The Andy Griffith Show* to make a film or television show, as was done with *The Beverly Hillbillies* and *Gilligan's Island*. Several of the actors have indicated they would be pleased to make a return to Mayberry if the opportunity ever arises. When I asked Andy about the prospects of such a reunion, he paused and said he would have to think about it, that there would have to be just the right script. He mused farther and said, "Perhaps it could open with a funeral—say, Floyd's—and people would be returning. . . ." Andy's disappointment with the quality of the other reunion shows, however, dampened his spirits on the subject. There would be a great deal at stake in such an undertaking. First of all, someone like Bullock or Greenbaum would have to come up with a first-rate script; then someone else would have to finance a pilot or preview of such a production and convince the networks and potential sponsors that the show would be competitive in the ratings. Given the present state of television comedy, such a venture would be no easy task. Furthermore, one has to consider the possibility that an attempt to return to the good old days simply might not work. Such a show could, in fact, disappoint our best memories. Andy is not interested in exploiting his past success and has reasonable grounds for fearing that such a reunion could become a sad caricature of the eight years of Mayberry that he crafted through hard labor into a work of art.

There seems to be little chance, in my judgment, that this talented group of actors will ever gather together again. While some of them might be lured back into Mayberry, most of them have chosen not to look back. They share a common psychological and financial need to advance their careers into new areas and, at the same time, they share a common memory of friendship, laughter, warmth, family, and artistic integrity from their years together on *The Andy Griffith Show*. That shared memory, embodied in the show, has moved well beyond the set at the Desilu Studios to envelope the hearts and imaginations of millions of people. I don't think any of us wants to risk losing that subtle link to a magical past for the sake of one more hour of looking back.

CHAPTER 10

Mayberry in the 1980s

Since this book was first published in 1981, I have received telephone calls and letters from people all around the nation. These people give many different reasons for getting in touch with me, but the basic impetus for their communication is simply to talk about *The Andy Griffith Show* and to share with someone their favorite moments from the show. "Remember the time Floyd punched Charlie Foley in the nose?" Or, "Do you recall when Andy asked Barney to go up to the old haunted house, the Rimshaw place, to retrieve Opie's ball? When Barney looked frightened, Andy quoted President Roosevelt's famous line to him, 'You have nothing to fear but fear itself,' and Barney, exasperated, yelled back, 'Well, that's what I have, fear itself!'" All of the characters—Andy, Barney, Floyd, Gomer, Goober, Aunt Bee, Opie, and the rest of the town—are as real to these people as members of their own town or family. Old-time fans of the series, who have been watching it since the 1960s, have had over twenty-five years to get acquainted with the characters, and such a long involvement naturally breeds a genuine and deep feeling of attachment.

A writer in *The Atlanta Journal* observed, "It's with a sense of relief that one *Andy Griffith Show* fan recognizes another; after all, shouldn't grown-ups be a little embarrassed to admit they love such a corny embodiment of life as it never was? That we love to watch Andy tease Barney about his one bullet, that we wish we lived in Mayberry, that we wish we had an Aunt Bee to cook for us? Well, we're out there . . ." Indeed, they are, in the tens of thousands, and the writer of that notice has put his finger on an interesting detail. Many people have for years been embarrassed about their strong feelings for the show. It is acceptable to wax enthusiastic about the comedies of Shakespeare, or even the humor of James Thurber, the Marx Brothers, S. J. Perelman, and Woody Allen. But *The Andy Griffith Show?* It is not respectable to love a television "sitcom." Well, all that is changing. The revolution is upon us: people are coming out of the closet in droves to assert their allegiance to the small town that never was. Mayberry is a state of mind and its citizens number in the millions. People from all states, all professions, and all social classes share a common mythical hometown, and like Andy himself, who learned that he could not hide his small-town life from his rich country club friends, the faithful followers of the show no longer need to disguise their affection for their simple, old friends from Mayberry.

There is, after all, the wonderful chance that one day, in *Twilight Zone* fashion, we shall take a wrong turn while driving down a North Carolina interstate and wind up in Mayberry. Floyd will still be sitting there with his whimsical smile and will give us an approving wave of the hand, but he will be watching us with the intensity of a bird of prey. Aunt Bee, of course, will be at home cooking supper. We might catch Barney finishing up his duties as crossing guard at the school. The town will always be there, suspended in time like an unfulfilled dream. But the urge to return lingers, and again and again we move back towards the elusive comfort of its quiet streets, its colorful and gentle citizens, its music, its whiskey-drinking mountain men. Such comfort, of course, is pleasantly disrupted on occasion by an explosion of a loaded goat and or by the plaintive cries of Ernest T. Bass, like a rogue elephant, calling for his Romeena.

Many people are trying to make their dream of Mayberry a reality, something tangible to remind them of those good old days. One of my colleagues at the univer-

sity has named his son after Andy Griffith and calls him
"Ange" for short. I have heard from other people who
have named their children after characters from the town
(no Opies yet—nobody seems to know where in the world
that odd name came from). Countless cats, dogs, and
other pets with names like "Barney," "Ernest T.," and
"Gomer" roam the suburbs or sleep on plush furniture,
ready to leap at a moment's notice of "Hey Barney, it's supper time!" In fact, in 1966 I named my rather stuffy, business-like black and white cat "Howard," after Howard
Sprague. Although he didn't meow through his nose, he
made a wonderful cartoon version of the county clerk for
more than sixteen years.

A man from Virginia who restores old cars wrote me
about his project to rebuild an old Ford to duplicate—in-
signia and all—the one Sheriff Taylor and Barney drove
in Mayberry. Some people are content to videotape all of
the 249 episodes of the show, thereby capturing the whole
world of Mayberry in 7,470 minutes, commercials included. Of course they lose some of the small treasures,
such as seeing Andy and Barney worked into the original
commercials for General Foods, and local stations frequently cut away actual segments of the show in order to
insert extra commercial time. Insensitive editors sometimes cut the scenes in which Andy and Barney are chit-
chatting, apparently to avoid cutting into the plot, but in
so doing they often destroy the soul of the episode. In any
event, videotape machines have helped to fix *The Andy
Griffith Show* in the electronic scrapbook of the 1980s. A
recent issue of *The Video Review*, in fact, gave national attention to the importance of the show and to the thousands of people who are taping it.

Ultimately, of course, the joy of Mayberry lies within us
as it grows and sweetens our imaginations. A woman from
Aliquippa, Pennsylvania, for example, wrote me to say
that she watches *The Andy Griffith Show* each day at noon.
Her letter, in part, reads:

I must say Andy and Barney are really my consolation in this terribly troubled world. Since I enjoy living a very simple life, I appreciate watching the show—it seems that for one half hour each day the world stands still and I can feel secure and at peace. And best of all, there seems to be a feeling of God's presence in each episode simply because of the harmony and friendliness of all those in the show.

Other people describe the "consolation" differently but this woman sensitively understands how the show is affecting her. The power of a skillful work of art to induce a compelling fantasy has been experienced by generations of people. *The Andy Griffith Show* provides the same feeling of warmth and goodness that one enjoys in Dickens' *A Christmas Carol* or Twain's *Tom Sawyer*. When Andy's in the courthouse, all's right with the world.

The good citizens of Mayberry in the 1980s, scattered around the country, enjoy nothing more than meeting one of their kind. One such citizen from Union City, New Jersey, wrote that he was nine years old when the show first aired in 1960: "I've had nothing but heartache when the reruns were discontinued twenty years hence." And so, he continues, "Discovering your book about *The Andy Griffith Show* on the shelves of my local bookstore made me feel the way the late anthropologist Dr. Louis Leakey must have felt when he first unearthed Zinjanthropus."

However, the problem of being a lonely, isolated Mayberrian has at last been solved. We can all renew our citizenship in that mythical town through two interesting organizations that have recently formed.

Perhaps the most important event after the founding of Mayberry for contemporary lovers of that immortal town was the creation of *The Andy Griffith Show* Rerun Watchers Club, better known as *TAGSRWC*. This organization, now grown to several thousand members, began in the fall of 1979 as an informal group of students who shared a fondness for watching *The Andy Griffith Show*. The founding members are Jim Clark, Lyell Asher, Dan Auter, and Brook Alexander. A group of Vanderbilt University undergraduates, they gathered daily at the Phi Kappa Sigma fraternity house to view the show. Articles by the Associated Press and by the Nashville *Tennessean* gave the club national attention and its membership began rapidly to grow.

On October 3, 1982, *TAGS*RWC published its first newsletter, named *The Bullet* after the bullet that Barney carries in his shirt pocket. The newsletter, which is published about twice a year, features interviews with the actors and other principals from the show. It also carries updates on what members of the cast are doing now, quizzes, and other articles to enhance the pleasure of loyal watchers of *The Andy Griffith Show.*

With voluntary dues of only one dollar a year, the club strongly encourages its members to promote the airing of the show in their communities, since there obviously cannot be a watchers club without a show to watch. Unlike the traditional fan club, with its teen-age cult of personality, *TAGS*RWC is, in Jim Clark's words, "mostly just a network of people who enjoy watching—and, when possible, promoting—*The Andy Griffith Show.* Still, at heart, we want the club to be just plain fun. . . . I try to operate the club much like the folks of Mayberry might have."

John Mayberry, Mayberry's founding father, would have been proud of Jim Clark because he appears to embody the contemporary spirit of Mayberry. Born in 1960 in Greensboro, North Carolina (only a short drive from Andy's home town in Mt. Airy), and a dedicated follower of the show since he was nine years old, Jim was an Eagle Scout and holds the Gold Palm and the Order of the Arrow. In fact, his vita reminds one of the entries in Andy's and Barney's high school annual, *The Cutlass.* Six-foot six, he played varsity basketball in high school, clearly an achievement superior to Barney's claim to fame as a member of the Volleyball Court Maintenance Crew. At Vanderbilt University, Jim majored in American Studies and managed to work his love of the show into a term paper on the small American town.

Jim has been variously described by newspaper reporters as "a grown Opie Taylor," "like one of Opie's school chums grown up," as if "he just stepped off the bus from Mayberry," and as having "a face squeaky-clean and an all-American grin." Now that he has graduated from Vanderbilt, Jim is working in the promotions and marketing department of Opryland in Nashville. Still, the heart of this talented writer and editor of *The Bullet* continues to beat to the lively tune of *The Andy Griffith Show*.

*TAGS*RWC now has over sixty chapters throughout the country and continues to grow at a rate that would have exasperated Mayors Pike and Stoner. Perhaps attracted by Mayberry's famous and infamous musicians—remember Bobby Fleet and His Band with a Beat?—several well-known musicians have recently joined *TAGS*RWC: the Oak Ridge Boys, the Statler Brothers, Lester Roadhog Moran and his Cadillac Cowboys, Doug Dillard (the banjo-playing Darling boy), Ronnie Milsap, and Merle Haggard. Mayberry's charms have also brought into the club such notable people as Jim Hunt, the former governor of North Carolina; Ted Turner, the owner of the Atlanta Braves and station WTBS (which has faithfully aired *The Andy Griffith Show* for years); Paul Harvey, the commentator and columnist; and Jack Dodson (Howard Sprague). Andy Griffith himself wrote to the club: "I don't know how anybody could be more flattered not only to know people watch my old show, but that you put out a newsletter about it and have an organization. . . . I tell you what . . . why don't I join and watch along with you."

The inventiveness and good fun of the modern generation of Mayberrians are nowhere more apparent than in the names of the various chapters of *TAGS*RWC. The first chapter founded was the Andy chapter, organized by Jim Clark. It continues to have mostly an administrative role.

Here is a list of the current chapters:

"Citizen's Arrest"	Birmingham, Alabama
The Esquire Club	Cullman, Alabama
"Get a Bottle of Pop"	Gadsden, Alabama
Mayberry Minuteman	Graysville, Alabama
Fearless Fife Fanatics, M.D.	Huntsville, Alabama
"How Do You Do, Mrs. Wiley?"	Madison/Decatur, Alabama
Floyd	Russellville, Alabama
"There's Andy, There's Me and Baby Makes Three"	Sylacauga/Auburn, Alabama
"He's A Nut!"	Tuscaloosa, Alabama
Floyd's Barbershop	Little Rock, Arkansas
Wally's Filling Station	Searcy, Arkansas (Harding College)
The Loaded Goat	Los Angeles, California
Rafe Hollister	San Francisco, California
The Squad Car	Whittier, California
"Shakedown!"	Wilmington, Delaware
Goober	Gainesville, Florida
Opie	Orlando, Florida
Juanita	Pensacola, Florida
Malcolm Merriweather	Tallahassee, Florida
"Pipe Down, Otis!"	Atlanta, Georgia
Salty Dog	Atlanta, Georgia
Leonard Blush	Doraville, Georgia
JL 327	Lumpkin, Georgia
"Checkpoint Chickey"	Savannah, Georgia
Maximum Security Cell #1	Valdosta, Georgia
Barney's Bird Dogs	Hayden, Indiana
The Darlings	Louisville, Kentucky
Mayberry Marketplace For Brides	Madisonville, Kentucky
"Sarah, Get Me My House"	Metairie, Louisiana
Howard Sprague	Framingham, Massachusetts

"There Went the Duck Pond"	Detroit, Michigan
Helen Crump	Gulfport, Mississippi
Otis Campbell	Jackson, Mississippi
Thelma Lou	Jackson, Mississippi
"Shazzam!"	Lincoln, Nebraska
"Hey, Paw!"	Brooklyn, New York
Malcolm Tucker	Asheville, North Carolina
"It's Me; It's Me; It's Ernest T."	Buies Creek, North Carolina (Campbell College)
"Boy, Giraffes Are Selfish!"	Chapel Hill, North Carolina
The Courthouse	Chapel Hill, North Carolina (University of North Carolina School of Law)
Sarah	Charlotte, North Carolina
"Kerosene Cucumbers"	Concord, North Carolina
Ernest T. Bass	Durham, North Carolina
Barney	Greensboro, North Carolina
Eagle-eye Annie	Greensboro, North Carolina
"Judy, Judy, Judy"	Hickory, North Carolina
Bluebird Diner	High Point, North Carolina
"I Remember Poindexter"	Lenoir, North Carolina
Gomer	Lexington, North Carolina
"Nip It in the Bud!"	Madison-Mayodan, North Carolina
Asa Breeney	Montreat, North Carolina
The Corner Room at the Raleigh Y	Raleigh, North Carolina
Ernest T. Bass Brick and Rock Brigade	Salisbury, North Carolina
The Rock	Tulsa, Oklahoma
"Poor Old Horatio"	Clemson, South Carolina
"You Beat Everything, You Know That?"	Greer, South Carolina
"All God's Children Got A Uvula"	[Undesignated city] South Carolina
The Bud Nippers	Chattanooga, Tennessee
Aunt Bee	Cookeville, Tennessee

Mayberry	Knoxville, Tennessee
Mr. McBeevee	Memphis, Tennessee
Andy	Nashville, Tennessee
Burt Miller	Nashville, Tennessee
"Goober says 'Hey'"	Dallas/Fort Worth, Texas
Mayberry Union High	Longview, Texas
The Miracle Salve	Richmond, Virginia
Two Fun Girls From Mount Pilot	Charleston, West Virginia
Mount Pilot	Madison, Wisconsin
"My Darling Romeena"	Neenah, Wisconsin
Bloody Mary's Rock	Wausau, Wisconsin
Dingo Dog	Desmarals, Alberta
"Watch It, Al"	Saudi Arabia

In addition to these named chapters, there are several groups which still have not settled upon appropriate names for their chapters, and they are located in such cities as Columbia, South Carolina; Bristol, Virginia; Columbus, Ohio; Clemmons, North Carolina; Charleston, West Virginia; Norman, Oklahoma; Fountain, North Carolina; Wilmington, Delaware; and Greenville, North Carolina. Some of these chapters have even started their own newsletter, like the Gomer chapter, which publishes "The Filling Station." Wally's Filling Station at Harding College also publishes its own chapter newsletter called "The Pocket" (the one, of course, which carries Barney's famous bullet). The "Hey, Paw!" chapter in Brooklyn has been campaigning to get those Big Apple city slickers to put *The Andy Griffith Show* back on the air. The Andy chapter hosted its first formal gathering in June of 1984 by featuring "An Evening with Goober." George Lindsey spoke to an enthusiastic group of members at the Bluebird Cafe in Nashville, where Jim Clark and all his fellow "goobers," enjoyed a return to Mayberry through the reminiscences of one of the town's most colorful citizens.

These numerous chapters have become a vital lobbying force not only for seeing to it that the show continues to be aired, but for protecting the show against such unwarranted attacks as those which were recently launched by the National Sheriff's Association. This organization apparently felt that television was presenting a poor image of the sheriff in America and protested against such shows as *Carter Country* and *The Andy Griffith Show.* Hearing this slander of their beloved Sheriff Taylor, many of the chapters responded vehemently and pointed out that Andy enhanced the idea of the lawman and that he exercised common sense and handled most of the town's problems with good judgment, understanding, and firmness, and not with a gun. Instead of condemning Andy, the association should have presented him with a plaque.

The Otis Campbell chapter is now the largest one in the network. One wonders, of course, if Otis' favorite pastime has anything to do with the popularity of this group. After their meetings, do they all go to the courthouse and lock themselves in jail? Like many chapters, they have contacted their namesake (a.k.a. Hal Smith) and invited him to join in the festivities.

The Andy chapter is seriously considering holding a convention in Nashville in the summer of 1985, and if successful, the group will undoubtedly continue to hold such national meetings in the future. Nashville, after all, was the city to which Floyd threatened to flee in "Floyd, the Gay Deceiver" if Andy did not help him in his pretense that he was a rich businessman. And so, perhaps it is only a matter of time before the thousands of contemporary Mayberrians gather together, perhaps to sing the old school song, "Mayberry Union High":

> Mayberry Union High
> Victory is yours well nigh
> We'll hit the line for points every time
> The Orange and Blue will try, try, try

And when the victory's won
You'll be our favorite son
Proud waves your banner in the sky
Mayberry Union High.

The Bullet recently conducted a poll of its readers to determine their favorite episode and their favorite scene. Given the difficulty of choosing favorites among such an array of riches, members nevertheless bit the bullet and voted as follows:

The Ten Favorite Episodes
1. "Barney's Sidecar" (Episode 112)
2. "My Fair Ernest T. Bass" (Episode 113)
3. "The Pickle Story" (Episode 43)
4. "Man in a Hurry" (Episode 77)
5. "Mountain Wedding" (Episode 94)
6. "Goober and the Art of Love" (Episode 147)
7. "The Education of Ernest T. Bass" (Episode 133)
8. "Ernest T. Bass Joins the Army" (Episode 99)
9. "The Sermon for Today" (Episode 100)
10. "Dogs, Dogs, Dogs" (Episode 93)

Considering the relatively few appearances of Ernest T. Bass in Mayberry, he did very well in this poll, appearing in four of the ten favorites. Perhaps his popularity can, in part, be explained by seeing him as Andy's alter ego, a comic sort of Mr. Hyde set loose upon the peaceful, well-ordered, civilized town. A child in a man's body, he follows his instincts. He represents pure energy, freedom from restraint, an animal joy, and as such, his appeal is powerful.

"Barney's Sidecar" is not a surprising first choice because it contains both the visual and the oral aspects of comedy. Barney's preposterous highway patrol costume, the sidecar separating from the motorcycle when Barney attempts to take Andy to lunch, and Barney riding over Aunt Bee's bag of groceries all combine with the wonderful dialogue (especially when Barney tells Andy how he plans to set up "Checkpoint Chickey") to make this one of the most memorable episodes. And again, as with Ernest

T. Bass, Barney embodies a child's view of the world: he plays at being a lawman, infatuated with equipment, uniforms, rules and regulations, and lacks common sense. The latter is for Andy to enforce.

The Ten Favorite Scenes

1. Any of the scenes in which folks are just quietly sitting on the Taylors' front porch. Perhaps they will gossip about one of the townspeople, reminisce about an old girlfriend, or talk about going down to the drugstore to buy some ice cream.
2. Andy and Barney getting locked in a jail cell.
3. Barney's romantic conversations on the telephone with Juanita, or anybody's conversations with Sarah.
4. Andy's good-natured teasing of Barney and Barney's classic, perturbed responses.
5. The music of the Darling family.
6. Any scene with Otis letting himself in or out of his cell, especially in "The Loaded Goat" (Episode 81).
7. Scenes with Floyd, especially the times he fidgets around the barbershop or sits outside the shop talking with Andy or others about what Calvin Coolidge might say about the weather. One such memorable scene is when Floyd is sitting on his bench next to his prize pansies, which he plans to enter in the annual flower contest. When Andy stands in front of him, blocking the sunlight, Floyd tells him to move out of the way because "pansies need all the rays they can get."
8. Barney's gun going off accidentally and his checking to see if he has his bullet.
9. Andy's and Opie's father-son discussions, and family talks including Aunt Bee, as in "Wedding Bells for Aunt Bee" (Episode 58).
10. Barney's testimony on behalf of Andy in "Andy on Trial" (Episode 61).

This list testifies to the good taste of the Rerun Watchers and their love of good, solid dialogue as well as visual comedy. The chit-chat on the front porch, the ludicrous conversations between Floyd and his friends, Barney's suave overtures to Juanita, and Andy's fatherly wisdom for his son are all unique features of this show. The current television situation comedies no longer seem to have many

talented writers like Harvey Bullock and Everett Greenbaum to create such wonderful dialogue. Is it any surprise,
then, that millions of people have reverted to old shows,
such as this one, to rejoice in the charm of the spoken
word?

If all of the riches one can derive from *The Andy Griffith
Show* Rerun Watchers Club are not enough, one can also
join a newer organization called *The Andy Griffith Show* Appreciation Society, founded in 1982 by the enterprising
and dedicated fourteen-year-old, John Stanley Meroney,
who lives in the small town of Advance, North Carolina.
John is among the millions of people who, because of their
age, saw the show only in reruns. But young as he is, he
has become a diligent historian and promoter of the series.
In his monthly newsletter, entitled *Mayberry*, he issues frequent reports on the recent activities of the actors from
the show, selected trivia, quizzes, and interviews with and
articles about such people as Ron Howard, George Lindsey, and Aneta Corsaut. A recent issue of *Mayberry* contains
an interview with Ed T. Mickey, a Moravian minister who
while living in Mt. Airy taught Andy Griffith to play the
trombone. John recently went to Los Angeles to hold interviews with Hal Smith, Aneta Corsaut, Betty Lynn, and
Rance Howard for *Mayberry*.

Though only a few years old, *The Andy Griffith Show* Appreciation Society has a growing number of members, approaching one thousand spread over half the states in the
country. Notices about this society in *USA Today*, *Video Review*, *Satellite Dish Magazine*, and on the Associated Press
wires have given it national status. Like *The Andy Griffith
Show* Rerun Watchers Club, the Appreciation Society
boasts a number of celebrity members, including Hal
Smith, Aneta Corsaut, Jim Nabors, Sheldon Leonard,
Earle Hagen, Senator Jesse Helms, and Vice President
George Bush.

The Appreciation Society is a bit more structured and
business-like than the Rerun Watchers Club. The latter,
for example, has offered for sale only bumper stickers.

(One reads "I'd rather be watching *The Andy Griffith Show*" and the other "Nip It in the Bud.") The Appreciation Society offers a variety of items for sale, including such things as back issues of *Mayberry*, scripts, photographs, and videotapes. There is a membership fee of nine dollars, not much more than the price of a movie and much more fun. The dual purpose of the Appreciation Society is to promote the airing of *The Andy Griffith Show* and to provide through its newsletter a forum in which the show's fans can come together and communicate.

Like Jim Clark, John is also interested in trying to assemble a convention to bring together fans of the show. He recently hosted a small gathering of his membership in Winston-Salem, at which I showed the pilot for *The Andy Griffith Show*. Shortly after Andy announced in that film that his Aunt Lucy won the shirt-washing contest at the county fair, everyone in the audience knew they were back home again, in that best of all simple towns.

Anyone interested in joining these excellent clubs may do so by writing to the following addresses:

> Mr. Jim Clark
> TAGSRWC
> 27 Music Square East
> Suite 146
> Nashville, Tennessee 37203

> Mr. J. Stanley Meroney
> *The Andy Griffith Show* Appreciation Society
> Box 753
> Bermuda Run, North Carolina 27006

Before the popular game "Trivial Pursuit" was even conceived, many followers of *The Andy Griffith Show* were lovingly compiling their own array of trivia from Mayberry. It would take a trivia expert, in fact, to recognize all of the names of the chapters in the Rerun Watchers Club. How many people could identify "JL 327," "Miracle Salve," "Eagle-eye Annie," or "Watch it, Al"? *The Bullet* regularly features "Miss Crump's Mayberry Quiz," and frustrated readers have to await the next issues to discover that Barney's address is 411 Elm Street, that the troop number of the Mayberry Boy Scouts is 44, that the highly regarded and unseen Mt. Pilot radio personality is Leonard Blush (and that Howard Morris did his voice), that the last name of Barney's waitress friend, Juanita, is Beasley, and that she worked at the Junction Cafe before coming to the Bluebird Diner.

In 1981 *Trivia Unlimited*, a publication of The United States Trivia Association in Lincoln, Nebraska, featured an issue dedicated to *The Andy Griffith Show*. The editor, Steve Tamerius, noted that although he has seen each episode of the show at least four times, he never was able to learn the last name of Thelma Lou. Jim Clark, who has seen every episode at least ten times, is probably one of the leading trivia experts on *The Andy Griffith Show* today. Here, then, are some of the interesting details from the show that only a faithful and true "goober" could know, courtesy of Jim and the many people who wrote and telephoned me.

Being a small town, Mayberry did not need a seven-number telephone exchange, and, indeed, many small towns in the past used only three or four digits. Here are some of the more popular telephone numbers in Mayberry: 431, Barney's number; 363, Wally's Service Station; 242, the Bluebird Diner; 247, Thelma Lou; and 327, Skippy, in Mt. Pilot. Sometimes the writers failed to keep such details consistent, as when Andy has a home address of 14 Maple Street in one episode and 332 (or 322) Maple Road in another. Since the house was the same, one assumes he did not move. Similarly, Barney is identified as Bernard P. Fife, Bernard Milton Fife, and Bernard Oliver Fife. Clara Edwards, Aunt Bee's good friend, was Clara Johnson in the early episodes. Goober Pyle, Gomer's cousin, was a Beasley in the beginning, a detail that makes one wonder if he was related to Juanita. Surely Barney would not find a girl who looked like Goober to be such a temptress! Floyd the barber was Floyd Colby in the beginning and had a wife and a son, but later, as Floyd Lawson, he had no family, except his unfortunate nephew Warren (Barney's replacement as deputy). During the early years of the show there were also two different actors who played Ben Weaver, the mean-tempered owner of the local department store. Will Wright was the first Ben, and later the role was taken over by Jason Johnson. Wright, who played a cranky businessman in the pilot film, is the Ben Weaver who played the Scrooge role in the only Mayberry Christmas episode. Johnson is best remembered for the episode in which Barney attempts to capture a shoplifter in the department store by disguising himself as a dummy.

Sometimes the inconsistencies can be observed only by the highly trained eye. When Otis Campbell got his first automobile, for example, its license number was AY321, the same license number that later appeared on Aunt Bee's first car. That sounds like something for Sheriff Taylor to look into.

The show sometimes used character actors in more than one role, and for those in the audience who recognize this, the effect is rather remarkable. The woman who played the formidable character of Big Maud, one of the three escaped women convicts who hold Barney and Floyd captives in O'Malley's cabin, appeared in a later episode as Barney's voice teacher, Miss Poultice. Her claim to fame is that she trained Leonard Blush. Another of the escaped convicts, played by the deep-voiced Jean Carson, reappears in later episodes as Daphne, one of the "fun girls" from Mt. Pilot. With the reruns showing daily, such inconsistences show up more dramatically than they did when the show was being aired over a period of eight years. One does not want to think that either Miss Poultice or Daphne had a police record. Even Howard Morris appeared in two roles, as Ernest T. Bass, of course, but also once as a television repairman. And Jack Dodson played an insurance salesman named Ed Jenkins before he established his role as Howard Sprague, the county clerk.

An unusual piece of trivia was supplied to me by Paul

Gereffi of Fort Lauderdale, Florida. He observed that within a thirty-mile radius of Andy's birthplace in Mt. Airy, North Carolina, are the following towns: Lawsonville, Walkertown, Crumpler, and Taylorsville. The names of such characters as Floyd Lawson, Ellie Walker, Helen Crump, and Andy Taylor all naturally come to mind. Is this simply coincidence? More likely, when Andy was reaching back in his mind during the script sessions, these names, which he remembered from his childhood, seemed appropriate for characters who were to be rooted in the fictional history of a North Carolina town.

There are probably few who can recall that the full name of Ernest T. Bass' girlfriend is Ramona Ancrum (he called her "Romeena") and that she was played by Jackie Joseph. He met Ramona in the episode called "My Fair Ernest T. Bass," in which he attended a party at the home of stuffy Mrs. Wiley (played by Doris Packer). During a conversation between Barney and Andy we discover that Ramona's grandfather burned down most of the town of Mayberry in the 1880s and then decided to go into the charcoal business. Trivia of this sort actually helps to flesh out the fascinating history of the town and its people.

The list of trivia is seemingly endless and has a compelling interest for thousands of fans—Barney wears a 7½B shoe; actor Skeets Gallagher was his boyhood idol; he likes his coffee with three lumps of sugar and a little cream; he attended (along with Andy and Thelma Lou) Mayberry Union High, where he was a member of the Spanish Club; he once lived in Mendelbright Park Apartments where he paid six dollars a week, could not cook in his room, and could not use a light bulb of more than forty watts; his favorite place to neck with Thelma Lou is down at the duck pond; and he is accustomed to eating a candy bar for a late afternoon pick-me-up.

One reason why so much of the so-called trivia (some details are more trivial than others) is memorable has to do with the engaging manner in which it is presented. For

example, the following dialogue not only answers the
question, What did Barney buy for his parents on their
anniversary, but also asserts Barney's good-hearted naivete
and his grotesque sense of decorum:

Barney: The last big buy I made was my Mom's and Dad's an-
niversary present.
Andy: What'd ya get 'em?
Barney: A septic tank.
Andy: For their anniversary?
Barney: They're awfully hard to buy for. Besides, it was some-
thing they can use. They were really thrilled. It had two tons
of concrete in it. All steel reinforced.
Andy: You're a fine son, Barn.
Barney: I try.

As Jim Clark says, "After you've seen the shows ten
times, you become sort of obsessed with the details." Perhaps it would be more accurate to say that when one is
obsessed with the show, the details become an almost natural part of one's thinking. *The Andy Griffith Show* is one of
the few television series that has created in its viewers such
a widespread preoccupation with detail. One may, of
course, treat trivia as a mere game, an exercise in memory,
but the question remains why so many people like to recall
the seemingly insignificant details of this show. Perhaps it
is for the same reason that people enjoy remembering details of their happy pasts: the sweet syrup in the little wax
jugs at the candy store, the colored dots of sugared candy
on long strips of paper, the first day of school, a day at the
lake, or the visits to the neighborhood restaurant. The recent motion picture called *Diner* was a success largely because it captured those early feelings and dwelled on them
at length. A group of boys, verging on manhood, sit
around in a diner in Baltimore shooting the breeze, bragging, teasing, arguing, laughing, and sometimes worrying
about their futures, but mostly just talking. The real subject of that film is what it was like to "hang out." That is

what the people in Mayberry do better than anyone else in television—they hang out—though on a front porch or in the courthouse more frequently than in a diner.

A knowledge of trivia seems to assume an obsession with and a love for the material from which it derives. If people did not care about Barney, Ernest T., Andy, and the other characters, then the trivia would be irrelevant. Trivia need not be trivial. Surely there is as much reason to know that the writer for the show has Ben Weaver misspeak himself when he says he sells spirits at his store (Mayberry is dry) as there is to know that John Keats errs in one of his sonnets when he attributes the discovery of the Pacific Ocean to Cortez instead of to Balboa. The scholarly habit of mind has begun to fall upon Mayberry and its people and, so long as this habit does not emulate the absurdities of pedantic scholarship, it does not seem a bad one to acquire. As Jim Clark wisely says, "We're serious about watching *The Andy Griffith Show*, but we try not to take ourselves too seriously." That is a sound approach to the study of comedy.

Late-night watchers of television may have noticed that the finer details of *The Andy Griffith Show* have not been lost on the satirists and impersonators. *Second City Television* parodied the show, with Eugene Levy performing a near flawless imitation of Floyd. And when Ron Howard was the guest host of *Saturday Night Live*, the cast put on a skit in which Opie returned to Mayberry. Floyd's barbershop has become a bizarre sex parlor containing life-sized, inflated plastic figures of women. Floyd is played as a gay barber by Eddie Murphy, the black comedian. It should be noted that the episode of *The Andy Griffith Show*, "Floyd, the Gay Deceiver," has no connection with Murphy's impersonation. Even Andy Griffith "appeared" on this show (his head inserted at the top of the screen as he talks to Opie from the past). Surely this skit proves once and for all that you can't go home again. Finally, on the *Late Night* show, host David Letterman, on a whim, wanted to know the name of the actor who played Floyd. Sad to say, no one in the audience knew, and he had to wait until the next night to get an answer. Floyd has become something of an institution recently, despite Letterman's ignorance. A testimony to this fact is that Harvard University, America's oldest and most prestigious school, has a snack bar at Cabot House called "Floyd's Grill." Managed by my nephew, David Garza, and his associate, Andy Collins, both Harvard undergraduates, the grill serves either a "Floyd Frank" or a "Floyd Frank with Cheese." And that may be the last word in trivia.

PART 4

Viacom

(Preceding page)
Andy Griffith and Producer Aaron Ruben review a script.

CHAPTER 11

The Script: "The Sermon for Today"

Sermons may be found in stones, as Shakespeare says, but those found in Mayberry are a bit more outspoken. At least that is the conclusion one comes to after seeing "The Sermon for Today," a hilarious episode written by John Whedon, originally aired on October 21, 1963. Besides featuring the Reverend Breen's ironic sermon, "What's Your Hurry?" the script itself is a sermon of sorts, one that sets down the fundamental values of *The Andy Griffith Show*.

The reprinting of this script allows the reader to see for himself exactly what the actors, directors, and cameramen had to work with. Like a play script, a television script is broken into acts. In this case, there are two acts and a tag. After acts one and two General Foods inserted commercial breaks. Each episode has such a tag, a final brief segment in which the story line is resolved.

The narrative portions of the script, or stage directions, are there to help both the director and the actors in establishing appropriate physical details for each scene. This particular script is especially rich in this respect. Because the camera can provide close-ups of the actors' faces—something impossible to see in most stage productions—the directions are sometimes very precise. For example, in the scene at church, the writer carefully orchestrates a number of small gestures, such as Andy and Aunt Bee slapping at a bothersome fly, Barney being caught in the midst of a yawn, and Aunt Bee removing a piece of lint from Andy's lapel.

The numbers in the left margin of the script indicate changes in camera positions or angles. There were twenty-three different camera shots planned for act one; four were omitted after the first draft of the script was revised. There were only four camera shots in act two and one in the tag. Every time there was a change of scene, the camera had to be repositioned and refocused. Even though there is only one set for the church scene, there had to be several different shots to present the interaction among the congregation and between the congregation and the Reverend Breen. There is a quiet visual drama that begins with the shot of the church billboard. The camera then moves to the interior of the church and focuses upon the front pew containing Barney, Andy, Opie, Aunt Bee, and Clara. Next it shifts to a medium shot of the pew across the aisle, then to a close-up of Aunt Bee smiling in response to the welcome nod of her neighbor. As Reverend Tucker introduces Reverend Breen, the focus again moves rapidly between the minister and the congregation, with the close-ups of yawning faces and nodding heads reinforcing the comic gap between Reverend Breen's message to slow down and the congregation that is already slowed down to the point of sleep.

There are three basic camera shots used in this production: the close-up, the medium, and the long shot. The two shot, as its name suggest, is a close-up of two characters. It is used to emphasize a physical relationship between two characters, a relationship that might be lost in a medium shot. Thus in shots #15 and #17 we see the quiet exchanges between Aunt Bee and Andy and Andy and Barney as the characters nod to each other and Andy "catches" Barney's contagious yawn. The long shot (#21) over the congregation to the preacher is a fitting visual conclusion to the church scene, since it embraces the entire group and yet focuses upon the Reverend Breen, whose presence and sermon ironically set the town off in a burst of activity.

The fact that there are more than four times as many camera shots in act one as there are in act two suggests what is happening in the script itself. In act one the writer is busily establishing a relationship between the visiting minister and the residents of Mayberry. Consequently, the viewer needs not only to hear the dialogue but to see the psychological reaction of the congregation to the sermon. In Barney's yawn and Gomer's nodding head we see clearly that the Reverend Breen's sermon, while appropriate to his New York parishioners, is comically unsuited to Mayberrians. In act two, the writer shows the town in action as it attempts to put on an old-fashioned band concert in order to recapture "the joy and serenity of just sitting and listening." In their eagerness to arrange the concert, the townspeople manage to rush and scramble about, argue, yell, and in general, turn the peace and quiet they previously enjoyed into a chaotic din. Since the focus in act two is upon the whole town, there is no need for the number of camera shots used in act one. Instead, we simply see a few representative group scenes—the ladies working on the uniforms, the men building the bandstand, and the band practicing "The Skater's Waltz." There is one camera shot for each of the three groups, plus one quick shot of Andy entering his house with a sewing machine. In act one it is as if we are watching the winding of a top; in act two we see it spinning down; and in the tag we see it resting on its rim—pooped out. It requires more camera shots to establish the tension than it does to release it.

The terms "fade in" and "dissolve to" appear at several points in the script. In the opening of the episode there is a fade in to a shot of the exterior of Andy's front porch. This simply means that the image of the porch gradually becomes visible on the screen instead of appearing abruptly. After Andy and Aunt Bee get ready to head to church, there is a dissolve to the exterior of the church.

This process is similar to a fade in, except that it is used to shift scenes. The picture of Andy and Aunt Bee fades out while the scene of the church appears behind it and grows clearer as the first dims.

The actors were committed to follow the words of the script very closely. Sometimes the writer provided small interpretative cues to help them with their lines. Opie is to look and sound "startled," for example, when he asks if Little Orphan Annie is forty-two years old, and Andy is to sound weary when he asks Aunt Bee, "Can we go now?" The writer hears a tone of voice in his lines that he communicates to the actors by words and phrases such as "reminiscing," "inspired now," "disgruntled," "impatiently," "hesitant," and "testy." On the other hand, all of the actors had ample time to rehearse their lines and work out questions of delivery well in advance of the actual filming, so these cues are not definitive.

The director used the narrative directions as a visual aid in arranging each scene. He had to get the right people in the right places for the cameraman and see to it that the lighting was proper and the lines were spoken to his satisfaction. His main concern was with the physical placement of the actors in each scene, and so he depended upon the script much as a military commander would depend upon a map to guide his soldiers into battle. Furthermore, he had to flesh out the skeleton of the script with physical details of setting, dress, and props—to place the words into a believable, physical world, a world that is only vaguely suggested by the script.

"The Sermon for Today" is an important script in the development of *The Andy Griffith Show* because it firmly establishes the tempo of life in Mayberry. It accomplishes this by the clever use of an outsider—the visiting preacher from New York—who, by misunderstanding what life in Mayberry is really like, temporarily destroys its peaceful and harmonious atmosphere. The scene on Andy's front porch, in which Andy and Barney drowsily debate who should go to the drugstore to buy the ice cream, is not only an excellent piece of comedy, but it demonstrates that in Mayberry time is not very important. This is a world where clocks move slowly and residents do not constantly attend to their wrist watches. The ritual of relaxing after dinner is a vital part of the good life.

It is interesting to note that Aunt Bee is the instigator of all the turmoil in this drama. Andy and Barney, their stomachs full and their minds dreaming, simply recall with nostalgia the old band concerts that Reverend Breen talked about. It is Aunt Bee who argues for actually trying to get such a concert put on again. She tells Andy, "I bet you could do it if you put your mind to it." Everything goes downhill after that.

And so we witness the wonderful comic irony of the script unfold. The quiet contentment seen on Andy's front porch is quickly replaced by the noise of construction and arguments and poorly played musical instruments. The exchange between Barney and Gomer is especially well written. After repeatedly reassuring Gomer that there are no spiders under the old bandstand, Barney loses his patience and screams, "Gomer, get down there with them spiders and start workin'!" In the tag we see Gomer was right. He looks at his hand and says, "Spider bite!"

The tag is important because it shows us that life in Mayberry has returned to its usual slow-paced tempo. The only difference is that everyone is sitting quietly because he or she is exhausted. As Gomer says to Reverend Breen, "We ain't relaxed. As a matter of fact, we're pooped." The script ends with a final touch of irony as the Reverend Breen announces that he has to "rush back to New York," to which Andy rejoins, "What's your hurry?" And thus the visitor leaves without having permanently scarred the fundamental serenity and village character of Mayberry. Mayberrians may be aroused and altered for a time, but their essential natures never change. It is that reassuring assumption upon which most of the episodes of the entire series of The Andy Griffith Show happily rest.

The following script of "The Sermon for Today" comes

from Andy Griffith's personal collection. Since it is a working script, I have revised some of the printed dialogue to
make it reflect what the actors actually spoke in the final
filmed version.

THE
ANDY GRIFFITH SHOW
"THE SERMON FOR TODAY"
#5-D (100)

Written by John Whedon
Directed by Dick Crenna
Produced by Aaron Ruben

MAYBERRY ENTERPRISES
846 No. Cahuenga Blvd.
Hollywood 38, Calif.

Revised
August 9, 1963

THE ANDY GRIFFITH SHOW

Subtitle: "The Sermon for Today"

CAST

ANDY TAYLOR .... ANDY GRIFFITH

OPIE TAYLOR .... RONNY HOWARD

BARNEY FIFE .... DON KNOTTS

AUNT BEE .... FRANCES BAVIER

GOMER PYLE .... JIM NABORS

CLARA .... HOPE SUMMERS

GUEST STARS: DAVID LEWIS, FORREST LEWIS, WILLIAM KEENE, ROY ENGEL, AND JOE HAMILTON

THE ANDY GRIFFITH SHOW
Subtitle: "The Sermon for Today" #100

FADE IN:

1 EXT. ANDY'S FRONT PORCH – DAY   1

OPIE lies on his stomach, listening to Andy reading Sunday comics aloud. Andy wears an open shirt and his Sunday trousers. Opie is still in his pajamas and bathrobe.

ANDY: And Orphan Annie she says: "Jumpin' Jehosaphat. The crooks are headin' for that nice Mr. Deacon's ranch!! . . . We better go tell the Chief of Police!! . . ." And Sandy, her dog, says "Arf."

OPIE: What?

ANDY: "Arf" . . . You know, when he agrees with her he says "Arf."

OPIE: Oh . . . Paw, how old is Little Orphan Annie?

ANDY: Oh, about forty-two, forty-three, I reckon.

OPIE (*startled*): Little Orphan Annie??

ANDY: No, the comic strip's that old. Little Orphan Annie's about your age, I guess. (continues to read) So anyway, the dog Sandy says "Arf" and . . .

AUNT BEE sticks her head out the door.

AUNT BEE: Opie! You should be getting dressed. And Andy . . . you're not going to sit there reading the paper. We should get started.

ANDY: Aunt Bee, preachin' don't begin till eleven o'clock.

AUNT BEE: But we want to get a good seat. And it's bound to be crowded with that visiting preacher.

ANDY: Just 'cause he's from New York?

AUNT BEE: It's because he's famous, and everybody's read his book.

ANDY: I ain't.

AUNT BEE: Well, you. All you read . . .

ANDY: Aunt Bee, I hold with Reverend Tucker. He's good enough for me.

AUNT BEE: Andy . . .

ANDY: We been takin' from Reverend Tucker a

(CONTINUED)

1   (CONTINUED)   1

good many years now, and I ain't about to change.
AUNT BEE: Andy, they're on the *same side.* Reverend Tucker invited him. And he wants a big turn-
out so we'll make a good impression. Opie, go get
dressed now.

Opie obeys.

AUNT BEE (*continuing*): —Andy . . . You, too.
ANDY: All right.

With resignation, he drags himself up.

AUNT BEE: I'll tell Clara we'll pick her up. I want
to find out what she's going to wear.
ANDY: Now you know what she's going to wear.
AUNT BEE (*crossing to door*): I know, but I want to
find out if she's going to wear it.

*Andy considers the logic of this, finds none. Aunt Bee shoos
him into the house.*

QUICK DISSOLVE TO:

2   INT. LIVING ROOM – DAY   2

*Aunt Bee is on the telephone. She is dressed for church and
wears a hat and pearl earrings, and carries gloves. Andy is
coming down the stairs, wearing his Sunday suit.*

AUNT BEE (*into phone*): . . . She didn't . . . But how
could she deny it? Everyone knows she's been
henna-rinsing for years . . . Oh, natural red-head
my foot. Why, she's been rinsing so long her *tem-
ples* are henna-colored.
ANDY: Aunt Bee . . . You still on with Clara?

Opie comes down the stairs. He, too, is all slicked up.

AUNT BEE (*into phone*): Let's see, what was it I
called you about? Oh yes . . . We're going to
church and we'll pick you up. By the way, Clara,
what are you going to be wearing?
ANDY: Come on Aunt Bee . . .
AUNT BEE (*into phone*): Clara, what do you think
about earrings? Do you think they're too much?

(CONTINUED)

2   (CONTINUED)   2

ANDY: Come on Aunt Bee.
AUNT BEE (*ignoring him*): Of course, it *is* Sunday.
But this preacher's from New York.
ANDY: Come on, Aunt Bee.
AUNT BEE (*into phone*): Well I haven't been there
either, but I always *imagine* them with earrings.
ANDY: Aunt Bee, let's go.
AUNT BEE (*into phone*): Well, I don't want to wear
them if you're not going to wear them.
ANDY: Me and Opie ain't wearin' any.
AUNT BEE (*into phone*): Well, what do *you* think? I
know Reverend Tucker wants us to make a good
impression.
ANDY: Play it safe and just wear one.
AUNT BEE (*into phone*): You're right. And if we see
the others don't, we'll go behind the bushes and
take them off. Now what about perfume?
ANDY: Aunt Bee! You can talk it over at church—if
you ever get there!
AUNT BEE (*into phone*): Excuse me, Clara. Andy's
shouting at me.

She turns to Andy.

ANDY: I'm goin' to preachin'. You coming?
AUNT BEE (*into phone*): I have to go, Clara. Call me
later in the week, Clara. Oh, no! I'll be seeing
you. We'll be coming right over.

She puts the phone down.

ANDY (*wearily*): Can we go now?
AUNT BEE: Well, I've been sitting here waiting for
you.

DISSOLVE TO:

3   EXT. CHURCH – DAY   3

CLOSE SHOT – CHURCH BILLBOARD

*From the church come the voices of the CONGREGATION
singing a hymn, accompanied by the organ. The billboard
reads:*

(CONTINUED)

3   (CONTINUED)   3

ALL SOULS CHURCH
Rev. Hobart M. Tucker, D.D.

Sermon:
"What's Your Hurry?"

Dr. Harrison Everett Breen
of New York City

4   INT. CHURCH – DAY – CLOSE SHOT – FRONT
     PEW   4

*Barney is next to the aisle, sharing a hymnal with Andy.
Beside them in the pew are Opie, Aunt Bee, and Clara.
Behind them is Gomer. All are singing earnestly. Clara
nudges Aunt Bee and points across the aisle, without pausing in her singing. Aunt Bee turns to look.*

5   MED. SHOT – PEW ACROSS AISLE – AUNT
     BEE'S POINT OF VIEW   5

*An ACQUAINTANCE smiles and nods to Aunt Bee, and
in pantomime compliments her on her hat—without missing a word of the hymn.*

6   CLOSE SHOT – FRONT PEW   6

*Aunt Bee smiles in acknowledgment, and returns the com-
pliment. Barney is distracted by woman across aisle, loses
his place in hymnal. Andy helps him find it.*

7   OMITTED   7

8   OMITTED   8

9   OMITTED   9

10   MED SHOT – DR. TUCKER   10

*DR. TUCKER, the local minister, has crossed to the lec-
tern. He is easy-going, benign. Congregation sits.*

DR. TUCKER: We are greatly honored today. It is
     our happy privilege to welcome to our midst a
     very dear friend of mine, Dr. Harrison Everett
     Breen, of New York City.

He turns to bow to DR. BREEN, who is seated at one side

(CONTINUED)

10 (CONTINUED) 10

of the chancel. Dr. Breen nods and smiles. He is younger than Dr. Tucker, and a more forceful type.

DR. TUCKER (*continuing*): Dr. Breen has inter-rupted his vacation to join us in worship this morning and to bring us, I know, an inspiring message. Dr. Breen . . .

Dr. Breen rises and crosses to the pulpit, as Dr. Tucker withdraws.

11 CLOSE SHOT – FRONT PEW – BARNEY AND ANDY 11

Barney is about to applaud. Andy catches his hand and shakes his head.

12 MED. SHOT – DR. BREEN 12

Dr. Breen enters the pulpit, grasps it with both hands, and pauses impressively.

13 CLOSE SHOT – FRONT PEW – ANDY AND AUNT BEE 13

Andy and Aunt Bee slap at a fly that is annoying them, then settle back to give Dr. Breen their earnest attention. Aunt Bee fans herself with her program.

14 MED. SHOT – DR. BREEN 14

He waits for the throat-clearing to stop and the congrega-tion to settle down. Then he begins. His delivery is dy-namic. Every word is significant. He makes the pauses count, too.

DR. BREEN: As I stood here, during the singing of the hymn, I asked myself, "What message have I to bring to these good people of Mayberry?" And I was reminded of an incident. A young man came to me recently, and said he, "Dr. Breen . . . what is the meaning of it all?" And I said to him, "Young man . . . I'm glad you asked!"

15 TWO SHOT – AUNT BEE AND ANDY 15

They turn to each other and nod. Aunt Bee notices a bit of

(CONTINUED)

15   (CONTINUED)   15

lint on Andy's lapel and picks it off, then turns back to give her attention to Dr. Breen. During this:

DR. BREEN (*over congregation*): My friends, I wish more of us found the time to ask that question!

16   MED. SHOT – DR. BREEN   16

DR. BREEN: Whither? Whither are we headed? And why? Why this senseless rush, this mad pursuit, this frantic competition, this pace that kills? Why do we drive ourselves as we do?

17   TWO SHOT – ANDY AND BARNEY   17

Andy turns to Barney and nods emphatically. Barney is caught in the midst of a yawn, but he stifles it and nods in agreement. Andy frowns, but the yawn is contagious, and he struggles with it himself. This bounces it back to Barney, who lets go with a real jaw-stretcher. Andy frowns again and shakes his head. Barney pantomimes his innocence. Through all this the voice of Dr. Breen continues:

DR. BREEN (*over congregation*): In our furious race these days to conquer outer space, are we not, perhaps, neglecting inner space? Shall we hope to find the secret of the universe by hurtling through it? Shall we find the true meaning of life by fleeing from it?

18   CLOSE SHOT – GOMER   18

Gomer is sound asleep. He lets out a loud snore. Opie turns around to look. The man next to Gomer, whose head has been nodding too, snaps it up. He jabs Gomer with his elbow. Gomer comes to with a start and almost falls out of his seat. Through this the voice of Dr. Breen continues without interruption:

DR. BREEN (*over shoulder*): Consider how we live our lives today. Everything is "run, run, run!" We bolt our breakfast, we scan the headlines, we race to the office. The full schedule and the split second—these are the gauges of success. We *drive ourselves* from morn to night.

(CONTINUED)

19   MED. SHOT – DR. BREEN   19

DR. BREEN: My friends, we've forgotten the meaning of the word, "Relaxation!"

*He pauses to survey the congregation, and slows down his
tempo. His delivery becomes soothing and mellifluous.*

DR. BREEN: What has become of the old-fashioned
ways . . . the simple pleasures of the past? Who
can forget, for example, the old-fashioned band
concert at twilight on the village green? The joy
and serenity of just sitting and listening?

20   OMITTED   20

21   LONG SHOT – SHOOTING OVER CONGREGA-
TION TO PREACHER   21

*Andy folds his arms and leans back reminiscently, with his
eyes on the ceiling. Barney's head is nodding.*

DR. BREEN: This is lost to us today, and this we
should strive to recapture. A simple, innocent
pleasure. And so I say to you dear friends: "Relax, slow down, take it easy. What's your hurry?
What, indeed, friends, is your hurry? . . ."

DISSOLVE TO:

22   EXT. CHURCH – DAY   22

*Inside, the organ is still playing the recessional. Dr. Tucker
stands at the door, with Dr. Breen, greeting the parishioners as they come out. Aunt Bee, Clara, Opie, and Barney exit church. Gomer leads Opie off.*

AUNT BEE: A lovely service, Dr. Tucker. Just lovely.
(turns to Breen) And I thought the sermon was
magnificent.
CLARA: Simply magnificent.
DR. BREEN: Well, thank you.
DR. TUCKER: Dr. Breen, may I introduce Sheriff
Taylor . . . his aunt, Miss Bee . . . Mrs. Johnson
and Deputy Fife.

They ad lib greetings and shake hands.

(CONTINUED)

22   (CONTINUED)   22

AUNT BEE: Oh, Dr. Breen, your sermon has such a
wonderful lesson for us.
ANDY: Yes, sir, you really hit the nail right on the
head there.
BARNEY: Yes, sir, that's one subject you just can't
talk enough about . . . SIN.

They all look at him. Barney shifts uneasily.

DR. BREEN: Well, thank you.
AUNT BEE: Will you be around long? We'd be very
honored to have you come to dinner.
DR. BREEN: I wish I could but I did promise to
drive over to Mt. Pilot this afternoon to preach a
service. But on my way back this evening, I'll stop
and have coffee with you, if I may.
AUNT BEE: Oh, we do hope you will.
ANDY: Oh, that'd be mighty nice. We'll look forward to seeing you.
DR. BREEN: Bye.

*Ad lib goodbyes. They start out. Bee and Clara comment
about Dr. Breen to themselves. As Andy and Barney pass
Camera:*

ANDY: Talk about sin!
BARNEY: Huh?

They exit shot.

                                      DISSOLVE TO:

23   EXT. ANDY'S FRONT PORCH – DAY   23

Andy and Barney seated in rocking chairs.

BARNEY: Man, we really packed it away, didn't we?
ANDY: Yeah, boy.
BARNEY (*pats tummy*): Fortunately, none of mine
goes to fat. All goes to muscle.
ANDY: Does, huh?
BARNEY: It's a mark of us Fifes. Everything we eat
goes to muscle. (*pats tummy*) See there?
ANDY: I see.

                                      (CONTINUED)

BARNEY: My mother was the same way. She could
  eat and eat and eat . . .
ANDY: Never went to fat . . .
BARNEY (*nods*): Know where it went?
ANDY: Muscle?

Barney nods.

BARNEY: It was a mark of us Fifes . . .
ANDY: You know what I believe I'll do? Run down
  to the drugstore and get some ice cream for later.
BARNEY: You want me to go? I'll go.
ANDY: No, I'll go.
BARNEY: I don't mind going.
ANDY: I don't either. I can go.
BARNEY: You're probably tired . . . Why don't you
  let me go?
ANDY: No, I'm not tired. I'll go.
BARNEY: I sure don't mind going.
ANDY: Why don't we both just go?
BARNEY: Okay.
ANDY: You ready?
BARNEY: Uh huh.

Now both rise slowly.

BARNEY (*continuing*): Where we goin'?
ANDY: Down to the drugstore to get some ice
  cream for later.

Aunt Bee comes out on porch.

AUNT BEE: Andy, where you boys going?
ANDY: We thought we'd run down to the drugstore
  to get some ice cream for later.
AUNT BEE: Well, why do you want to run to the
  drugstore, as if it can't wait . . .
ANDY: Huh?
AUNT BEE: That's exactly what the preacher was
  talking about this morning. Seems as if nothing
  can wait. Everything is rush rush rush!

Both sit down.

(CONTINUED)

GOMER (*over shoulder*): Hey Andy!

Andy spies Gomer over shoulder.

ANDY: Hey Gomer! Where are you headed?

Now Gomer comes up on porch, his jacket slung over his shoulder.

GOMER: Oh, I just thought I'd run over to Cousin Goober's and watch him wash his car.

AUNT BEE: See? There's another example. Run run run. Exactly what Dr. Breen was talking about this morning. People just don't know how to relax.

ANDY: She's right, you know that?

BARNEY: Yeah.

ANDY: Sit down, Gomer!

GOMER: Crazy. I guess I just wasn't thinking.

ANDY: 'Member when we used to have them band concerts Dr. Breen was talkin' about?

AUNT BEE (*reminiscing*): Yes, that was relaxing, wasn't it? Sitting around on a Sunday evening listening to music . . .

ANDY: Yeah . . . I'm kind of sorry we don't have the town band anymore.

BARNEY: Sure wish we had it again.

AUNT BEE (*beat*): Andy, do you think you could?

ANDY: Could what?

AUNT BEE: Organize the band again?

ANDY: Well, I don't know.

AUNT BEE: I bet you could if you put your mind to it.

ANDY: You know, the boys might enjoy getting together again.

BARNEY: Of course they would.

AUNT BEE: Uniforms need a bit o' repairin', but I could call Clara to help me fix them up.

ANDY: I'd hafta get the boys together.

AUNT BEE: Fine.

ANDY: Well, the band stand's all busted and layin'

(CONTINUED)

23 (CONTINUED) 23

over there in the junk heap. It'll need some car-
penterin'.
GOMER: I'll lend you a hand with it.
ANDY (*inspired now*): You know the way we're
talkin', we're talkin' about gettin' up a band con-
cert by tonight.
AUNT BEE: Why not?
BARNEY: Yeah, why not? If we all pitch in,
Gomer'n me'll get started on the stand.
GOMER: I'll borrow us some tools.
AUNT BEE: I'll call Clara. We can get started on the
uniforms.
ANDY: I'll just go out to the garage and get my
horn.

*Now they are all up and buzzing with excitement over their
new project.*

AUNT BEE (*on way to the door*): Oh, we're actually
gonna have a band concert tonight.

And they scurry to their tasks in different directions, as we,

FADE OUT.

END OF ACT ONE

ACT TWO

FADE IN:

24 EXT. AREA BEHIND SHERIFF'S OFFICE – DAY 24

*The bandstand is a smallish platform, big enough to ac-
commodate about six musicians. Andy is sawing a two-by-
four. Barney walks into scene carrying a large poster. Andy
wipes brow.*

BARNEY: Bandstand's gonna be a lot more work
than we thought, huh?
ANDY: Yeah, but if we stick with it, we can get 'er
done. Then we'll just haul 'er over to the
square . . . Whatcha got?

(CONTINUED)

24   (CONTINUED)   24

> BARNEY: Poster I made to put on the back of the
> squad car. You know—let folks know.

Andy turns poster around and reads:

> "CONCERT TONIGHT –
>
> RELAX TO
>
> MUSIC UNDER THE STARS."

> BARNEY: Ya like that? I made it up.
> ANDY: Good . . . (*looks up at sky*) Might be cloudin'
> up, though.
> BARNEY: Well . . . I could change it to "Music Un-
> der the Clouds"?

Andy shakes his head.

> BARNEY (*continuing*): "Music Under the Sky"?
> ANDY: It's outdoors . . . That's obvious.
> BARNEY: How about I just leave that part out alto-
> gether?
> ANDY: Well, what have ya got left here: "Concert
> Tonight Relax To"?
> BARNEY: How about just "Concert Tonight"?
> ANDY: When they hear the music, they'll know it's a
> concert.
> BARNEY: And they'll know it's tonight too, right?
> ANDY: Right.
> BARNEY: Forget the poster, huh?
> ANDY: I would.

Now Gomer comes into scene carrying hammer and saw.

> ANDY (*continuing*): You get Goober?
> GOMER: Goober wouldn't come, but he borrowed
> us these tools. Only thing is I'm the only one can
> use 'em. He don't want strangers usin' 'em. Only a
> relative.
> BARNEY (*rolls eyes*): Oh, brother.
> GOMER: No . . . it don't hafta be. Can be a cousin
> like me.
> BARNEY: I meant—oh, skip it.

                                              (CONTINUED)

24   (CONTINUED)   24

ANDY: Why wouldn't Goober come? He still
washin' his car?

GOMER (*nods*): I begged him but him and his maw
are goin' vistin', and he said he wouldn't put his
mother in a dirty car.

ANDY (*shakes his head*): Just like Dr. Breen said—
everything's rush, rush, rush, rush.

GOMER: Goober says hey, though.

ANDY (*disgruntled*): Hey to Goober . . . Come on,
grab hold. Lend us a hand.

GOMER: Grab hold o' what?

Andy crosses to the bandstand.

ANDY: Well, we've got to prop up those timbers,
and get that sag out o' the middle.

BARNEY: Yeah, if she's goin' to go, that's where
she's goin' to go.

ANDY: Have to crawl in under there somehow and
heave up on those timbers, so's to wedge this in.

He indicates the two-by-four he has cut.

BARNEY: Why don't we use a jack. We got one in
the car.

ANDY: Barn! That's an inspiration! Here, I've got
to go see how Aunt Bee's comin' with the uniforms. I promised I'd get her another sewing machine. Take charge here.

*Andy departs, and Barney takes over. He folds his arms
and leans against the bandstand, prepared to supervise.*

BARNEY: Okay, Gomer, you heard what Andy said.
I'm in charge. Let's get cuttin' here . . . You crawl
in under there, and I'll go get the jack.

*Gomer squats down and peers dubiously under the band-
stand.*

GOMER: Damp under there. Could be spiders.

BARNEY (*impatiently*): Now what makes you think
there's spiders under there?

(CONTINUED)

24   (CONTINUED)   24

> GOMER: Cause . . . if I was a spider, that's where
> I'd go.
> BARNEY: Gomer, there are no spiders under there.
> Now let's get movin'.
> GOMER (*hesitant*): I don't know. Sure looks spidery
> to me.
> BARNEY: There are no spiders under there. Now
> will ya stop worryin'?
> GOMER: But, Barney, if I crawl under there . . .
> BARNEY: Look . . . Are we gonna do this or ain't
> we? We all agreed we wanted to have a band con-
> cert tonight. Well, it ain't gonna happen if you
> just stand around. Now let's get moving.
> GOMER: But, Barney, I'm sure that . . .
> BARNEY: Gomer, get down there with them spiders
> and start workin'!

QUICK DISSOLVE TO:

25   EXT. ANDY'S PORCH – DAY   25

Andy enters to go into house. He carries a portable sewing machine.

CUT TO:

26   INT. ANDY'S LIVING ROOM – DAY   26

Aunt Bee and Clara are busily and noisily engaged in fitting uniform on a model. They part as Andy enters and we see they have been covering Opie, who stands on a footstool acting as a model. Opie wears a jacket that reaches to his ankles, also a cap that covers his eyes.

> ANDY: Somebody I know under there?

He lifts cap off Opie's eyes.

> OPIE (*wearily*): Paw, can I go now? I'm tired of bein'
> a tailor's dummy.
> AUNT BEE: In a little while . . . Land sakes, don't
> be so impatient.
> ANDY: Got ya another machine over at Louise Pal-
> mer's.

(CONTINUED)

26 (CONTINUED) 26

AUNT BEE: Well, I hope it'll do some good.
ANDY: Whatsa matter?
AUNT BEE: These uniforms are in terrible shape. But we'll do the best we can.
ANDY: You need me for anythin' else, Aunt Bee? I got to get on with band rehearsal.
AUNT BEE: No, you run along.
ANDY: Call me if ya need anything.

He exits. Clara comes to her.

CLARA: Bee, I think we're going to have to restitch every one of those seams. Cheap thread, that's what it is.

Clara holds up jacket.

CLARA (*continuing*): And will you look at that: mildew. You can't expect me to do anything about mildew.
AUNT BEE (*testy*): Well, don't blame me for it. It's not my fault these uniforms are in such bad condition. I didn't store them, you know.
CLARA: Well, neither did I, Bee.
AUNT BEE: I didn't say you did . . . But we aren't going to get any work done if we stand around arguing like this.
CLARA: We *have* been working, Bee. We just can't perform miracles.
OPIE: Can I go now, Aunt Bee?
AUNT BEE (*turning on him*): No you cannot! Now just hold still!

And they fall to work again.

QUICK DISSOLVE TO:

27 INT. COURTHOUSE – DAY 27

Andy in front of desk playing tuba faces four musicians seated in front of music stands. They are just finishing "The Skater's Waltz," which is hardly recognizable. At finish Andy sighs.

ANDY: I knew we was outa practice, but I didn't

(CONTINUED)

know we was *that* much outa practice. (*to saxophon-ist*) Luther, you're a little late now and then.

LUTHER (*cups hand*): What say?

ANDY (*louder*): I say you're late . . . you're draggin'.

LUTHER: Sounded real good to me, too.

ANDY: No . . . it was off, way off.

LUTHER (*hand to ear*): How's that?

ANDY: It was off. Boys, we just got to get with it. Let's take "The Skater's Waltz" once more. And let's do it better this time.

LUTHER: What'd ya say, Andy?

ANDY (*patiently, louder*): I say let's do it again, and do it better . . .

LUTHER: Sounded real good to me.

ANDY: Ready? One, two . . .

They play. It sounds horrible. Andy stops. He waves his hands to stop the others. Intent on their music, and unable to hear him, they keep right on.

ANDY (*continuing*): Hold it! . . . Whoa! . . . Fellers!

All stop except saxophonist, who blissfully plays on.

ANDY (*continuing; shouts*): Luther! Hold it! Hold it!

Luther stops, looks around.

LUTHER: What'd ya say, Andy? What'd ya stop us for? We was goin' real good that time.

ANDY: We got the spirit all right. We just got to get together on the tune.

CLARINETIST: I'm together. It's him.

He points to the trombonist.

TROMBONIST (*indignantly*): Don't tell me! I'm playing what's wrote here. Look at the notes!

CLARINETIST: You read 'em. You're the one that's missin' 'em.

TROMBONIST: Don't tell me!

Ad lib argument. During this Aunt Bee and Clara enter arguing as they come in. Aunt Bee holds the torn, mil-dewed jacket.

(CONTINUED)

27   (CONTINUED)   27

CLARA: Bee, I told you before we started, we
   couldn't do it.
AUNT BEE: I know what you told me, Clara. But it
   didn't hurt to try, did it?
CLARA: If you ask me, it was just a waste of time.
AUNT BEE: Well, I don't think so.
ANDY: Wait a minute, ladies, wait a minute. Whatsa
   matter?
AUNT BEE: Oh, it's no use, Andy. These uniforms
   are just too far gone. Look at this. (*holds up jacket*)
   And the others are even worse.
CLARA: I told you it was a waste of time.
AUNT BEE: Yes, I know you said that, Clara. (*to
   Andy*) We worked and worked, but we just
   couldn't do it.
ANDY: That's a shame, boys . . . looks like no uni-
   forms.
TROMBONIST: Well, I wished I'd a known, Andy.
   I sure can't play without a uniform.
CLARINETIST: You sure can't play *with* one.
TROMBONIST: That supposed to be funny?

*Ad lib argument. During it, Barney and Gomer enter,
quarreling.*

GOMER: Wasn't my fault. It was you and your jack.
BARNEY: Oh, pipe down, Gomer. Just pipe down!

*The others have stopped their argument and now turn to
Barney and Gomer.*

ANDY: Don't tell me you got bad news, too.
BARNEY: Well, it's about the bandstand.
ANDY: What about it?
BARNEY: You tell him. You did it.
GOMER: I didn't do nothin'.
BARNEY: You and Goober's hammer.
GOMER: You and your jack! I told you I heard
   somethin' give.

Ad lib argument between them.

ANDY: Wait . . . Hold it! What happened?

                                    (CONTINUED)

27   (CONTINUED)   27

GOMER: Well, we was under there, see, and you know how dark it is. Spiders and all . . .

BARNEY (*to Andy*): I don't know what he hit, but it musta' been holdin' up the whole shebang.

GOMER: I didn't go to hit nothin'! Just took a whack at a spider. I told ya there was spiders under there.

BARNEY: Anyways, she begun to creak and rumble . . . and (*makes crashing sound*)

ANDY (*appalled*): The *whole* thing?

Barney nods.

ANDY (*continuing; desperately*): Well, is there any chance of proppin' it up again?

GOMER: It's a whole day's work, and I'm just too pooped to start.

BARNEY: Well, I'm too pooped, I'll tell you that. I don't see how you're going to have a band concert without a bandstand.

AUNT BEE: And then, I've no uniforms.

CLARA: Oh, I knew they weren't going to have uniforms.

Now all parties fall to arguing with each other. Andy tries to stop them.

ANDY (*shouting*): Wait a minute, wait a minute! Hold it! We can still practice! Listen!

LUTHER: Practice? You ready to go again, Andy?

And Luther starts to play his saxophone to add to the din. Andy sags defeated.

FADE OUT.

END OF ACT TWO

TAG

28   EXT. ANDY'S PORCH – DAY   28

Opie lying on stomach with one arm hanging over edge of porch. Barney sits soaking feet in pail of water. Aunt Bee

(CONTINUED)

28   (CONTINUED)   28

sits exhausted fanning herself. Clara is there. Andy is
spread out on chair and rubs salve in palms of his hands.
Gomer sits on top step with head propped against porch
post. He rubs his neck.

ANDY: Well . . . nobody can say we didn't at least
    try to have a band concert.
BARNEY: Sure can't say that.

Gomer is looking at his hand.

GOMER: Spider bite! (*he looks at Barney about to say*
    something—)

At this point Dr. Breen drives into driveway, gets out,
crosses to porch.

DR. BREEN: Good evening, folks . . .

All ad lib weary greetings.

DR. BREEN (*continuing*): Well, I said I'd stop by on
    my way back and have coffee with you, but now
    I'm afraid I won't even be able to do that.
AUNT BEE: Oh—what a shame!
DR. BREEN (*surveying them*): Well, it seems as if my
    sermon this morning had some effect.
ANDY: Scuse me?
DR. BREEN: Look at you all . . . nice and relaxed. A
    picture of contentment. Yes, you all look as serene
    and relaxed as if . . . as if you just finished listen-
    ing to a pleasant band concert . . . yes.

All look at each other.

DR. BREEN (*continuing*): Good, good . . . I'm happy
    to see it. Well, if you'll all excuse me, I have to
    rush back to New York now . . . Goodbye,
    again . . .

He starts toward car. Gomer calls after him.

GOMER: Oh, Reverend, we ain't relaxed. As a mat-
    ter of fact, we're pooped . . . See, we tried to or-
    ganize a—
ANDY: Gomer!!

                                        (CONTINUED)

28   (CONTINUED)   28

Dr. Breen has stopped and taken a step back to them.

DR. BREEN: I beg your pardon?
ANDY: Oh, nothin', Reverend . . . Gomer was uh
    . . . Gomer was just sayin: "What's your hurry?"
DR. BREEN: Hm? . . . Oh . . . Yes . . . yes.

He smiles, slows his move to the car, as all wearily wave goodbye.

FADE OUT.

THE END

CHAPTER 12

An Unfilmed Script

The following script, "The Wandering Minstrel," was written by Harvey Bullock and Ray Saffian Allen for the 1962–63 season. The character of Wally Jordan is based upon a mountain man that Andy knew as a boy, an old man who would come to town and win the affection of the kids, a sort of pied piper figure. Unfortunately, due to the passage of more than twenty years, none of the people I talked to connected with the show could remember exactly why they chose not to use the script. Andy said he loved the story, but for "some reason" they never got around to using it.

Whatever the reasons may have been for not using the script, it is still a fine piece of work which is rich with the small details that were characteristic of *The Andy Griffith Show*. In the opening scene, for example, Aunt Bee is typically fussing about Andy's clothes, and Andy accepts her attentions with his usual, mildly ironic patience. We also find Andy never too busy to share a bottle of pop with an old friend, and we see yet another example of Andy's humane dispensation of the law, which, as always, is more concerned with the moral consequences than the letter of the law.

This episode is rather unique in the fact that it is Andy, not Barney, Aunt Bee, Opie or even Ernest T. Bass, who brings about the conflict that has to be resolved. But even in this new role of agitator, Andy remains true to character, for it is his heart that suggests trying to get Wally to settle down in Mayberry: "Y'know, maybe it's about time we all stopped *taking* from Wally and got around to doing a little *giving*."

This "giving," however, consists of getting a job for Wally that changes him from a happy, carefree wanderer, always with time and a lollipop for the kids, into a harried, money-conscious grouch. It is when Wally abruptly dismisses some children that Andy fully sees the mistake he has made in coercing Wally into taking the job as clerk. Andy convinces Wally that he doesn't need the job, for which he is ill-suited, in order to have the love and respect of the people of Mayberry. And once again the natural order of things is restored to Mayberry.

THE ANDY GRIFFITH SHOW

Subtitle: "The Wandering Minstrel"

FADE IN:

1   INT. JAILHOUSE–DAY   1

Opie is an interested spectator as Aunt Bee holds up a new (white) shirt in front of Andy and critically inspects to see if the size is right. A shopping bag is on the desk nearby. Andy is impatient.

ANDY: It's fine, Aunt Bee.

Aunt Bee squints her eyes to get the over-all effect.

ANDY (*cont'd.*): Seems to be my size all right.

AUNT BEE (*comes to conclusion, nods*): Yes, it's perfect. (*She starts folding up shirt to put into shopping bag*) All I have to do is shorten the sleeves, stitch the collar seams stronger, let out the pleat and take in the sides.

ANDY: That's all, eh? Uh . . . wouldn't it be easier just to get a bunch of thread and buttons and make a new one from scratch?

AUNT BEE: You want a shirt that's right when you go out with Peggy, don't you?

ANDY: Oh yes'm . . . Wouldn't be proper going out with Peggy less'n my collar seams was *good* and strong . . . they'd be talk.

AUNT BEE: I should get you another while they're on sale, but it takes forever for George to wait on you. I don't know why he doesn't get some extra help in that store.

ANDY (*gently tries to usher Aunt Bee toward door*): Yes, well—one's plenty . . . Now if you'll excuse me, I am on the busy side what with Barney off on vacation.

AUNT BEE: You're *sure* you don't want another?

ANDY (*still ushering*): No need to bother, Aunt Bee.

AUNT BEE: Man can't have *too* many white shirts . . . and the store's right on my way.

ANDY: This'll do me fine.

(CONTINUED)

1   (CONTINUED)   1

AUNT BEE (*disappointed*): Oh. (*she starts out door, stops, turns back*): Well, I believe I *will* get you another. (*now she pretends it's an afterthought*) And while I'm there I suppose I might as well pick up a couple of little house dresses, too . . . I'm down to nothing.

Andy comprehends the gambit. He nods soberly.

ANDY: While you're there, you might as well.

Aunt Bee gladdens, exits. Andy turns back amused, shaking his head.

OPIE: Pa, why are girls and ladies always so interested in clothes?

ANDY: Well, you saw that sign in George's window what says "It Pays To Look Your Best." Girls buy lots of clothes figuring it'll make 'em popular.

OPIE: Oh. (*new thought*) And does buying lots of clothes make them popular?

ANDY: Well, it sure makes them popular with George.

A boy Opie's age sticks his head in the door.

BOY: Hey, Ope, guess what—Wally Jordan's coming!

Opie reacts.

OPIE: No fooling . . . ! (*runs out door*) See you later, Pa.

Andy is amused, walks over and looks out window up the street.

QUICK DISSOLVE TO:

2   EXT. STREET SCENE–DAY   2

The residential street. Down the sidewalk strolls Wally Jordan. He wears his comfortable old clothes, his battered hat, and over his back is slung a musette bag and a vintage guitar. Here is a man without a care, without a worry,

(CONTINUED)

2   (CONTINUED)   2

*without an enemy. He lives a completely unregulated life
drifting about the countryside, and every year he makes an
appearance. To the children, it's the circus coming to town.*

*It's a Pied Piper scene. Children appear from bushes, out
of houses and from around corners. Soon he is leading a
happy jabbering entourage of children and barking dogs.
Some of the youngsters are in baseball suits, some barefoot,
some with fishing poles. Whatever they were doing they
have interrupted at the word Wally was coming. It's an occasion not only for the young. An old timer on a porch
waves at him, a man in a passing truck honks his horn and
waves. Wally returns it all and has a salutation for every
new addition to the throng.*

                                          QUICK DISSOLVE TO:

3   EXT. BENCH AREA–DAY   3

*Wally now reaches a bench. Obviously this has traditionally
been his headquarters and the children all stop in anticipa-
tion. Wally regards the bench as though he'd never seen it
before, then he goes over and carefully sits down. He lets a
sigh of pleasure escape and then he looks about at the
group. Now begins his ritual which never varies.*

WALLY: Let's see now, this here town is . . . lemme
    think . . . oh sure . . . Mudville.
GROUP: No no no.
WALLY: It's not? (*he looks around in amazement*)
    Hmmm, then . . . I know . . . it's Pokey Corners.

*Once again the delighted shout to tell him he's wrong. Now
Wally acts completely flabbergasted.*

WALLY: You *sure* it isn't Pokey Corners?

They shout affirmation.

WALLY: Then where in the world am I?
ALL: Mayberry!
WALLY: Well, I'll be, this big place? It can't be May-
    berry! But I guess it has to be 'cause there's

                                          (CONTINUED)

3   (CONTINUED)   3

Denny Sargent there . . . that new tooth ever
grow back, Denny?

*Denny Sargent, a seven-year-old, nods, shows teeth in big
grin and points to a tooth.*

WALLY (*cont'd.*): . . . And Rusty Finch, you get the
bike you wanted for your birthday?

Rusty indicates the bike he's on.

WALLY (*cont'd.*): And Snuffy Pierson . . . Snuffy, you
learned how to get to school on time yet?

The group laughs, Snuffy shakes his head.

WALLY (*cont'd.*): And there's Ginny Parker . . .
Ginny, I been wondering and wondering . . . that
black cat of yours have kittens?

GINNY: Six of 'em, just like you said.

WALLY: No! Reckon now you'll have to stop calling
her "Walter".

*The crowd laughs approval. Wally is now unlimbering his
guitar.*

WALLY (*cont'd.*): Now there's a few little things I'd
like to inquire about . . . (*strikes a chord and talks in
cadence*) First tell me something, since I been here
last—Has everyone behaved just as good as they
dast?

All nod heads.

WALLY (*cont'd.*): No one's chased a dog nor teased a
cat? . . . Or anything at all faintly resemblin' that?

All shake heads. Wally shows mock amazement.

WALLY (*cont'd.*): No one's slammed any doors, nor
took any dares? You been busy reading your lessons and saying your prayers?

He stands straight, talks proud.

WALLY (*cont'd.*): Y'all showed the flag on the Fourth
of July? (*whispers*) No one's told a whopper . . .

(CONTINUED)

3   (CONTINUED)   3

> (*softer*) . . . or a fib . . . (*softer yet*) . . . or a lie?

Group shakes its head.

WALLY (*cont'd.*): There's been no squabblin' and no sassing back? You ain't been playing on that railroad track?

Group shakes its head again.

WALLY (*cont'd.*): Well, seems you've been so good, I might as well stop and see what we got in the way of a lollipop!

There is a chorus of approval. Wally puts down guitar, fishes in musette bag and produces a handful of lollipops. Andy has approached behind, unnoticed. Wally passes out lollipops to all the children. Andy comes forward.

ANDY (*a bit formal*): Wonder if you'd come 'long with me a minute.

WALLY: What? . . . Oh, sure thing, Sheriff. (*to children*) See you later.

He and Andy walk off.

QUICK DISSOLVE TO:

4   INT. JAILHOUSE–DAY   4

Andy and Wally enter. Andy walks to his seat behind the desk and looks up at Wally appraisingly.

ANDY (*still a touch severe*): Now Wally, you remember the little talk we had last time you was in town.

Wally nods soberly.

ANDY (*cont'd.*): Anything changed since then, do you have any visible means of support?

Wally shakes his head. Andy pulls book out from rack, opens it to illustrate a point.

ANDY (*cont'd.*): Well, there are laws in this state about vagrancy . . . and it's my job to carry them out. I told you plain that if you showed up again this was bound to happen.

(CONTINUED)

4   (CONTINUED)   4

Wally nods his understanding.

ANDY: And since you give me no choice in the matter—(*picks up gavel*) As Justice of the Peace I hereby sentence you to serve five nights in the jail there. (*he indicates*) You understand?

Wally nods. Andy pounds the gavel on the desk.

ANDY (*cont'd.*): The court's adjourned.

Andy snaps the book closed, now the mood changes, he jumps to his feet and grabs Wally's hand.

ANDY (*cont'd.*): Wally, you ol' son of a gun, what kept you 'way so long?

WALLY (*indicating guitar*): It was mostly 'cause of Lila-Belle here. Now I'm just spry as ever, but she's getting kinda old and tired . . . so I had to slow down so she could keep up with me.

ANDY: Well, we're tickled to see you. Now, you probably got folks to call on, so I'll get busy and fix up the cell for whenever you're ready.

WALLY: Certainly most obliging of you, Andy.

Andy turns stern again.

ANDY: Obliging? Nothing of the sort. It's the law . . . and I'm sworn to uphold same. Plain as that—(*he points to the book on desk*) You may not realize it, but you have just been duly sentenced.

WALLY: Well, naturally, I wouldn't want to go against the law.

ANDY (*relaxing*): 'Course as you know the *real* law in this town is Aunt Bee . . . and she'd skin me alive if I didn't bring you home to dinner tonight.

WALLY: Be pleased and proud to oblige. Reckon first I'll run over and see Widow Scully . . . she still shut in with her Sciatic, I s'pose.

Andy nods. The door opens and Peggy enters.

PEGGY: Hi Andy. (*Stops as she sees Wally*) Am I interrupting?

(CONTINUED)

4   (CONTINUED)   4

ANDY: Come right in . . . just in time to meet an old
    friend . . . Miss Peggy Cartwright, this is Wally
    Jordan.
WALLY: My extreme pleasure, Miss.
PEGGY: How do you do.
WALLY (*injured tone to Andy*): How come I never met
    this lovely girl before?
ANDY: It's nobody's fault, Wally, Peggy's new here in
    town.
WALLY: (*Stage whisper to Andy*): She's the prettiest
    thing in nineteen counties. If I was you, Sheriff,
    I'd lock up this angel before she climbs on some
    pink cloud and floats right back up to heaven.

Peggy smiles, nods her appreciation.

ANDY: I see *all* the sugar you pass out ain't just in
    the lollipops.
WALLY (*laughs*): See you both later . . . oh, just one
    thing. (*He produces an envelope from his shirt pocket*)
    Wonder if I might borrow a stamp?

Andy reaches in desk drawer.

ANDY: Sure thing, one enough?
WALLY: Just fine. (*He takes stamp*) Thanks very
    much . . . see you tonight.

*Wally exits, Andy moves to window to watch Wally cross
street.*

ANDY: That Wally is really something.
PEGGY: What does he do?
ANDY: Oh, little bit of everything, not much of any-
    thing. Mostly just travels around.
PEGGY: But he must have some kind of job.
ANDY: Nope, oh he'll do anything he can to help
    someone . . . and he'll play that ol' guitar if there's
    just a crowd of one . . . but he'll never take a
    penny for it. No sir, Wally's not a beggar . . . he's
    more kind of a wandering minstrel.
PEGGY: But how *does* he get along?

                                        (CONTINUED)

4   (CONTINUED)   4

ANDY (*playfully mysterious*): Confidentially, I happen to know he *does* have a little bitty income.

PEGGY (*intrigued*): I know, that letter he wrote, that has something to do with it, doesn't it?

ANDY: Wellllll, yes, you might say it does.

DISSOLVE TO:

5   INT. POST OFFICE–DAY   5

There are two wickets marked "STAMPS"—one empty, but behind the second is Postal Clerk Lyle Fenton. A woman stands in front of his wicket. As Wally enters, she pushes some coins across the counter. Lyle takes them and gives her some stamps. Wally has moved up to stand behind the woman, and as she leaves, he steps up to the wicket.

LYLE (*warmly*): Well, now the things you see when you ain't got a gun. How are ya, Wally?

WALLY: Couldn't be better, Lyle. Your sister over to Oxford sends regards.

LYLE: She wrote me you come by and did some wood-chopping for her. Mighty nice of you.

WALLY: Needed the exercise.

LYLE: What'll it be today?

WALLY (*taking some envelopes from his pocket*): Two air-mail, seven regular and a three-center.

Lyle has been jotting figures rapidly on scratch pad.

LYLE: Comes to exactly forty-five cents.

WALLY (*nods*): 'Bout what I figured.

Now occurs a reverse of the usual transaction. From the coins loose on the counter Lyle shoves forward a quarter and two dimes.

LYLE: Here's your money.

WALLY (*giving him stamps inside one envelope*): And here's your stamps.

Lyle very calmly takes the stamps. Wally picks up money, has a sudden thought.

WALLY (*musing*): Forty-five cents . . .

(CONTINUED)

5   (CONTINUED)   5

LYLE: What is it?

WALLY: Invited over to Aunt Bee's for dinner tonight, was hoping to take her a box of licorice
drops . . . that's her favorite.

LYLE: Guess that could run you six bits.

There is a pause, Wally looks at his letter, then back to Lyle.

WALLY: Say, Lyle, wonder if you could let me have
a stamp?

LYLE (*plays it straight*): Sure thing. If it's important,
you probably want a special delivery.

WALLY: Yes, s'pect so.

*Lyle hands a special delivery stamp to Wally who nods his
thanks. Wally turns, walks slowly to the empty wicket. Now
Lyle has moved over behind the counter and appears at the
second wicket. Wally hands the stamp through the window.
Lyle takes it, inspects as though this is a completely separate
transaction.*

LYLE (*businesslike, takes coins from pocket*): It's worth
thirty cents.

*Wally takes the money, nods perfunctorily and departs, his
pride intact. Lyle looks after him, a warm grin growing.*

DISSOLVE TO:

6   INT. LIVING ROOM–NIGHT   6

*Andy and Wally each with his guitar, picking and tuning.
Peggy holds a box of candy toward Aunt Bee.*

PEGGY: More candy, Aunt Bee?

AUNT BEE: Gracious no. (*pushing it away*) Not one
more piece. They're delicious, but I have to think
of my diet.

*Peggy puts the box down within reach of Aunt Bee and
turns toward the two men. Aunt Bee looks at the un-
guarded box, her lips tight with determination. Nobody is
looking her way.*

WALLY: In memory of that delicious bird we had

(CONTINUED)

6   (CONTINUED)   6

for dinner, how about a few choruses of "The Old
Gray Goose is Dead"?

Aunt Bee's hand drifts toward the candy box.

ANDY (*considers the suggestion*): Ummmm. 'Course if
we wanted to be even *more* up to date. . . .

Aunt Bee has picked up a licorice drop.

ANDY (*cont'd.*): . . . we could play something like
maybe . . ."Music To Steal Just One More Licorice
Drop By."

*Everybody turns and catches Aunt Bee just about to pop
the candy in her mouth.*

AUNT BEE: Oh, Andy!
WALLY: You go right ahead, Aunt Bee, you're a
growing girl.
ANDY: And we'll do our best to drown out all the
lip-smacking. (*to Wally*) Maybe a touch of (*SONG
TITLE*).
WALLY: I'll try to keep up.

Aunt Bee eats the candy as the two men do their song. Applause from Aunt Bee and Peggy.

WALLY (*putting guitar aside*): But what am I sitting
here for? Aunt Bee, let me give you a hand with
the dishes.
AUNT BEE (*rising*): Now Wally, you're not here to
work.
WALLY: There's no work to it, the way you cook a
meal, them dishes get all cleaned up at the *table*.
C'mon.

They exit.

PEGGY: I'd say he's about the nicest man in the
world.
ANDY: Truth is I been thinking on him all day.
Y'know, maybe it's about time we all stopped *taking* from Wally and got around to doing a little
giving.

(CONTINUED)

6 (CONTINUED) 6

PEGGY: But what can you give him? He seems to have everything he really wants.

ANDY: There is one thing he doesn't have that we *can* give him . . . that's a chance to hang up his walking shoes and settle down.

PEGGY (*excited at prospect*): Settle down? Here in Mayberry? Do you think he'd do it?

ANDY: Yep, if it was handled right. Wally'd be glad to stay put here in town if he thought he was needed and useful . . . and we can make him feel useful by getting him some steady work, a good job.

PEGGY: But what sort of a job could he do?

ANDY (*smugly*): Got it all figured out. Aunt Bee was saying how short-handed George is at the store. Now let me ask, can you think of anyone in the world who'd be a better salesman than Wally?

PEGGY: He'd be marvelous! What a wonderful idea!

ANDY: It'd help George, help the town, and at the same time finally give Wally the chance to stop the drifting and better himself for a change.

PEGGY (*smiles fondly at Andy*): I've changed my mind about something . . . maybe Wally's only the *second* nicest man in the world.

ANDY: Now it isn't done yet, I still don't know what George is gonna say to the idea.

FLIP OVER TO:

7 INT. THE EMPORIUM STORE–DAY 7

It's an area of the store near the front door. George has a desk against the wall. A few counters are nearby, one with cleaning aids, vacuum cleaners, carpet sweepers, brooms, mops—also a row of kitchen chairs. An archway in the wall is labelled: "To Men's Wear Annex". The opening shot, however, is fairly close on the dyspeptic George. He has an expression of stunned disbelief. Finally he finds the words to match.

(CONTINUED)

7   (CONTINUED)   7

GEORGE: Are you out of your mind?

*Full back to reveal Andy is talking to him, both near the
desk.*

ANDY: Just give it a minute more thought . . . you
    are short-handed, everybody knows and likes
    Wally, and he's honest as the day is long . . .
GEORGE: Now I don't know, Sheriff. For one thing,
    I couldn't have a clerk in the store dressed like he
    is . . .

*Aunt Bee sweeps in from annex, carrying a man's suit on a
hanger, and a shirt under her arm.*

AUNT BEE: You don't have to worry about that . . .
    This suit should fit him fine.
GEORGE (*rises*): But I can't just give him . . .
AUNT BEE: Be a wonderful ad for your men's de-
    partment.
GEORGE: Now hold on . . . Look, I don't have any-
    thing against the man, but . . .
ANDY: Good, then we'll have him here this after-
    noon ready for work. Congratulations, George.
    You've made a wise decision.

Andy and Aunt Bee exit before George can answer.

                                QUICK DISSOLVE TO:

8   EXT. STORE FRONT–DAY   8

*Aunt Bee and Andy coming out of the store, Aunt Bee car-
rying the suit on a hanger and the shirt.*

AUNT BEE (*looks at suit*): It's perfect! Just a little
    taking-in here and there. (*she notices Andy pausing
    reflectively*) I thought you'd be rushing right off to
    tell Wally the good news.
ANDY: Well, there's still one little problem.
AUNT BEE: What problem? I'm sure George will
    give him the job.
ANDY: Yep, he'll give him the job. But now I have

                                (CONTINUED)

8 (CONTINUED)   8

to figure out the tough part . . . how to make
Wally *take* it.

On Aunt Bee's puzzled expression—

DISSOLVE TO:

9 EXT. STREET SCENE–DAY   9

*Wally and Andy saunter along, man in passing car toots
horn, waves at Wally who waves back.*

ANDY: You sure have lots of friends 'round here,
Wally.

WALLY (*casually picking up an empty pop bottle and slid-
ing it into musette bag where it clinks against others*):
Nice of you to say so.

ANDY: Uh, fellow wanting to settle down could sure
do a lot worse.

WALLY: I s'pect so.

ANDY: You ever think about it?

WALLY: About what?

ANDY: Settlin' down.

WALLY (*shakes head*): Me? Why should I live in just
one town when I can live in fifty?

*Casually Wally reaches around corner of building and
without looking pulls out a pop bottle hidden from sight.*

WALLY (*cont'd.*): There's allus one there.

He pops it into musette bag.

ANDY: But it would be easy for you to settle here,
even bet you could find a job.

WALLY: What would I want a job for?

ANDY: Lots of things . . . fellow can always use a
little pocket money.

WALLY: Don't need a job for that . . . there's
enough money just lying around.

*They have come to a bench on the grass near a curb. Wally
stops Andy.*

WALLY (*cont'd.*): Now you take a bench like this. I'd

(CONTINUED)

9   (CONTINUED)   9

like to shake hands with the fellow who invented it. (*he's circling carefully*) The seat is built at just the perrrrfect angle so a fellow sitting down'll have a dime walk right back out of his pocket.

He kneels and squints, reaches down, and in the grass he pulls up a coin. He shows it to Andy proudly.

QUICK DISSOLVE TO:

10   EXT. SIDEWALK AREA–DAY   10

Andy and Wally are walking down the sidewalk, approaching a soft drink cooler in front of a store. A boy is seated nearby.

ANDY: . . . 'Course with a regular job you'd be able to live better . . .

WALLY: Excuse me, but would you care for a cold drink?

ANDY: No thanks, but—(*reaching into pocket*)—if you'd like one . . .

Wally restrains his arm.

WALLY: My treat. You sure you don't want one?

Andy shakes his head.

WALLY (*cont'd.*): Well, I'm just dry as a bone . . . lessee . . . (*he starts pulling the empty bottles from bag*) Deposit on five empties is worth one full, ain't it?

ANDY: That's right.

WALLY (*putting five empties into rack*): The price of living nowadays, I 'member used to get one for only three empties.

Wally takes a full bottle from the cooler, opens it, about to drink when he is suddenly aware of envious scrutiny of the boy who has moved to stand near the cooler. Wally passes the bottle over to him.

ANDY (*he has an idea*): Say, Wally, something I'd like to show you over here in the window.

QUICK DISSOLVE TO:

(CONTINUED)

11   INT. MUSIC STORE WINDOW–DAY   11

A gorgeous new guitar stands prominently displayed in the center of the window.

ANDY (*Voice Over*): And like you said, Wally, your old guitar is in mighty bad shape . . . 'bout time you bought yourself a new one.

                           QUICK DISSOLVE TO:

12   EXT. STORE WINDOW–DAY   12

Andy and Wally looking in, Wally transfixed.

WALLY: I could never get the money.

ANDY: Unless of course, you were to get on a pay-roll somewhere.

WALLY: You mean . . . take a job?

ANDY: Say now, you've got a *good* idea there. Come to think, George over to the Emporium is losing his health trying to keep up with the work . . . be a great favor if you could help him out as a salesman.

WALLY: But these clothes . . .

ANDY: Well, you'd wear your new suit.

WALLY: What new suit?

ANDY (*casually*): The one you get when you leave jail.

Wally looks at Andy, puzzled. Andy goes on to explain.

ANDY (*cont'd.*): Haven't you seen it in the movies? Fellow leaves prison, the state has to provide him with a suit of clothes?

WALLY: But I been in your jail lots of times, never got a suit before.

ANDY: But that was different . . . Y'see, now you're a six-time loser. The state don't give clothes to just an occasional wrongdoer, it's only the repeat customers . . . the hardened criminals, who get the free clothes.

Wally is at the point of decision.

                               (CONTINUED)

12   (CONTINUED)   12

WALLY: But me taking a job . . . hardly know what to say.

ANDY (*off-hand*): Up to you . . . (*he turns back toward window, his voice lowers to an enticing whisper*) Think, Wally . . . if a guitar *looks* that good, can you imagine what it'll *sound* like?

Wally's eyes widen, he eyes the guitar wistfully.

ANDY (*continuing same hushed, coaxing tones*): Shall we go see George about that job?

Wally pauses, then, still hypnotized, eyes on the guitar, he nods assent slowly, then turns to look at Andy.

ANDY: You're doing the right thing, Wally, you really are.

Andy leads Wally away as we,

                                                    FADE OUT.

END OF ACT ONE

ACT TWO

FADE IN:

13   EXT. STORE–DAY   13

Andy walks along sidewalk, nods to passerby and enters store.

                                        QUICK DISSOLVE TO:

14   INT. STORE–DAY   14

Andy comes in door, walks to counter where Wally, in new suit, is rifling through some letters to be mailed. His back is toward Andy.

ANDY: Pardon me, where could I find Mr. Wally Jordan?

Wally turns.

                                                (CONTINUED)

14 (CONTINUED)   14

WALLY (*not quite his old exuberance*): Oh, hi Andy.

ANDY (*mock surprise*): Well I'll be . . . I thought you
were the president of the bank or something.

WALLY (*grins, stands erect in suit*): What do you think
of it?

ANDY: Mmmm-umpf! I'll never be able to arrest
you as a vagrant no more. How's the job coming?

WALLY: Doing my level best. I appreciate what you
done, Andy, and I'm gonna make you proud
of me.

ANDY: I am proud of you and I bet George is too.

WALLY: Do you think so? Has he said anything?

ANDY: No, but if he *wasn't* happy, I sure would
have heard about it.

Wally is pleased.

WALLY: Well, I gotta run and get these in the mail.

ANDY: Oh, I understand, I know how busy you executives are.

*Wally takes letters, Andy turns, sees a woman browsing
among merchandise.*

ANDY: You got a customer, Wally.

WALLY: Customer, hmpf! She's here every day,
never buys a thing, no sense wasting any time
with her. Never make a nickel on it.

*Wally waves letters at Andy and departs. Andy looks after
him somewhat thoughtfully, then continues on toward back
of store.*

DISSOLVE TO:

15 INT. GEORGE'S DESK AREA–DAY   15

A harried George is on the phone.

GEORGE: You tell her that if she don't pay by the
end of the week, I'll get the law after her.

George slams the phone down, fuming.

GEORGE (*cont'd.*): Customers! How are you, Sheriff?

(CONTINUED)

15   (CONTINUED)   15

ANDY: Fine. How's Wally coming along?

GEORGE: Well, the first day was awful, he talked to a hundred customers, but the cash register didn't ring once. But now he's catching on, he may work out after all.

ANDY: I'm glad to hear.

GEORGE: How'd you ever get him to take a job in the first place?

ANDY: I just let him feast his eyes on a new guitar down to the music store, next minute he wanted a job to earn money for it. Ol' Wally turned capitalist right in front of my eyes.

GEORGE: Guitar, eh? That's not so good. Soon's he's earned enough for the fool thing he'll quit.

ANDY: No, I don't believe so. By then he'll find lots other things to work for. I doubt he'll ever go back to what he was.

GEORGE: I hope not. Y'know Sheriff, you did a good turn for him, you deserve a lot of credit for it.

Phone rings.

GEORGE (*cont'd.*): 'scuse me. (*to phone*) Emporium . . . no sir, absolutely not! I don't care about your problems, I got problems of my own! (*he slams phone down*) Yep, if Wally stays at it, no reason why someday he couldn't be just what I am . . . and he'd owe it all to you.

Andy looks at George, thoughtful once again.

DISSOLVE TO:

16   INT. POST OFFICE–DAY   16

Aunt Bee is at the table addressing a parcel. Wally enters with letters in his pocket. She sees him first.

AUNT BEE: Hello Wally. My don't you look nice.

WALLY: Thank you, Miss Bee.

AUNT BEE: I should have let out that sleeve a touch more.

(CONTINUED)

16 (CONTINUED)   16

WALLY (*impatient*): It's fine, just fine.

AUNT BEE: Tell you what, you come by tonight, I'll
fix it and give you a good dinner too.

WALLY: I can't tonight . . . we got inventory.

AUNT BEE: Then tomorrow.

WALLY: Well, maybe tomorrow.

Wally nods and continues to window, Aunt Bee resumes addressing. Clerk Lyle Fenton at window.

LYLE: Hi Wally, how's tricks?

WALLY: Not bad.

Wally takes letters from pocket.

LYLE: How many stamps you sellin' today?

WALLY: I'm not here for that, I want these to go
out right away.

LYLE (*takes them*): Sure, sure, say—I got a postcard
from my sister, she was asking . . .

WALLY (*interrupting*): You know those packages I
brought in Tuesday?

LYLE: Uh, yes, what about 'em?

WALLY: Customer called and said she hasn't gotten
'em yet.

LYLE: They were going way out to the county line,
deliveries are a little slow up there.

WALLY: Oughta be some way to get a little better
service. We got a business to run, you know.

LYLE: I'll look into it right away.

WALLY: You'd better just do that.

Lyle nods quietly, Wally tries to make amends.

WALLY: I know you're kinda busy and all, Lyle, . . .
but they are important . . . honest they are.

*Lyle nods again, Wally a little embarrassed turns away and
leaves. Aunt Bee comes over to window. She has heard and
is a little embarrassed too.*

AUNT BEE: Wally sure looks nice doesn't he.

Lyle nods in agreement.

(CONTINUED)

16   (CONTINUED)   16

AUNT BEE: Just starting a new job, naturally he's
    anxious to get things done, that's all.

*Lyle nods, unconvinced, Aunt Bee looks toward where
Wally exited. She too is a little troubled.*

DISSOLVE TO:

17   EXT. SIDEWALK AREA–DAY   17

*This is the same place where Wally used to bring his empty
pop bottles. Andy is standing there just finishing a bottle of
pop as Wally comes by.*

ANDY: Hi Wally, care to join me?
WALLY: Oh sure, I guess so.

Andy fishes a bottle from the cooler.

ANDY: I can personally recommend the sarsparilla.
    (*He displays bottle elegantly on his arm like a posh wine
    steward.*) This is a very good year.
WALLY: Well, I dunno . . . sarsparilla . . .

Wally fishes in cooler.

ANDY: The grape soda is very nice too . . . im-
    ported all the way from Mt. Pilot.
WALLY: They're kinda' warm. You'd think Bert'd
    keep a little more ice in his cooler.
ANDY: They're cool enough—and at least they're
    wet.
WALLY: But a body paying good money for an ice
    cold drink is entitled to just that. This is kind of a
    gyp.
ANDY (*grins*): Never used to bother you when you
    was bringing back empties . . . remember that?
WALLY (*a little embarrassed*): Well, those days are
    over . . . Don't you think as Sheriff, you oughta
    make him take care of this a little better.

Peggy enters.

ANDY (*glad at the interruption*): Oh, hi Peggy.
PEGGY: Hi Andy, Wally . . . haven't kept you wait-
    ing long, have I?

(CONTINUED)

17   (CONTINUED)   17

ANDY: Mmmmmwell, not too long, only about two
and a-half bottles.

PEGGY (*to Wally*): Seen my pink cloud anywhere?

WALLY (*he's not with it*): Your what?

PEGGY: My angel's pink cloud. I was sure I parked
it around here.

WALLY (*still dense*): Pink cloud?

ANDY: It's nothing . . . just a little joke.

WALLY: Oh, well, I gotta get back to the store . . .
(*indicates cooler*) I still think Bert oughta do something about that ice.

Wally nods to both and exits. Peggy looks after him approv-
ingly.

PEGGY: You'd hardly know him now, would you?

Andy nods.

PEGGY (*cont'd*): Never saw such a change in a man.
It was a wonderful thing you did, Andy, and I'm
so glad it's working out this well.

ANDY: But *is* it working out so well?

DISSOLVE TO:

18   INT. STORE–SIX P.M.   18

George putting on his jacket ready to leave, closes desk
drawer, steps over to counter where Wally is sorting out pile
of shirts all jumbled up, and putting them back in order on
shelf according to size.

GEORGE: Don't forget to bring in the sign from the
sidewalk.

WALLY (*testy*): All right, I won't forget it.

George turns toward door, Wally slams shirts into proper
places angrily. As George opens front door, Andy enters.

ANDY: Wally gone home yet?

GEORGE: No, he's over there closing up. (*raises voice*
to Wally) See you in the morning.

Wally grunts a reply.

GEORGE: And don't forget that sign.

(CONTINUED)

18 (CONTINUED) 18

WALLY: All right, all right.

George grunts and exits. Andy walks to where Wally is sorting.

WALLY (*mutters*): Signs, him and his signs.

ANDY: How's it going Wally?

WALLY: Darn customers, so inconsiderate . . . look at the way they messed this place up.

ANDY (*experimentally*): You don't seem too happy about the work, Wally.

WALLY (*walks toward door to reverse a stringed placard from "Open to "Closed"*): A job's a job . . . and this one ain't no picnic. But don't worry, Andy, I'm not gonna let you down, I'll do it right if it kills me.

Outside a woman appears and raps on the glass in the door.

WALLY (*shouts—without opening door*): We're closed . . . can't you read! Come back tomorrow.

Woman, a little taken back, leaves. Wally turns back to Andy and parroting George's favorite epithet:

WALLY (*cont'd*): Customers!

ANDY: Well, leastwise won't be long 'fore you can buy that shiny new guitar.

WALLY: Uh huh.

ANDY: Speaking of which, how 'bout you and I having us a little musicale tonight . . . your ol' guitar's still at the jailhouse.

WALLY: Thanks Andy, but just don't feel much like playing it.

ANDY: But Wally, don't seem much point in working to get a guitar if the working keeps you from enjoying it.

Wally looks at Andy, shrugs, opens front door and exits.

QUICK DISSOLVE TO:

EXT. STORE FRONT–SIX P.M.

19 *Wally comes out of the store and goes to pick up a sign on a*

(CONTINUED)

19   (CONTINUED)   19

*stand—"Special Clearance Sale Today." Four youngsters
on the sidewalk rush over.*
FIRST BOY: What kind of lollipops you got Wally?
WALLY: I don't have any.

*One of the children reaches toward Wally's coat pocket imp-
ishly. Wally brushes his hand aside.*

WALLY: I don't have any . . . how many times I
   gotta tell you!
SECOND BOY: You gonna sing us a song Wally?
WALLY: Why aren't you kids home having supper?
FIRST BOY: 'Cause we'd rather have lollipops!

All the children laugh.

WALLY: Well, for the last time, I don't have any . . .
   go along . . . let me be!

Wally picks up sign and carries it toward door.

                              QUICK DISSOLVE TO:

20   INT. STORE–SIX P.M.   20

*Andy, at open door, has been observing. Wally brings in
sign and stands it behind door.*

WALLY: They sure can be pesky when they want to.
ANDY: It's only that you're kind of a special honor-
   ary uncle around here.
WALLY (*relaxing*): Didn't really mean to yell at them
   . . . I'm a little tired . . . had a hard day.

Andy nods noncommittally, Wally looks at him keenly.
WALLY (*thoughtfully*): But I never used to act this
   way, did I?
ANDY: No Wally, you didn't.
WALLY: Guess I'm edgy, what with the job being so
   new to me. I'll get over it after I been here a
   while.
ANDY (*innocently*): Uh huh, then you'll have a nice
   easy going disposition, like George has.

Wally looks at him sharply, Andy explains—

                                      (CONTINUED)

ANDY: He's been here a *good* while.

Wally is silent.

ANDY (*Picks up item on counter and scrutinizes*): It
    might help if you was to take tomorrow morning
    off . . . give you a chance to kinda unwind.
WALLY: Gee, I dunno . . .
ANDY: And the afternoon too . . . make it the whole
    day . . . or why not take a week.
WALLY: A week!
ANDY: You're right, a week's no good . . . make it a
    month. Better still, a year . . . two years . . . ten
    years.

Wally now comprehends.

WALLY: I don't want to be a quitter, Andy. I want
    everyone to be proud of me.
ANDY: Wally, the truth is we *always* were proud of
    you just the way you were.
WALLY: But I sure didn't amount to much.
ANDY: Depends on how you figure. You were a
    happy man . . . and you made folks around you
    happy. I'd say that amounts to a whole lot.
WALLY: I dunno Andy . . . I admit I still feel the
    wandering bug, but . . . well, I just don't want to
    make any mistake.
ANDY: The mistake has *already* been made . . . and
    I'm the fellow who made it . . . trying to change
    you (*indicates store*) into this.

Wally is silent, troubled.

ANDY: Wally, maybe someday you sould settle
    down, but *you'll* know when that time comes. All
    I'm saying is that you don't have to rush it . . . the
    town'll always be here. The main thing Wally, is
    that it's up to *you* to decide.

Wally is thoughtful, unsure.

DISSOLVE TO:

(CONTINUED)

21   INT. JAILHOUSE–DAY   21

Peggy is talking to a somber Andy.

PEGGY: What do you think he'll do?
ANDY: I don't know. I really don't.
PEGGY: You can't blame yourself too much, Andy,
    who ever thought he'd become such a . . .

*Andy stops her with a warning gesture as Opie enters from
the back room with an empty waste basket.*

OPIE: It's all cleaned out Paw.
ANDY: Good, good.

*There is a moment of constrained silence. Opie glances
from Andy to Peggy. Finally—*

OPIE (*innocently*): Am I interrupting something?

Peggy smiles.

PEGGY: No of course not.

The front door bursts open, a small boy sticks his head in.

SMALL BOY: Hey, Opie, c'mon. It's Wally.
OPIE (*shakes his head, not interested*): I got some
    things to do here.
SMALL BOY: Ok, but you'll be sorry!

*The small boy slams out. Peggy and Andy look at each
other wondering, they walk over to the door and open it to
investigate. Through the open door Wally's back is seen as
he stands handing out lollipops to his group of children.
And it's the old Wally, in his old clothes, with his old musette bag.*

WALLY: And remember, whoever gets a red one'll
    live to be a hundred and eight.

*Wally tosses the rest of them to the group with a laugh.
Opie scoots out to join group, Wally turns and enters the
jailhouse passing in front of Andy. Andy closes the door
and he and Peggy look at the new, old Wally.*

WALLY: Just stopped by to say so long, leaving on a
    vacation.
ANDY (*casually*): Is that right.

                                            (CONTINUED)

21   (CONTINUED)   21

WALLY: I figured an executive like me is entitled to
    a little six month vacation . . . twice a year.

Peggy smiles.

WALLY (*cont'd.*): What I really want to do Andy, is to
    thank you for what you did . . . both times.

Wally shakes Andy's hand.

PEGGY: Oh, Wally, it's wonderful.

Andy reaches next to desk and produces Wally's old guitar.

ANDY: Shame you couldn't have gotten that new
    guitar, but ol' Lila-belle here's still got a few more
    miles left on her.
WALLY: Oh, but I did get that new one . . . lemme
    show you.

Wally opens the front door again.

                                          QUICK FADE TO:

22   EXT. JAILHOUSE–DAY
*Wally steps out and picks up the new guitar he'd left leaning
on the outside wall. Andy, carrying the old guitar, and
Peggy are next to him. He displays guitar.*
WALLY: It's a beauty, ain't it. (*he strums a chord*)
ANDY: But how in the world . . .
WALLY: Worked out a little deal with the music store
. . . I'm their new advertising manager . . . this here's
my year's salary.
PEGGY: An advertising manager?

Wally nods.

WALLY: Yep, the arrangement is . . . when I'm not
    playing . . . I'm *dis*playing.

*Wally flips guitar over. On its back is painted in large block
lettering: "Shop at The Mayberry Music Store". Peggy and
Andy chuckle. Andy slaps Wally on the back in appreciation.*

WALLY: You can give my old one to George. Well,
    see you later.

                                          (CONTINUED)

22 (CONTINUED)   22

*Wally starts off. The children reappear and follow him as
he strolls away.*

23 ANOTHER ANGLE   23

*Peggy and Andy stand together watching. George rushes
up from opposite direction.*

GEORGE: Sheriff, something's happened. Wally
  didn't show up for work this morning . . . he left
  his new suit there but . . .

*George's eyes widen as he looks down the street past Andy,
he turns to Andy—*

GEORGE: It can't be . . . is that him?

Andy nods.

GEORGE: You mean . . . he's leaving . . . passing up
  a job in my store?
PEGGY: Sure seems like it.
ANDY: But he didn't forget you, George. (*thrusts
  guitar into George's hands*) He left you this.
GEORGE (*shakes his head*): I can't believe it . . . and
  just when he was . . . (*sighs*) Oh I tell you it's a pity
  . . . a pity.
ANDY: You know George, I agree with you . . . it *is*
  a pity . . . (*turns to look after Wally*) But the pity is
  that we can't go with him.

                                          DISSOLVE TO:

24 EXT. STREET SCENE–DAY   24

*It's Wally again, guitar slung over shoulder and followed
by his full entourage walking away up the street, pausing
just to pick up a pop bottle, slide it in his musette bag without breaking stride as he saunters away. Once again, a
man without a care, without a worry.*

                                          DISSOLVE TO:

25 EXT. JAILHOUSE–DAY   25

                                          (CONTINUED)

25   (CONTINUED)   25

Andy and Peggy smiling, look at each other, and then back down the road with the disgruntled George still standing by, shaking his head in disapproval.

FADE OUT.

END OF ACT TWO

TAG

26   INT. LIVING ROOM–DAY   26

Andy comes in front door.

ANDY: Anybody home? This here restaurant open for business?

Aunt Bee sticks her head out of kitchen.

AUNT BEE: Lunch'll be ready in just a jiffy.

Aunt Bee ducks back into kitchen. Andy stretches out in chair, phone rings and he answers.

ANDY: Andy Taylor . . . (*suddenly he tenses*) Yes George, what is it? You sure? When'd it happen? Hold everything, I'll be right over.

Andy slams down the phone, calls toward the kitchen—

ANDY: Hold off on the lunch Aunt Bee.

Aunt Bee comes out of kitchen. Andy races out of front door.

DISSOLVE TO:

27   EXT. STORE FRONT–DAY   27

The sheriff's car comes screeching to a halt. Andy jumps out and runs into the store.

QUICK DISSOLVE TO:

28   INT. STORE–DAY   28

Andy enters door and strides to George's office section where an excited George stands awaiting.

(CONTINUED)

28   (CONTINUED)   28

GEORGE: What took you so long?
ANDY: Came as fast as I could . . . was you telling
    me the truth?

George nods vigorously.

ANDY: Well show me.

*George turns, picks up Wally's old guitar, not seen til now,
puts a foot on his chair and now haltingly, but enthusiastically picks out the unmistakable chords of the beginning of
"Home On The Range". The phone rings, George impatiently picks up the phone.*

GEORGE: What? She can't pay . . . well then tear up
    the bill . . . don't bother me, I'm busy.

George slams down phone, takes posture with guitar again.

GEORGE: What do you think Andy, not bad eh?
ANDY: No, not bad at all, George. In fact . . . I'd say
    Wally'd be real proud of you.

                                        FADE OUT.

                THE END

PART
5

Summaries

The Andy Griffith Show appeared on CBS at 9:30 on Monday nights and ran for a total of 249 shows between October 3, 1960, and April 1, 1968. The show continued another three years as *Mayberry, R.F.D.*, with Ken Berry replacing Andy Griffith as the star. Produced by Griffith and Linke, the new series ran from September 22, 1968, to September 6, 1971. At the outset, Andy Taylor finally marries Helen Crump and they move away with Opie, leaving Aunt Bee behind to become the new housekeeper for Sam Jones (Ken Berry), a widower, gentleman farmer, and city councilman. Several of the actors from *The Andy Griffith Show* continued into the new series: Francis Bavier, George Lindsey, Jack Dodson, Paul Hartman, and Arlene Golonka. Sam Jones's son, Mike, played by Buddy Foster, proves to be an amiable substitution for the departed Opie. Sam's girlfriend, Millie, is played by Arlene Golonka, who previously was Howard Sprague's girlfriend (also Millie) in the *Griffith Show*. The characters of Howard Sprague, Goober, and Emmett continue as they were in the original series. Before *Mayberry, R.F.D.* concluded, Frances Bavier retired from acting and was replaced by Alice Ghostley, who played Sam's new housekeeper.

The Andy Griffith Show had two main producers during its eight-year run: Aaron Ruben from 1960 to 1965, and Bob Ross from 1965 to 1968. There were many directors, but the most important one was Bob Sweeney, who directed all of the episodes (except the first) during the crucial early years, 1960 to 1963. Other important directors included Alan Rafkin, Richard Crenna, Coby Ruskin, and Lee Philips. Among the numerous writers for the series were Jack Elinson and Charles Stewart, Leo Solomon and Ben Gershman, Jim Fritzell and Everett Greenbaum, John Whedon, and Harvey Bullock and William Idelson.

The first season of *The Andy Griffith Show* established the small-town nature of Mayberry and developed the relationships among Andy Taylor, Barney Fife, Aunt Bee, Opie, and Otis Campbell. In the fourth show, "Ellie Comes to Town," Ellie Walker (Elinor Donahue) was introduced, and she became Andy's chief romantic interest. The character of Floyd Lawson was introduced in the thirteenth show, "Mayberry Goes Hollywood."

Donahue left the show at the end of the first year, and the second season brought in new women for Andy to court. The most important female character was Mary Simpson, the county nurse, played by Sue Ane Langdon.

In the third year the character of Mary Simpson disappeared and was replaced by Peggy McMillan, played by Joanna Moore. Parley Baer appeared this season as the new mayor, and the Darling family, Ernest T. Bass, and Gomer Pyle also made their debuts. Andy finally got a permanent girlfriend in Helen Crump, played by Aneta Corsaut, who was introduced in "Andy Discovers America" (episode 86).

The fourth season allotted several episodes to Gomer Pyle and Ernest T. Bass and introduced the fun girls from Mt. Pilot. Episode 107, "Gomer Pyle, U.S.M.C.," became the pilot for Aaron Ruben's own series of the same name. Jim Nabors finished the season and was replaced the following year by George Lindsey, who played his cousin, Goober.

There was a general mix of shows during the fifth year. All of the main characters and some of the supporting ones had episodes built around them. Don Knotts made his last appearance in "Opie Flunks Arithmetic" (episode 157).

Jack Burns replaced Don Knotts in the sixth year by playing the role of Deputy Warren. He made his first appearance in "The Bazaar" (episode 162). For the first time the Taylors are removed from Mayberry when, in three consecutive shows, Andy, Opie, and Aunt Bee visit Hollywood. Don Knotts made two return appearances that year (for which he won Emmies) in "The Return of Barney Fife" and "The Legend of Barney Fife" (episodes 176, 177). Jack Dodson put in his first appearance as an insurance salesman in "Lost and Found" (episode 178), and in "The County Clerk" (episode 185) he was first introduced as the county clerk, Howard Sprague. Jack Burns left the show in midseason and was not replaced.

The seventh year focused upon the characters of Howard Sprague, Floyd, and Goober in order to compensate for the vacancy left by Knotts and Burns. Jack Nicholson made two brief appearances this year: first, as the husband who abandons a baby on the Taylors' doorstep in "Opie Finds a Baby" (episode 202); and later as a burglar on trial in "Aunt Bee the Juror" (episode 223). Howard McNear appeared for the last time in "Goober's Contest" (episode 219). Don Knotts made two more guest appearances and won two more Emmies for his performances in "A Visit to Barney Fife" and "Barney Comes to Mayberry" (episodes 211, 212).

The last season was devoted to a variety of shows featuring Jack Dodson, Opie, and Emmett. Andy Griffith appeared in all of the episodes, but it became clear toward the end of the season that he was grooming Ken Berry to take his place the next year. Don Knotts made his final guest appearance in "Barney Hosts a Summit Meeting" (episode 240) and won his fifth Emmy.

Here, then, are brief summaries of all 249 episodes, listed in the order of their first appearance on television, with official script titles. The order in which the shows were originally filmed is indicated by the episode numbers. Since the shows were filmed months in advance of their presentation, the producers had the opportunity to rearrange the order in which they were put on the air. In a sense, this reordering comprised the final "editing," and, therefore, the definitive order in which to discuss the shows. The order of filming, on the other hand, is a more expedient one, determined by practical matters, such as the availability of actors and writers and the efficient use of sets.

The two shows introducing Ellie Walker, for instance, were moved up in the sequence in order to add the important element of romance earlier in the season. "The Christmas Story," of course, had to be aired on December 19 because of its timeliness. The basic motive behind the reordering of the original sequence in which the episodes were filmed was to provide a variety of shows each month. The first month, for example, presents four very different subjects: a change in the Taylor household, Andy's and Barney's hunt for an escaped convict, a local guitar player makes good, and Ellie's move to Mayberry.

1. "The New Housekeeper"   *October 3, 1960*
Aunt Bee comes to live with the Taylors after their housekeeper leaves to get married. Unhappy at first, Opie finally comes to accept her, and the Taylor household is established for the rest of the series. Don Knotts appears briefly as the new deputy who thanks "cousin" Andy for giving him the job. This and "The Bazaar" (episode 162) were the only two directed by Sheldon Leonard. (Episode 1)

2. "The Manhunt"   *October 10, 1960*
Andy and Barney are ridiculed by the state troopers for their small-town police tactics during a search for an escaped convict. Andy's horse sense, however, leads him to capture the convict by allowing him to steal a boat with a hole in it. (Episode 2)

3. "Guitar Player"   *October 17, 1960*
In order to give Jim Lindsey, a home-town guitar player (played by James Best), the opportunity to audition for Bobby Fleet's Band with a Beat, Andy arrests Jim and puts him in a cell adjacent to the one containing Bobby Fleet and the band (arrested for a parking violation). Jim plays for his captive audience and is hired into the group. (Episode 3)

4. "Ellie Comes to Town"   *October 24, 1960*
Ellie Walker, an attractive young pharmacist, moves to Mayberry to help her uncle out in the local drugstore. Rigidly professional, she refuses to sell Emma Watson, one of the town's senior citizens, medicine without a prescription. Emma's aches and pains grow and she demands that Andy make Ellie sell her the pills she needs. It turns out that Ellie's uncle had been giving Emma sugar pills over the years, and Ellie learns to accommodate her professional standards to the common sense needs of the townspeople. (Episode 6)

5. "Irresistible Andy"   *October 31, 1960*
Andy rashly assumes that his asking Ellie to the church picnic is a signal to her that he is thinking of getting married. He thus tries to interest her in three eligible bachelors in order to regain his sense of freedom, but she discovers his plan and confronts him with the absurdity of his assumption that the picnic date will entrap him into marriage. They reach an understanding, and he finally takes her to the picnic. This is the first episode to establish a romantic relationship between Andy and a woman. (Episode 7)

6. "Runaway Kid"   *November 7, 1960*
Andy lectures Opie on the importance of keeping promises and then gets into trouble when Opie appears with a runaway boy who has made Opie promise not to tell where he lives. Andy finally convinces the boy that his parents will be worried about him and gets him to return home. The show raises an interesting ethical question, but Andy's allowing the boy to spend the night at his house violates adult common sense. (Episode 4)

7. "Andy the Matchmaker"   *November 14, 1960*
Andy arranges a date between Barney and Miss Rosemary, the dressmaker. Although they have walked to church together on Sunday mornings, Barney and Rosemary are too shy to express their feelings for each other, and Andy happily brings them together for a date. This was the producers' first attempt to find a suitable girlfriend for Barney, but Miss Rosemary did not appear in subsequent episodes. Several weeks later Thelma Lou (played by Betty Lynn) is quietly introduced into the show as Barney's steady girlfriend. (Episode 9)

8. "Opie's Charity"   *Nov. 28, 1960*
Andy misjudges Opie when the boy refuses to give his allowance money to a charity drive in favor of spending it on a present for his girlfriend. It turns out that his girlfriend is from a poverty-stricken family and Opie bought her a new coat. (Episode 5)

9. "A Feud Is a Feud"   *Dec. 5, 1960*
Andy ends a feud between two mountain families by arranging for the marriage of their children. In this episode Andy tells Opie a Southern, down-home version of the story of Romeo and Juliet. This story was part of Griffith's repertoire when he was a stand-up comic, and this was the only episode from the series that used old Griffith material. The tale, however, so well matched the theme of the show that the writers had no trouble working the monologue into the story. (Episode 8)

10. "Ellie for Council"   *Dec. 12, 1960*
Ellie Walker divides the town into two hostile camps—the men and the women—when she decides to run for the office of city council. Andy finally supports her election and she wins the seat. (Episode 12)

11. "Christmas Story"   *Dec. 19, 1960*
Andy and Barney capture the spirit of Christmas by helping a prisoner and his family celebrate the holiday in the Mayberry jail. In the process, they teach the town scrooge, Ben Weaver, the true meaning of Christmas. (Episode 11)

12. "Stranger in Town"   *Dec. 26, 1960*
The townspeople of Mayberry become suspicious when a stranger arrives who knows not only their names but also seems to know all about their personal lives. Their distrust proves to be embarrassment when they finally learn that the stranger's knowledge grew out of his association with a Mayberry resident and that he has come to Mayberry to enjoy the friendship of the people he has admired vicariously. (Episode 10)

13. "Mayberry Goes Hollywood"   *Jan. 2, 1961*
When the people of Mayberry hear that a Hollywood producer is coming to film a movie there, they decide that the town and the people need a new image better suited to the silver screen. But the new store fronts and changed personalities are not what the producer had seen in Mayberry, and the people learn that

their town's true value lies in its honest, simple characteristics. (Episode 13)

14. "The Horse Trader" *Jan. 9, 1961*
When Andy discovers that Opie has falsely traded some seeds for a cap pistol by claiming they are licorice seeds, he talks to the boy about the importance of honest dealing. But Andy himself learns a lesson when he tries some "dealing" of his own in an attempt to sell the town cannon. Opie's naive questions reveal to Andy that it is not easy for a parent to practice what he preaches. (Episode 14)

15. "Those Gossipin' Men" *Jan. 16, 1961*
Andy laughs at Aunt Bee and her friends for being such gossips, and Bee decides to show him that men are worse gossips than women. She starts a rumor of her own among the men, and they quickly begin to gossip among themselves, not hesitating to exaggerate. Andy is forced to swallow his pride when Bee and her friends finally tell him about the trap they set to catch those "gossipin'" men. (Episode 15)

16. "The Beauty Contest" *Jan. 23, 1961*
Andy is selected to judge the Mayberry beauty contest, and he finds himself in a touchy situation. Various citizens attempt to influence Andy to select their favorite contestants, and he realizes that if he picks any of the girls, he is in trouble with the townspeople. At the very moment when Andy must choose, he realizes that the true winner is an older lady who has worked hard to make the contest a success. Andy not only selects a popular winner, but also suggests that true beauty lies in the heart, not in outward appearance. (Episode 20)

17. "Alcohol and Old Lace" *Jan. 30, 1961*
Andy and Barney work hard to discover who is selling moonshine in Mayberry, and Otis certainly doesn't help them. Much to their surprise, Andy and Barney learn that the moonshiners are two sweet old ladies, the Morrison sisters, who naively sell liquor to Otis and others. (Episode 17)

18. "Andy, the Marriage Counselor" *Feb. 6, 1961*
In an attempt to solve the apparent marriage problems of a local couple, Fred and Jennie Boone, who constantly fight with one

another, Andy plays the role of a marriage counselor. But Andy discovers that the couple's love for one another is really expressed through their fighting. (Episode 18)

19. "Mayberry on Record"   *Feb. 13, 1961*
A record promoter comes to Mayberry and gives the citizens a chance to show their musical talents and to make some money in the process. Barney, Floyd, and other members of the town invest their money, but Andy suspects the promoter is a con artist who is taking advantage of the trusting nature of the people. The trust bestowed by the people proves to be rewarded, for the promoter sends a check to Mayberry, proving that Andy's suspicions are unjustified. (Episode 19)

20. "Andy Saves Barney's Morale"   *Feb. 20, 1961*
While Andy is out of town, Barney becomes overzealous in enforcing the law and arrests most of the people in town, only to have Andy release them all (including Aunt Bee and the mayor!) upon his return. Humiliated, Barney vows to quit his job, but Andy informs the townspeople who, to restore Barney's morale, agree to arrest themselves and return to jail. (Episode 16)

21. "Andy and the Gentleman Crook"   *Feb. 27, 1961*
A famous confidence man is held temporarily in the Mayberry jail, and Aunt Bee, Opie, and Barney are taken in by him, seeing him as a gentleman and a kind of hero. Andy is not so easily fooled by the con man and finally is forced to protect everyone's feelings. (Episode 21)

22. "Cyrano Andy"   *March 6, 1961*
Barney gets into trouble with Thelma Lou, and Andy decides to help him regain her good favor. But Barney misinterprets Andy's actions and thinks Andy is out to steal his girl. He accuses Andy of being a turncoat, but Andy finally is able to absolve himself of guilt and reunite the lovers. (Episode 22)

23. "Andy and Opie, Housekeepers"   *March 13, 1961*
Aunt Bee leaves Mayberry for a few days to visit relatives, and Andy and Opie discover that they can't keep house as well as they had thought. Andy finally gets Bee's friend, Clara, to help him, but when Bee returns home Andy realizes her feelings will be hurt if she thinks they don't need her. Andy sends Opie to

"wreck" the rest of the house, and Aunt Bee is happy to discover that they really do need her. (Episode 23)

24. "The New Doctor" *March 27, 1961*
Andy becomes disturbed when a new doctor comes to town and works closely with Ellie. Thanks to Barney's inept spying and Aunt Bee's prodding, Andy is convinced that he must fight for Ellie's hand. He rushes to propose to her, only to discover that the doctor is really not interested in Ellie. Andy finds himself trapped into an untimely marriage proposal, but Ellie, who sees the humor of the situation, turns down his proposal. (Episode 24)

25. "A Plaque for Mayberry" *April 3, 1961*
The mayor and town council become disturbed when they learn that the recipient of an award for being the only descendant of a Revolutionary War hero is to go to Otis, the town drunk. Pressure is put on Andy to prevent Otis from receiving the plaque, but Andy believes in him, and Otis comes through proudly as he receives the award. (Episode 25)

26. "The Inspector" *April 10, 1961*
A state inspector comes to Mayberry to review Andy's and Barney's police methods. He is appalled by their lack of "correct" police procedures, but he learns that the down-home policies of Andy are much more effective in Mayberry and that knowing the people is a necessary part of being a good sheriff. (Episode 26)

27. "Ellie Saves a Female" *April 17, 1961*
Ellie takes it upon herself to help a farmer's daughter break free of an overprotective, domineering father by showing the girl how to look more appealing and by helping her become a kind of "Cinderella." Andy and Ellie succeed in saving the girl from a dull, lonely life on the farm. (Episode 27)

28. "Andy Forecloses" *April 24, 1961*
Andy finds himself faced with evicting a local man whom he does not feel should have to leave. Torn between personal conscience and civic duty, Andy finds a way to foil the eviction attempt supported by the scrooge-like businessman, Ben Weaver. Andy's concern helps save the local man's family from a desperate situation. (Episode 28)

29. "Quiet Sam"   *May 1, 1961*
Andy delivers a baby in a farmer's home because the town doctor is not available. Barney succeeds only in making Andy more nervous than he already is by reading directions from a medical handbook. Andy gets Barney and the prospective father engaged in conversation so that they relax while he successfully delivers a healthy baby. (Episode 29)

30. "Barney Gets His Man"   *May 8, 1961*
While writing a ticket to a stranger in town, Barney is suddenly entangled in a scuffle as two state patrolmen arrive on the scene to arrest the stranger, who, as it happens, is a wanted man. Barney accidentally trips the criminal and is credited with his capture. As the state patrolmen drive off with their prisoner, he vows revenge upon Barney. It is later reported that the man has escaped and is returning to Mayberry. Barney is terrified but, to save his self-respect, Andy arranges for Barney to make the final capture in an abandoned barn where he knows the convict is hiding. Barney becomes so excited when he sees the convict that he swallows his chewing gum and fires his gun off. Thinking Barney is shooting at him, the convict surrenders. All this occurs while Andy secretly watches over the situation from a window outside the barn. (Episode 30)

31. "The Guitar Player Returns"   *May 15, 1961*
When a local musician, Jim Lindsey, returns to Mayberry and acts as if he is enjoying all the rewards of success, Andy realizes that Jim is not the success he pretends to be and that he actually is in financial trouble. Andy helps Jim overcome his pride and face the reality of his situation. Jim, thanks to Andy, is able to regain his former position in the band by patching up his quarrel with the band leader, Bobby Fleet. (Episode 31)

32. "Bringing Up Opie"   *May 22, 1961*
When Aunt Bee decides that the jail does not provide a proper atmosphere for a young boy like Opie, Andy decides to keep Opie away from him at work. But Andy and Aunt Bee come to realize that Andy's and Opie's relationship is more important than worrying about the evil influences of the Mayberry jail. (Episode 32)

End of 1960–61 season

33. "Opie and the Bully" Oct. 2, 1961

Opie is victimized by a seven-year-old bully who demands his milk money on the way to school each day. Opie is afraid, and Andy has to make a very difficult decision. He decides that Opie must face the bully alone. The wait in the office is a long, hard one for Andy as Opie goes to meet the bully, but Opie returns heroically to show that a black eye is painless compared to his earlier fear. (Episode 34)

34. "Barney's Replacement" Oct. 9, 1961

Barney resigns as deputy because he believes that Andy is unsatisfied with his work. The trainee who replaces him, however, upsets everyone in town by exercising the letter instead of the spirit of the law. By allowing Barney to witness the incompetence of the trainee, Andy wins Barney back on the job. (Episode 33)

35. "Andy and the Woman Speeder" Oct. 16, 1961

When Andy jails a beautiful woman for speeding, she proceeds to turn Barney, Aunt Bee, and even Opie against him, bribing Opie with a baseball, telling Barney he looks like Frank Sinatra, and flattering Aunt Bee by complimenting her cooking. During her trial, the woman is made to feel bad when Andy expresses his disappointment in all concerned, especially in the woman for taking advantage of Opie. The woman repents and everyone apologizes to Andy. (Episode 35)

36. "Mayberry Goes Bankrupt" Oct. 23, 1961

The Mayberry Town Council pushes Andy to evict an older citizen for not paying his taxes. Andy discovers that the city apparently owes the citizen a huge sum of money for a century-old municipal bond which he has never redeemed. The council faces bankruptcy and is forced to help the citizen renovate his house rather than pay him. The bond is discovered to be worthless because it is a Confederate bond, but the citizen is saved from eviction, thanks to Andy's help. (Episode 39)

37. "Barney on the Rebound" Oct. 30, 1961

When a father and his daughter come to Mayberry to settle down, Barney goes crazy over the girl, breaks off with Thelma Lou, and courts the newcomer for two straight nights. On the second night she makes it seem that he has proposed to her. The news of the proposal appears in the newspaper and the whole town is buzzing. Barney finally gets Thelma Lou to forgive him, but the girl and her father threaten to sue Barney for breach of promise. Andy, who is suspicious of the newcomers, surprises them by pulling out a Bible and starting the wedding ceremony. The girl and her father admit that they are actually husband and wife and that they hoped to trick Barney out of some money. Andy, of course, kicks the two con artists out of Mayberry. (Episode 36)

38. "Opie's Hobo Friend"   *Nov. 13, 1961*
Opie becomes friends with a hobo (played by Buddy Ebsen), whose carefree life-style appeals to him, but the hobo encourages Opie to be irresponsible. Andy persuades the hobo to consider the bad influence he might have, and the hobo purposely exposes his dishonesty to Opie in order to correct his negative influence on the boy by pretending that he has stolen a pocketbook from Aunt Bee. (Episode 40)

39. "Crime-free Mayberry"   *Nov. 20, 1961*
A supposed FBI agent and his accomplice come to Mayberry to award Andy and Barney for their perfect record of crime prevention, but in reality the two men are out to rob the Mayberry Bank. Andy is not fooled by their trick (Barney is, of course) and captures the crooks at the scene of the crime. (Episode 41)

40. "The Perfect Female"   *Nov. 27, 1961*
Thelma Lou's cousin, Karen, arrives in Mayberry, and Andy becomes interested in her. But Karen resents Andy's placing her in a traditional female role, so she defeats Andy at the yearly skeet-shooting contest. Andy realizes his unfair actions and apologizes. (Episode 37)

41. "Aunt Bee's Brief Encounter"   *Dec. 4, 1961*
A handyman (played by Edgar Buchanan) stops at the Taylor residence, and Aunt Bee is attracted to him. Andy encourages him to stay around for more repair work so that Bee can enjoy his company, but Andy soon learns that the handyman is not sincere in his involvement with Aunt Bee. Andy subtly threatens him with the consequences of insincerity, and the handyman leaves in a hurry. (Episode 38)

42. "The Clubmen"   *Dec. 11, 1961*
Andy and Barney have an opportunity to be selected for membership in an exclusive club, but Barney's lack of social graces

causes him to be rejected. Andy tries to protect Barney's feelings, and Barney mistakenly believes Andy has been rejected. Andy never reveals the truth to Barney, and he turns down the club membership, realizing that his genuine friendship with Barney is the type of friendship he values. (Episode 42)

43. "The Pickle Story"   *Dec. 18, 1961*
Aunt Bee's homemade pickles prove to be too sour for Andy and Barney to eat, but in an attempt to protect her feelings they substitute store-bought pickles in her canning jars and discuss how good the pickles are. Aunt Bee, encouraged by Andy's and Barney's pickle eating, enters the pickle contest at the county fair and threatens to defeat Clara Edwards, the long-time champion. Andy and Barney are forced to eat all the substituted pickles to be sure that Aunt Bee's own pickles are entered in the contest, thus assuring Clara's winning the prize. (Episode 43)

44. "Sheriff Barney"   *Dec. 25, 1961*
Barney has an opportunity to become the sheriff of a neighboring town, but Andy is not convinced that Barney is ready for the responsibility. Andy cleverly allows Barney to be sheriff of Mayberry for one day, and Barney soon discovers that being sheriff is not as easy as he thinks. His lesson learned, Barney remains with Andy in Mayberry. (Episode 44)

45. "The Farmer Takes a Wife"   *Jan. 1, 1962*
When Jeff Pruitt (played by Alan Hale) comes to Mayberry seeking a wife, Andy and Barney are glad to help him until Pruitt's eye falls on Thelma Lou, whom he selects as his choice for a wife. Barney loses his self-control and decides to fight the much tougher Pruitt, but Andy saves Barney and gets rid of Pruitt by having Thelma Lou attempt to "civilize" the farmer. (Episode 45)

46. "The Keeper of the Flame"   *Jan. 8, 1962*
Opie joins a secret club and is designated "The Keeper of the Flame." He vows not to reveal club secrets, but when he is accused of burning a barn, Andy pressures him to tell all. Opie does not understand, for his father seems to suggest that he go back on his word, but Andy tries to explain that sometimes circumstances require modifying absolute ideas. Opie is finally found to be innocent when Andy learns that the owner of the barn burned it himself while making moonshine. (Episode 46)

47. "Bailey's Bad Boy"   *Jan. 15, 1962*
Andy teaches a wealthy young man (played by Bill Bixby) the
satisfaction of self-reliance. Accustomed to his father's pulling
him out of difficulties, Ron Bailey learns from Andy that the
only way to deal with his problems (in this case, to work off a
fine), is to handle them himself. (Episode 47)

48. "The Manicurist"   *Jan. 22, 1962*
A lovely young lady (played by Barbara Eden) becomes a manicurist in Floyd's barbershop, and the men of Mayberry, reluctant at first, accept her enthusiastically. The women of Mayberry
are not convinced they approve and pressure their husbands to
"cool" their interest. The manicurist's feelings are hurt, but the
people of Mayberry finally warm up to her when they realize
that she is not deserving of their unfair treatment. (Episode 48)

49. "The Jinx"   *Jan. 29, 1962*
Andy is disturbed by the accusations of Barney and others that
a local resident is a jinx. Circumstances seem to prove that Barney and his friends are right, but Andy refuses to believe in
such superstitious ideas and attempts to restore the poor man's
self-confidence by "rigging" a lottery. The unlucky man loses
the drawing, but his confidence is restored because of his reali-
zation that the townspeople do care about him. (Episode 49)

50. "Jailbreak"   *Feb. 5, 1962*
The State Police arrive in Mayberry to capture an escaped convict and are condescending to Andy and Barney, who they assume are not capable of understanding complex police methods. Andy proves that "small-town" methods are more effective
and using common sense, he captures the criminal and wins the
respect of the State Police. (Episode 50)

51. "A Medal for Opie"   *Feb. 12, 1962*
Opie dreams of becoming the winner in the school race, and
when another boy comes in first, Opie needs Andy to help him
understand the value of being a good loser. (Episode 51)

52. "Barney and the Choir"   *Feb. 19, 1962*
Andy and his fellow members are faced with a dilemma when
Barney seeks membership in the town choir, for Barney's off-
key singing spoils their harmony, but they don't want to hurt
Barney's feelings by rejecting him. Andy cleverly proposes that

Barney be given the lead role in the choir, but unknown to Barney his microphone doesn't pick up his singing. A fine baritone sings Barney's part behind stage while Barney proudly believes the wonderful voice he hears is his own. Andy solves the problem for the choir and saves Barney's ego. (Episode 52)

53. "Guest of Honor"   *Feb. 26, 1962*
In a festive mood, the townspeople of Mayberry honor a nonresident by making him guest of honor for one day. But the guest proves to be a pickpocket, and Andy and Barney spring into action to foil his attempts and to protect the townspeople from the harsh truth. (Episode 53)

54. "The Merchant of Mayberry"   *March 5, 1962*
When Ben Weaver, the local merchant scrooge, pressures Andy to stop a competitor from selling his wares on the street, Andy supports the underdog merchant by helping him establish a "legitimate" store. Weaver is forced either to accept the competitor or to hire him to work in his own store. (Episode 54)

55. "Aunt Bee the Warden"   *March 12, 1962*
Andy finds that he is short of jail space, and so he brings Otis, the town drunk, home with him to serve his jail sentence there. Aunt Bee determines to play the role of a warden, and under her jurisdiction Otis discovers that he would much rather reform than serve any more time at "the rock," as he call Bee's home. (Episode 55)

56. "The County Nurse"   *March 19, 1962*
Rafe Hollister refuses to submit to a tetanus shot, and Andy helps the county nurse persuade him to give in by singing him a moving song about his death that will occur if he does not have the innoculation. (Episode 56)

57. "Andy and Barney in the Big City"   *March 26, 1962*
Andy and Barney take a trip to Raleigh and become involved in catching a potential jewel thief. Barney takes it upon himself to sniff out the thief, and in his usual way he mistakes the house detective for the crook. He unknowingly serves as the thief's accomplice, but thanks to Andy's watchful eye, he accidentally captures the thief and appears to be the heroic police officer. (Episode 57)

58. "Wedding Bells for Aunt Bee"   *April 2, 1962*
A misunderstanding leads Aunt Bee and Andy to believe that
they are both eager to get married. After encouraging each
other's pretense for several days, they both finally acknowledge
their happiness in being single and free, and promise that in the
future they will be more open with each other. (Episode 58)

59. "Three's a Crowd"   *April 9, 1962*
Andy becomes involved in a romance with Mary Simpson, the
county nurse, but Barney constantly intrudes, never seeming to
realize that three people make a crowd. Andy is frustrated by
Barney's lack of insight, but the situation finally becomes a comical one, for Barney is not easily put off. (Episode 59)

60. "The Bookie Barber"   *April 16, 1962*
Floyd Lawson, the local barber, is excited when a new semi-re-
tired barber comes to Mayberry and proposes a two-chair barbershop, but the seemingly ideal setup proves to be a real setup
for the new barber, who is actually a bookie. Barney attempts to
capture him by posing as a little old lady gambler, and chaos
follows, but Andy comes to the rescue and captures the bookie
ring. Meanwhile, Floyd is oblivious to the whole situation. (Episode 60)

61. "Andy on Trial"   *April 23, 1962*
Barney unknowingly gives information to a female reporter
about the unusual practices of Andy as sheriff, and she twists
the information so that Andy faces charges of malfeasance in
office. When Barney learns what is actually happening, he
makes a moving speech about Andy's honorable conduct, and
the charges are dismissed. (Episode 61)

62. "Cousin Virgil"   *April 30, 1962*
Barney's cousin Virgil (played by Michael Pollard) comes to
Mayberry, and Andy agrees to give him a chance to help around
the sheriff's office, but Virgil constantly makes foolish mistakes
and Barney rather harshly scolds him. Andy realizes that Virgil's
problem is a lack of self-confidence when he sees that Virgil can
do excellent woodcarvings when left to himself. Andy allows
Virgil to correct his own error, and Andy's trust helps the young
cousin restore his confidence. (Episode 62)

63. "Deputy Otis"   *May 7, 1962*
When Otis learns that his brother Ralph is coming to visit, he is

dismayed, for in an attempt to impress his relatives Otis has told them he is a deputy. Andy allows Otis to play this role during the visit, and Otis makes everyone proud of him. Ralph surprises them all by showing that he is actually a town drunk. Otis lectures Ralph about the concept of self-pride, and Ralph is inspired to better himself when he returns home. (Episode 63)

End of 1961–62 season

64. "Mr. McBeevee" *Oct. 1, 1962*
Opie seems to have a make-believe friend named Mr. McBeevee, and when Opie shows up with some money he claims Mr. McBeevee gave him, Andy accuses Opie of carrying his pretense too far. But Andy discovers that there is in fact a Mr. McBeevee, just as Opie described him. (Episode 66)

65. "Andy's Rich Girlfriend" *Oct. 8, 1962*
Andy enjoys his association with Peggy McMillan, an attractive lady, until he learns that her father is wealthy. Andy finds himself having problems trying to live up to a role he has imagined is necessary, but he learns a valuable lesson that true riches lie in being oneself. (Episode 67)

66. "Andy and the New Mayor" *Oct. 15, 1962*
When the new mayor of Mayberry (played by Parley Baer) takes over, he is critical of the job that Andy is doing as sheriff. Andy is hard-pressed to get along with him, but the mayor suddenly learns to appreciate Andy's home-spun methods. (Episode 69)

67. "Andy and Opie—Bachelors" *Oct. 22, 1962*
Aunt Bee leaves for a few days, and Andy and Opie are left to fend for themselves. Peggy McMillan gladly offers to assist them and comes to their home to cook for them each night. Andy listens to the gibes of the local male residents and feels threatened by Peggy's actions, falsely assuming she is trying to "hook" him. He tries to ward off her help and discovers that he has accused her unfairly. He apologizes and all is made well again. (Episode 65)

68. "The Cow Thief" *Oct. 29, 1962*
Several cow thefts in Mayberry baffle Andy, and the mayor impatiently demands that a crime expert be brought in from the city. Andy cleverly solves the mystery of the disappearing cows

by showing that the thief has been putting shoes on the cows to disguise their tracks. (Episode 70)

69. "Barney Mends a Broken Heart"   *Nov. 5, 1962*
When Peggy McMillan has to break a date with Andy, Barney assumes that Andy needs another girl and immediately lines one up for him, despite Andy's protest. Barney's scheme only causes Andy unnecessary humiliation, and Andy finally makes his peace with Peggy. (Episode 68)

70. "Lawman Barney"   *Nov. 12, 1962*
Barney warns some local farmers not to sell their goods along the roadside, but they bully him and scare him away. Andy learns the truth about the matter and helps Barney gain courage by tricking the farmers into believing that Barney is a tough, ruthless lawman who will not tolerate disobedience. Barney finally confronts them with the power of his badge and the law it represents, and they move on. (Episode 73)

71. "The Mayberry Band"   *Nov. 19, 1962*
Andy is called on to shape up the Mayberry band for its annual trip to the state band competition in Raleigh, but the band is anything other than harmonious. In an attempt to convince the mayor that funds should be appropriated, Andy gets a touring jazz group to mix with the town band long enough to win the mayor's approval. (Episode 72)

72. "Floyd, the Gay Deceiver"   *Nov. 26, 1962*
Faced with the visit of a wealthy widow to whom he falsely represented himself as a well-to-do gentleman, Floyd Lawson enlists the help of Andy and Aunt Bee to carry out the deception. The widow turns out to be a deceiver herself and, found out by Andy, heads out of town. Andy keeps her secret from Floyd, lest he hurt his feelings. (Episode 71)

73. "Opie's Rival"   *Dec. 3, 1962*
Opie becomes jealous of Andy's constant attention to Peggy McMillan. Even when fishing, Andy praises Peggy for catching a minnow and ignores Opie's large bass. Opie finally pretends to be sick to regain his father's notice, and Andy soon realizes that he has not been giving his boy enough attention and remedies the situation. (Episode 64)

74. "Convicts at Large"   *Dec. 10, 1962*
Three tough women convicts escape and hold Barney and Floyd

prisoners in a remote cabin. Floyd willingly cooperates with them while Barney attempts to deceive them with his pretense that he is attracted to Big Maud, their leader, in order to give Andy, who appears outside, a chance to capture the women. Andy finally arrests them, but not before Barney tangos Maud right through the door into Andy's hands. (Episode 74)

75. "The Bed Jacket" *Dec. 17, 1962*
Aunt Bee secretly suspects that she will receive a feminine bed jacket for her birthday, but Andy and Opie rather stupidly give her practical gifts: salt and pepper shakers and canning jars. Her reaction prompts Andy to seek the true object of her desire (which he learns about from Clara), only to discover that the mayor has purchased it and plans to use it to swap for Andy's favorite fishing pole, Ol' Eagle-Eye Annie. Andy turns the table on the mayor and secures the gift for Aunt Bee. (Episode 75)

76. "The Bank Job" *Dec. 24, 1962*
Barney is disgusted by the lack of security in the Mayberry bank and sets out to prove that the bank is an easy target for criminals. Meanwhile, genuine criminals do attempt to rob the bank, but by a coincidence their robbery attempt is foiled. (Episode 78)

77. "One-Punch Opie" *Dec. 31, 1962*
Opie is bullied by a new boy who moves to Mayberry and decides he must learn to fight. Barney tries to help him but proves to be a weak boxing coach. Opie finally faces up to the boy, who turns out to be a coward after all, and Opie's friends proclaim him a hero. (Episode 79)

78. "Barney and the Governor" *Jan. 7, 1963*
Barney places a ticket on an illegally parked car only to learn the car belongs to the Governor of the state. Barney refuses to tear up the ticket, but he worries about it. The question of the equality of the law is at stake, and Barney remains firm. The Governor personally commends Barney for his refusal to abandon his duty. (Episode 76)

79. "Man in a Hurry" *Jan. 14, 1963*
A high-powered businessman is forced to remain in Mayberry because his car breaks down. At first he is incensed about the slow-moving efforts to repair his car, but as he tastes the relaxed

Mayberry atmosphere, he learns that he does not want to hurry and actually prolongs his stay. (Episode 77)

80. "High Noon in Mayberry"   *Jan. 21, 1963*
An ex-con comes to Mayberry to see Andy about having sent him to prison. Barney is convinced that the ex-con is out to get Andy, and so he overreacts to the man's visit, especially when he sees him with a gun. Much to Barney's amazement, the ex-con has actually come to give Andy a shotgun as a gift for helping him get his life in order. (Episode 80)

81. "The Loaded Goat"   *Jan. 28, 1963*
A farmer's goat wanders into a storage shed and eats some dynamite. Andy and Barney discover the facts about the goat's meal and are faced with solving the explosive problem. After a series of comical events, the goat is safely led away from town. (Episode 81)

82. "Class Reunion"   *Feb. 4, 1963*
Andy and Barney are excited about seeing their high school sweethearts at the Mayberry class of 1945 reunion. Barney is disappointed when his old flame hardly even recognizes him, but Andy finds that his former sweetheart, Sharon de Spain, remembers him vividly. She and Andy realize that their lifestyles are now very different, and thus they part more satisfied about how their fates have worked out. (Episode 82)

83. "Rafe Hollister Sings"   *Feb. 11, 1963*
Andy discovers that a local farmer has a beautiful singing voice and urges him to audition for an upcoming concert. Some of the "more refined" citizens of Mayberry fear that the farmer is not quite proper, but Andy supports him. In a simple, charming way the singing farmer enchants the audience with his rustic ways and fine voice. (Episode 83)

84. "Opie and the Spoiled Kid"   *Feb. 18, 1963*
Opie meets a spoiled child who convinces him that he should use certain tactics to get Andy to triple his allowance. Opie tries these methods, without success at first, but Andy soon becomes aware that Opie's tantrums are simulated. Andy quickly corrects the problem, using his common sense methods, and both Opie and the spoiled kid learn a lesson. (Episode 84)

85. "The Great Filling Station Robbery"   *Feb. 25, 1963*
Gomer is left in charge at the filling station during the owner's

absence, and several burglaries take place there. A young man who has already been branded as "no good" is accused of the crime, but Andy believes in his good qualities. Barney attempts to capture the criminal on film, but manages to take a picture of himself instead. Finally, the accused young man captures the true criminal by wiring the cash register to a series of automobile batteries. When the thief, who is hiding in the trunk of a car parked inside the filling station, reaches for the cash drawer, he receives a shock, screams, and is arrested by Andy and Barney. (Episode 85)

86. "Andy Discovers America"   *March 4, 1963*
Andy finds himself in trouble with the new teacher for not properly encouraging Opie about the importance of learning history. Andy gets out of his dilemma by telling the boys interesting stories from the past and by suggesting a "history club" to Opie's gang. The boys learn to love their study of history, and Andy gains the teacher's favor. (Episode 86)

87. "Aunt Bee's Medicine Man"   *March 11, 1963*
A traveling medicine man comes to Mayberry, and Aunt Bee purchases some of his Indian elixir. Unfortunately, the elixir is alcoholic and causes Aunt Bee to become "tiddly." Andy is amused when he finds the happy Aunt Bee singing away merrily in her intoxicated state, but he brings her back to the ground and drives the peddler from town. (Episode 87)

88. "The Darlings Are Coming"   *March 18, 1963*
A family of mountain musicians, the Darlings, come to Mayberry to meet a bus, and Andy finds himself faced with a wily group of lively folks who constantly cause problems about town. But Andy, who understands their character and appreciates their music, takes the Darling family home and joins in with them to play some good mountain music. (Episode 88)

89. "Andy's English Valet"   *March 25, 1963*
Bernard Fox makes his debut in this episode as Malcolm Merriweather, an English tourist who comes to Mayberry and incurs a fine for reckless driving. Andy finds himself with a valet and chauffeur as Malcolm works off his fine. (Episode 89)

90. "Barney's First Car"   *April 1, 1963*
Barney decides he needs a car of his own, and so he purchases a used car with his life's savings. The car proves to be a lemon,

and Barney soon realizes he has been "taken." Andy prepares a trap for the little old lady who sold Barney the car and captures her and her dishonest crew. The crooked old lady is played by Ellen Corby, best remembered for her more recent role as Grandma Walton on *The Waltons*. (Episode 90)

91. "The Rivals"   *April 8, 1963*
Opie develops a puppy love for a little girl named Karen, and Barney attempts to teach him how to woo women. But Barney's teachings turn on him, for Thelma Lou becomes Opie's chief interest, and Barney finds that Opie is his rival. Fortunately for Barney, Opie realizes that he can't be happy with Thelma Lou and rejects her in favor of Karen. (Episode 91)

92. "A Wife for Andy"   *April 15, 1963*
Barney attempts to push Andy into marriage by presenting to him the eligible young ladies of Mayberry. Barney contrives several meetings where the girls are displayed, but Andy leaves in disgust when he learns of Barney's plan. Barney is left to try to explain the events to the angry ladies. (Episode 92)

93. "Dogs, Dogs, Dogs"   *April 22, 1963*
A visiting state official comes to Mayberry, and Andy attempts to impress him, but a pack of hunting dogs overruns the Mayberry courthouse. Much to Andy's delight, the dogs prove to be a blessing, for the somewhat tight-fisted official loves hunting dogs and is so impressed that he gives Andy extra funds. (Episode 93)

94. "Mountain Wedding"   *April 29, 1963*
Ernest T. Bass attempts to win Charlene Darling away from her true love, Dud Wash. Ernest T. is determined to prevent Charlene and Dud's marriage, and in an attempt to trick Ernest T., Barney is disguised as the bride and is stolen away by the eager Bass. Charlene marries Dud and Ernest T. loses his chance. (Episode 94)

95. "The Big House"   *May 6, 1963*
Barney starts his own rehabilitation program at the Mayberry jail when two thieves are kept there temporarily. But Barney's attempts to rehabilitate them prove to be an embarrassment, for he unknowingly provides the criminals with a means of escape. Fortunately Andy comes to the rescue and recaptures the crimi-

nals. George Kennedy guest stars as one of the detectives called in to help with the capture. (Episode 95)

End of 1962–63 season

96. "Opie the Birdman" *Sept. 30, 1963*
Opie accidentally kills a mother bird with his slingshot and must take on the responsibility of being foster-mother to her three young birds. He learns to love the birds (named Winkin, Blinkin, and Nod) but must make a tough decision about freeing them when they learn to fly. Opie realizes that he must let them go, and he proves to Andy how responsible he is. (Episode 101)

97. "The Haunted House" *Oct. 7, 1963*
Opie loses his baseball in a "haunted house," and Barney and Gomer are sent to retrieve it. They flee back to Andy, assuring him the house is indeed haunted. Andy goes with them, hears the ghosts himself, and finally captures them. The "ghosts" prove to be a moonshiner and Otis, who have set up a still in the basement. (Episode 98)

98. "Ernest T. Bass Joins the Army" *Oct. 14, 1963*
Andy has his hands full when Ernest T. Bass comes to Mayberry to join the Army in order to impress his girlfriend and is rejected by the recruiting sergeant. Ernest T. seeks revenge, and Andy is forced to try to stop him. Andy finally solves the problem by getting an old uniform for Ernest T. (Episode 99)

99. "The Sermon for Today" *Oct. 21, 1963*
A visiting preacher suggests that the Mayberry residents need to slow down and enjoy life. The residents take the sermon to heart and try to rejuvenate the Mayberry band for a Sunday afternoon concert. The efforts to repair and restore the band cause more pain than pleasure, and the Mayberry residents realize that they are already relaxed. (Episode 100)

100. "Briscoe Declares for Aunt Bee" *Oct. 28, 1963*
Briscoe Darling seeks Aunt Bee's hand in marriage, much to her dismay. Andy tries to help Aunt Bee out of her uncomfortable situation, but Briscoe kidnaps her. Aunt Bee escapes by pretending to accept Briscoe, but she assures him he must become

more civilized to meet her expectations. He quickly sends her on her way. (Episode 96)

101. "Gomer the House Guest"   *Nov. 4, 1963*
Gomer loses his job and dwelling at the filling station, and Andy allows him to move into his house. The result is unhappiness for Andy because of Gomer's irritating habits about the house. Gomer finally gets his job and room back at Wally's and frees Andy from his burden. (Episode 97)

102. "A Black Day for Mayberry"   *Nov. 11, 1963*
A gold shipment is secretly scheduled to pass through Mayberry on its way to Fort Knox, but Barney lets the secret out and the truck is met by a large crowd of Mayberrians. Barney then suspects the shipment is being hijacked and he "arrests" the F.B.I. agents. Later, it is revealed that the truck was a decoy and that the actual gold shipment went by another route. Ronny Howard's brother, Clint, and father, Rance, put in brief appearances in the episode. (Episode 102)

103. "Opie's Ill-gotten Gain"   *Nov. 18, 1963*
Opie is puzzled when he brings home an all-"A" report card, knowing that he doesn't deserve the grades. However, when Andy wants to reward him with a new bicycle, he doesn't protest. Later, his teacher calls Opie in to explain that she made a mistake on his report card. He tells Andy and gets the bicycle anyway. (Episode 103)

104. "A Date for Gomer"   *Nov. 25, 1963*
When Thelma Lou refuses to go with Barney to a dance unless her cousin Mary also has a date, Barney gets Gomer as a partner for Mary. The two make a rather awkward pair at first, but in the end Gomer succeeds in bringing Mary out of her shyness. (Episode 105)

105. "Up in Barney's Room"   *Dec. 2, 1963*
Barney is evicted from his room in a boarding house for illegal cooking and sets up his home in the back room of the jail. Andy finds the situation unbearable, but fortunately Mrs. Mendelbright, Barney's landlady, takes Barney back into her graces after she is nearly ruined by the dishonesty of the new boarder who replaced Barney. (Episode 104)

106. "Citizen's Arrest" *Dec. 16, 1963*
Barney gives Gomer a ticket for making a U-turn, and Gomer retaliates by making a citizen's arrest against Barney for the same offense. The result is a feud between the two since Barney considers himself exempt from arrest. Andy finally steps in and solves the dispute. (Episode 106)

107. "Opie and His Merry Men" *Dec. 30, 1963*
Opie and his pals befriend a hobo in Robin Hood fashion by taking from the rich pantries of Mayberry to give to the poor hobo. Andy discovers the tricks that the hobo is playing on the well-meaning boys and steps in to teach them all a lesson. When the hobo is offered a chance at honest earnings, he flees, and Opie learns that some men take advantage of charity. (Episode 108)

108. "Barney and the Cave Rescue" *Jan. 6, 1964*
Barney organizes a rescue party when he believes that Andy and Helen are trapped in a cave, but Andy and Helen escape through a back exit after the cave-in. Andy hears about Barney's rescue attempt on the radio and realizes that Barney will be ridiculed for his zealousness. He and Helen climb back into the cave and pretend to be saved by Barney, who is proclaimed a hero. (Episode 109)

109. "Andy and Opie's Pal" *Jan. 13, 1964*
Opie befriends a newcomer to Mayberry, but he becomes jealous when Andy gives much of his attention to the new boy. Opie at first cannot learn to hide his unhappiness, but Andy teaches him that true friendship involves sharing. (Episode 110)

110. "Aunt Bee the Crusader" *Jan. 20, 1964*
When a local farmer whose property has been condemned refuses to leave the premises, Aunt Bee starts a crusade to help the poor man, and Andy becomes the target of her abuse. Much to Bee's surprise, she learns the man's true reason for wanting to stay is that he has a moonshine operation in his chicken house. (Episode 111)

111. "Barney's Sidecar" *Jan. 27, 1964*
Much to Andy's dismay, Barney purchases an army-surplus motorcycle and begins to ride about Mayberry disturbing the peace of the town. Andy finally returns the cycle with Barney's bless-

ing by pretending that the cycle is of historical significance and must be put on public display. (Episode 112)

112. "My Fair Ernest T. Bass" *Feb. 3, 1964*
Andy and Barney update "My Fair Lady" by attempting to polish the crude manners of Ernest T. Bass to the point where they can pass him off as a proper Bostonian at Mrs. Wiley's swank evening party. He manages to pass muster for a few moments, but when someone takes away his dancing partner, he strikes him on the head with a vase and Mrs. Wiley discovers Andy's ploy. (Episode 113)

113. "Prisoner of Love" *Feb. 10, 1964*
A beautiful prisoner spends a day in the Mayberry jail, and Andy becomes attracted to her as she eagerly attends to his accounts of his past. A bit lovesick, he watches her leave town in the state patrol car and overhears her flatter the state trooper the same way she did him. (Episode 114)

114. "Hot Rod Otis" *Feb. 17, 1964*
Otis Campbell acquires a car, and the people of Mayberry appear to be in danger. Otis is suspected of driving under the influence, but Andy and Barney soon discover that Otis is not as irresponsible as everyone assumes, for he does not drive when he actually is intoxicated. (Episode 115)

115. "The Song Festers" *Feb. 24, 1964*
When Gomer is overheard singing while changing a flat tire, he is recruited to join the singing group. He outsings Barney and later pretends to have laryngitis so as not to hurt Barney's feelings. Gomer's white lie is discovered when he reveals himself accidentally before the group goes onstage. Gomer joins them and he, Andy, and Barney sing as a trio—the voices of Gomer and Andy drowning out Barney's faltering tenor. Andy Griffith's first wife, Barbara, appears in this episode as a member of the singing group. (Episode 116)

116. "The Shoplifters" *March 2, 1964*
An outbreak of thievery prompts Barney to disguise himself as a mannequin in the department store. Barney is recognized by many of the townspeople, but his disguise proves somewhat successful when he notices a woman concealing merchandise. When he accosts her and searches her purse, nothing is found and Barney is made to look the fool. But Andy later proves that

Barney was right by exposing the woman. She had hidden the merchandise under her coat. (Episode 117)

117. "Andy's Vacation"   *March 9, 1964*
Andy decides to take a week off and spend that time relaxing at home and fishing at Myers' Lake. Gomer is deputized, and he and Barney allow a prisoner to escape. On one occasion, Andy accidentally walks into the courthouse just as the prisoner is about to flee. When the prisoner is allowed to escape again, Andy must recapture him while Barney grapples with Gomer, whom he mistakes for the escapee. Andy's vacation thus becomes a disaster as it is repeatedly interrupted. (Episode 118)

118. "Andy Saves Gomer"   *March 16, 1964*
Andy finds Gomer asleep in Wally's gas station and makes the mistake of "saving" his life by putting out a small fire. Gomer refuses to let Andy forget his "heroism" and obsequiously attends to his every need, not realizing that he is preventing Andy from performing both office and household duties. Finally Andy arranges a situation to make Gomer think he has returned the favor by saving Andy's life. (Episode 119)

119. "Bargain Day"   *March 23, 1964*
Aunt Bee forsakes the local butcher when she buys a freezer of beef from another butcher in order to save money. Andy is upset when their old freezer shorts out and Aunt Bee won't allow him to call a repairman from Mt. Pilot because of the expense. Gomer's attempt to repair the freezer is only temporarily successful. And when the machine coughs for the last time, Aunt Bee must swallow her pride and ask the local butcher if she can store the meat in his meat locker. He agrees. In the end, Andy buys Aunt Bee a new freezer. (Episode 120)

120. "Divorce, Mountain Style"   *March 30, 1964*
The superstitious Darling family comes down from the mountains to arrange the marriage of Charlene and Andy. Andy is shocked and tries to reason with the Darlings but with no luck. Barney reads in a book about mountain folklore and superstition that a marriage may be called off and even cursed if the bride and groom see a man riding a white horse from east to west. Andy persuades Barney to don black clothing and ride the white horse at the proper moment. The Darlings see the sight and return to the hills, believing the marriage to be cursed. (Episode 121)

121. "A Deal Is a Deal" *April 6, 1964*
Opie orders salve from a dubious distributor and is stuck with it when it doesn't sell. Barney and Gomer pose as buyers and visit the "salve office." They act interested in buying all of the product, and the distributor recalls all of the salve that he has sent out. When the plan backfires, Barney and Gomer are themselves the recipients of several cases of salve. (Episode 122)

122. "Fun Girls" *April 13, 1964*
Barney and Andy cancel their dates with Helen and Thelma Lou so that they can work late. Their work is interrupted by two fun-loving blondes from Mt. Pilot. They get rid of the girls for a while, only to have them return as Helen and Thelma Lou, feeling sorry for the men, decide to drop by the office. They are surprised to find the "fun girls" there flirting with Andy and Barney. Confusion ensues and Andy and Barney finally explain the situation. (Episode 123)

123. "The Return of Malcolm Merriweather" *April 20, 1964*
Malcolm Merriweather, the Englishman, returns to Mayberry and upsets Aunt Bee because he is so efficient in organizing daily routines and keeping house. Malcolm purposely pretends to be intoxicated in order to lose his job. To protect Aunt Bee's feelings, Andy discovers what Malcolm has done and goes after him to bring him back into the good graces of the Taylor family. (Episode 124)

124. "The Rumor" *April 27, 1964*
Typically jumping to conclusions, Barney, anxious to see Andy with a wife and Opie with a mother, surmises that Andy and Helen will soon announce wedding plans when he sees them together in a jewelry store. Barney informs Thelma Lou and spreads his suspicions to the rest of the town. Throughout, Andy and Helen are met with approving smiles and gestures from the townspeople. Naturally the couple is confused. Barney's surprise party at the Taylor household is ruined when Andy and Helen dispel Barney's rumor. (Episode 125)

125. "Barney and Thelma Lou, Phfftt" *May 4, 1964*
Barney sees Thelma Lou innocently kiss Gomer Pyle in thanks for a favor—driving her to Mt. Pilot. Barney is jealous, for he assumed that Thelma Lou was his girl. Gomer mistakenly tries to prevent Thelma Lou from falling for him, but she plays a

trick on him and Barney by pretending to be attracted to Gomer. Finally Barney reconciles himself with her, understanding that he cannot take her for granted. (Episode 126)

126. "Back to Nature"   *May 11, 1964*
When Barney and Gomer become lost on a camping trip with Andy, Opie, and several of Opie's friends, Andy tries to save Barney and Gomer from embarrassment. He leaves the camp to look for them, finds Gomer, and tells him to follow Andy's imitation "lakeloon" call back to camp. Barney, hearing the "lakeloon," finds his way back to camp. After Andy makes a speech praising Barney's woodsmanship, Opie and his friends applaud Barney and Gomer, and Barney makes himself out to be the expert camper. (Episode 127)

127. "Gomer Pyle, U.S.M.C."   *May 19, 1964*
Gomer Pyle decides to join the Marine Corps, but even with Andy's able assistance he manages to run afoul of military regulations and tries the thin patience of Sergeant Carter (played by Frank Sutton). Written, produced, and directed by Aaron Ruben, this episode introduced Jim Nabors' own successful series, leaving his place on the *Griffith Show* to be filled the next year by George Lindsey (Cousin Goober). (Episode 107)

End of 1963–64 season

128. "Opie Loves Helen"   *Sept. 21, 1964*
Andy and Helen don't want to hurt Opie when they find out he has a crush on Helen. Opie, when he discovers that adult courting involves certain things he's not interested in and that grown-up women don't like to go fishing or catch frogs, goes to Helen and "tries to let her down easy." Helen acts hurt but tells Opie that she understands. Opie's innocence is preserved and Andy and Helen resume their relationship. (Episode 132)

129. "Barney's Physical"   *Sept. 28, 1964*
Barney isn't tall enough and doesn't weigh enough to meet the new requirements. Stretching himself by hanging in the closet, Barney meets the height requirement. At the time of the physical, in spite of Aunt Bee's good cooking, he still doesn't weigh enough. Andy has Barney wear his police whistle on a very heavy chain, thus conforming to the regulations and passing the

weight test. This is the first of eight episodes that Howard Morris directed. (Episode 131)

130. "Family Visit"   *Oct. 5, 1964*
To please Aunt Bee, Andy agrees to allow her to invite relatives to Mayberry. The obnoxious Uncle Ollie and his wife and kids invade and take over the Taylor household as Andy silently suffers the inconvenience. Ollie, fascinated by the patrol car, continually plays with the siren. With Andy at the end of his rope, Ollie borrows the squad car to go fishing. When Andy finds it gone, he is furious. As the family prepares to leave, Andy and Aunt Bee politely ask them to stay on. To their dismay, they do. (Episode 129)

131. "The Education of Ernest T. Bass"   *Oct. 12, 1964*
Ernest T. Bass goes back to school in Mayberry when his girl does not approve of his illiteracy. His classroom behavior disrupts the education process in Mayberry, but Andy solves the problem by holding a ceremony and awarding him with a special diploma. (Episode 133)

132. "Aunt Bee's Romance"   *Oct. 19, 1964*
When Aunt Bee's old beau shows up in Mayberry, Andy is at first friendly with him, tolerating his obnoxious practical jokes for Aunt Bee's sake. The courtship develops and Roger proposes to Aunt Bee. Realizing that Roger wants to marry only for material comfort and security, Andy "bribes" Roger into leaving. Upon discovering Roger gone, Aunt Bee is at first mildly shocked but admits to Andy that she's glad that the romance didn't work out. (Episode 130)

133. "Barney's Bloodhound"   *Oct. 26, 1964*
Barney purchases what he claims to be a bloodhound but what is actually a bedraggled mutt. The dog will respond only to a silent dog whistle, and then he responds by viciously attacking the blower of the whistle. Barney, using the dog to track an escaped convict, is taken in by the criminal posing as a fisherman. Andy arrives on the scene, allows himself to get caught, and tricks the convict into blowing the dog whistle. The dog attacks him and he is captured. (Episode 128)

134. "Man in the Middle"   *Nov. 2, 1964*
Andy finds himself in the middle of a spat between Barney and Thelma Lou. Talking privately to each, Andy for a time loses

both as friends when Barney finds out what Andy said to Thelma Lou and when Thelma Lou hears what Andy said about her to Barney. Andy finally arranges a situation to bring the two together, and the lovers patch up their differences. (Episode 134)

135. "Barney's Uniform" *Nov. 9, 1964*
When Barney is threatened by the town's bully, he begins wearing his uniform everywhere because the man promises to thrash Barney if he catches him out of uniform. Andy realizes what Barney is doing and hires a judo expert to pose as Barney. The man attacks the imposter, is badly beaten, and the threat to Barney is over. (Episode 135)

136. "Opie's Fortune" *Nov. 16, 1964*
Opie finds a wallet with fifty dollars, but Andy tells him he must hold it for seven days before Opie can claim it. The owner doesn't show up in Mayberry until after Opie has spent some of the money. When Opie overhears the owner express to Andy his need for the money, Opie goes to the store to return his purchase. Andy thinks that Opie knows the truth of the matter and that the boy refuses to return the money. When Andy finds Opie in the store, he furiously grabs his son only to find that Opie is planning to return the money. Andy learns another valuable lesson in child rearing. (Episode 136)

137. "Goodbye, Sheriff Taylor" *Nov. 23, 1964*
Andy goes to Raleigh for a job interview, and Barney acts as temporary sheriff, causing chaos in Mayberry, including a traffic jam in the usually calm town. When Andy returns, Barney acts as though all were well, but Floyd lets the truth slip. (Episode 137)

138. "The Pageant" *Nov. 30, 1964*
With Clara away attending to a sick relative, Aunt Bee assumes the starring role of Lady Mayberry in the Mayberry pageant. While Aunt Bee rehearses, Andy and Opie are left to fend for themselves. Clara returns and begins to take care of the Taylor men. Aunt Bee, whose acting "ability" distresses the director of the pageant, becomes uneasy when Clara invades her kitchen. Aunt Bee returns home when she realizes that Andy and Opie are "doing fine" without her, and Clara resumes the role of Lady Mayberry, which she had played for years. (Episode 138)

139. "The Darling Baby" *Dec. 7, 1964*
The Darlings come to town to claim Opie as the future husband of Charlene's new baby, but naturally Opie objects. Andy plays upon the superstition of the Darlings by using disappearing ink for the signing of a marriage contract, and the Darlings reject Opie as a suitable husband. (Episode 139)

140. "Andy and Helen Have Their Day" *Dec. 14, 1964*
Andy and Helen look forward to their day off and plan to spend it with a picnic lunch at a secluded spot near the lake. After assuring Andy that he can run the sheriff's office for the day, Barney continuously interrupts him with foolish problems, ruining the couple's outing. (Episode 140)

141. "Three Wishes for Opie" *Dec. 21, 1964*
Barney shows Opie the art of Gypsy fortune telling, and Andy is not convinced that such predictions are valid. But Barney grants three wishes to Opie, which seem to begin to come true. Opie finally learns that Barney is not actually able to grant wishes or predict the future. (Episode 142)

142. "Otis Sues the County" *Dec. 28, 1964*
At Barney's insistence, Otis hires a lawyer to present his case when the town drunk falls in the jail, sustaining only a minor injury. The lawyer proves crooked and urges Otis to sue the county. Andy and Barney disown Otis when they discover his intentions. During the trial, Otis realizes the error of his actions, the crooked lawyer is exposed, and Otis decides not to sue. (Episode 141)

143. "Barney Fife, Realtor" *Jan. 4, 1965*
Barney's attempts to earn some extra money as a realtor become a nuisance to Andy when Barney persuades him to sell his house and buy another one he has long admired. Andy discovers that his own home is the right place for him and that business and friendship do not mix well. Barney is disappointed, but he doesn't give up his "dealing." (Episode 143)

144. "Goober Takes a Car Apart" *Jan. 11, 1965*
His friend Gilly asks Goober, who is answering Andy's telephone for an afternoon, to work on his car. Goober's dilemma is that he must stay in the office to answer the phone—so he dismantles the car and assembles it in the courthouse. When Andy returns,

he is shocked to find the car in his jail; so Goober must once again dismantle Gilly's car. (Episode 144)

145. "The Rehabilitation of Otis" *Jan. 18, 1965*
Otis Campbell rides into town on a cow thinking it is a horse. Barney takes it upon himself to rehabilitate Otis, but his pseudo-psychological approach succeeds only in forcing Otis to the Mt. Pilot jail. Barney and Andy both come to realize how much they miss Otis and are delighted at his return, again on a cow. (Episode 145)

146. "The Lucky Letter" *Jan. 25, 1965*
Barney believes he is hexed for not continuing a "lucky" chain letter, but Andy assures him he isn't. Barney, unwilling to believe that he isn't hexed, seeks the disposed-of letter in the garbage dump. He finally discovers that the letter is not the true cause of his bad luck. (Episode 146)

147. "Goober and the Art of Love" *Feb. 1, 1965*
Goober is a constant nuisance to Andy and Barney when they're with Helen and Thelma Lou. So Andy and Barney fix Goober up with Thelma Lou's cousin, Lydia, and they believe their problems are solved. Goober, however, has different ideas. He enjoys their company and continues to make himself a pest around the couples, joining them at the diner and later for dancing. (Episode 147)

148. "Barney Runs for Sheriff" *Feb. 8, 1965*
Mayberry is shocked when Andy entertains the idea of taking another job. Andy, sure he will be leaving, convinces Barney that he is the best candidate for sheriff of Mayberry. After Barney gets caught up in the prestige of his potential position, Andy's job falls through. The Mayberry townspeople show their confidence in Andy by writing in his name on the ballot. For a time, tension exists between Barney and Andy, but the two resolve their differences. Barney realizes that Andy is best for the job even though his pride is hurt somewhat. (Episode 148)

149. "If I Had a Quarter-Million" *Feb. 15, 1965*
Barney finds $250,000 in cash from a bank robbery and decides to capture the robber himself. Pretending to be a civilian who has suddenly come upon considerable wealth, he lures the robber into a trap. He is outwitted by the crook, however, and Andy has to save the day by making the arrest. (Episode 149)

150. "TV or Not TV"   *March 1, 1965*
Under the guise of being a Hollywood film company, a group of
men come to Mayberry to make a picture about this crime-free
town. When they discover that Andy does not carry a gun and
that Asa, the bank guard, is usually asleep while on duty, they
plan to rob the Mayberry bank. When Barney finds the men in
the bank later that night, they convince him that they are filming a movie and Barney eagerly plays a supporting role. The
robbers hold Barney and Asa at gunpoint, but Andy arrives in
time to save them and the money. Gavin MacLeod plays the part
of one of the robbers. (Episode 150)

151. "Guest in the House"   *March 8, 1965*
Helen Crump becomes jealous when a pretty friend of the
family stays at the Taylor home. Helen's anger soon conveys itself to Andy, who learns that a woman wronged is a dangerous
creature and turns his affections back in the direction of his
steady girlfriend. (Episode 151)

152. "The Case of the Punch in the Nose"   *March 15, 1965*
Digging through old criminal records, Barney finds that a case
between two Mayberry residents in which one punched the
other was never resolved. Barney is determined to reopen the
case despite Andy's advice. Barney confronts those involved in
the long-forgotten skirmish and succeeds in creating bad blood
once again. However, in this instance, the entire town becomes
involved, some siding with Floyd, some with Charlie Foley.
Chaos results, and Andy must become involved to restore order.
(Episode 152)

153. "Opie's Newspaper"   *March 22, 1965*
Opie becomes interested in journalism on a minor scale, and
when he decides to print his own newspaper, Barney, Andy, and
Aunt Bee all approve until complaints begin to pour in over the
nature of the paper's subject matter. Opie takes literally Andy's
advice to report only the facts, and he prints everything he
overhears, regardless of how scandalous it is. The townspeople
find Opie's "Gossip Column" intriguing until their own names
appear. Opie learns a lesson in discretion and good judgment.
(Episode 153)

154. "Aunt Bee's Invisible Beau"   *March 29, 1965*
Aunt Bee pretends to have a beau in order to free Andy from

worrying about her, but the invented beau, the butter and egg man, is actually married, although Aunt Bee doesn't know it. Andy nearly makes a mistake in accusing the man of two-timing, but he finally realizes the truth and makes Aunt Bee understand that she need not pretend. (Episode 154)

155. "The Arrest of the Fun Girls" *April 5, 1965*
The "fun girls" from Mt. Pilot return to plague Andy and Barney. The girls are determined to get the men to take them dining and dancing. On purpose, they get themselves arrested for speeding and insist on being taken to jail. Suffering much embarrassment and inconvenience, Andy and Barney escape the girls once again. (Episode 155)

156. "The Luck of Newton Monroe" *April 12, 1965*
Newton Monroe (Don Rickles) comes to Mayberry to find work. Monroe is an itinerant peddler whose inability to do anything right has caused the people to avoid patronizing him. Andy and Barney employ him as a handyman around the courthouse and at the Taylor home. Newton's propensity for careless mistakes and bad luck prompt Andy and Barney to arrange it so that Newton will think his luck has changed and will thus repair his self-confidence. (Episode 156)

157. "Opie Flunks Arithmetic" *April 19, 1965*
When Opie's arithmetic grades fall below par, Barney uses his own methods to help Opie, and begins convincing Andy that Opie will not be prepared for a college career. Andy overreacts to Opie's grades and halts the boy's usual play. Helen convinces Andy that he is overreacting, and Opie returns to being a normal boy, even improving his grades. (Episode 157)

158. "Opie and the Carnival" *April 26, 1965*
Opie tries to win a razor for Andy at the carnival shooting gallery. The boy is puzzled when he can't hit the target, and finally spends all of the money he could have used to buy his father a gift. Opie doesn't realize that the sights on the guns are crooked. Andy becomes suspicious, visits the shooting gallery, and observes the proprietors switching guns. He makes them promise to give Opie the gun with no defect when he returns. Goober persuades Opie to try his luck one more time, and with the good gun he wins the razor. (Episode 158)

159. "Banjo Playing Deputy"   *May 3, 1965*
Jerry Van Dyke, brother of Dick Van Dyke, appears in this episode as a destitute carnival banjo player. Andy gives him a chance to be a deputy, but he proves to be quite inept. Andy helps him regain his self-respect and acts as a true friend to him. (Episode 159)

End of 1964–65 season

160. "Opie's Job"   *Sept. 13, 1965*
Opie and Billy Crenshaw arrive at Mr. Doakes' grocery store to apply for a job as delivery boy. Both boys are employed for a week's trial, but when Opie discovers that Billy needs to work to help pay his family's hospital bills, he loses the job on purpose. Andy reprimands him angrily until he finds out Opie's reason for "losing" the job. Once again, Andy learns that he shouldn't underestimate Opie. (Episode 161)

161. "Andy's Rival"   *Sept. 20, 1965*
A sophisticated teacher, well-educated and handsome, comes to Mayberry to work with Helen on a project for her school. Andy becomes jealous because Helen continually breaks their dates so that she can work. Andy finally comes to understand that his jealousy is ill-founded and accepts Helen's need to keep up with the demands of her profession. (Episode 163)

162. "Malcolm at the Crossroads"   *Sept. 27, 1965*
Ernest T. Bass is given a job by Andy as a school crossing guard and is made to feel important by both the job and the uniform that he is allowed to wear. When he is replaced by Andy's English friend, Malcolm Merriweather, he becomes furious and threatens Malcolm with physical harm. (Episode 164)

163. "Aunt Bee, the Swinger"   *Oct. 4, 1965*
Claiming that her life has no excitement, Aunt Bee meets a new boyfriend who enjoys going out on the town. Andy is amazed at Aunt Bee's new-found energy when she and her new boyfriend stay out late dancing and then begin other activities early the next morning. Pride overcomes the older couple, and neither is willing to admit that age is taking its toll until Andy points out to Aunt Bee that she is too tired to do her usual household duties. (Episode 160)

164. "The Bazaar"   *Oct. 11, 1965*
Warren Ferguson, Barney's replacement, is anxious to show
Andy that he is an efficient lawman. He proves overly ambitious,
however, when he arrests Aunt Bee and her friends for operating a Bingo table at the charity bazaar. When they refuse to pay
a simple fine, Warren refuses to drop the charges, and Andy
finds that his courthouse has become a boarding house for
women. This is the first appearance of Jack Burns as Deputy
Warren. (Episode 162)

165. "A Warning from Warren"   *Oct. 15, 1965*
Andy and Helen's picnic plans are spoiled when Warren warns
them that something ominous is going to happen. Andy and
Helen go on their picnic anyway, despite Warren's attempts to
prevent them. Warren accompanies the couple to the picnic spot
and himself brings on the disaster when he overturns the couple's boat. Andy is furious, and Warren sheepishly reminds
Andy of his ominous prophecy. (Episode 169)

166. "Off to Hollywood"   *Oct. 25, 1965*
Opie, Aunt Bee, and Andy leave for Hollywood to observe the
making of a movie about Andy entitled "Sheriff Without a Gun."
A large crowd turns out to see them off, and Andy and Helen
part reluctantly. The family is shown on the plane anticipating
their arrival in Hollywood and later as they arrive at their hotel
room. The movie studio has arranged for their accommoda-
tions, but Andy and Aunt Bee are uncomfortable in their new
plush surroundings. (Episode 166)

167. "Taylors in Hollywood"   *Nov. 1, 1965*
Included in the Taylors' sight-seeing of Hollywood is a trip to
the movie studio where the film about Andy is being made. The
family is shocked by the fast pace around the set, but are even
more amazed when they see the actors who are going to play
their roles in the movie. Andy is depicted as a fearless, romantic
hero (played by Gavin McLeod) and Aunt Bee is played by a
young, sexy blonde. (Episode 167)

168. "The Hollywood Party"   *Nov. 8, 1965*
Ruta Lee plays a beautiful Hollywood starlet who becomes
mildly interested in the shy Andy when the two pose for publicity photographs at the studio's insistence. She invites him to her
apartment, and Aunt Bee persuades the reluctant Andy to go.

When Helen sees one of the pictures in the Mayberry paper, she becomes jealous and calls the Taylor hotel room, only to find that Andy is at the starlet's apartment. Andy explains the situation to Helen, and she apologizes for not trusting him. (Episode 168)

169. "Aunt Bee on TV"   *Nov. 15, 1965*
Aunt Bee wins some modern appliances on a local game show, and by constantly bragging about the items to her friends she finds that they begin to resent her. Realizing her mistake, she returns all of the goods and regains her friends. (Episode 165)

170. "The Cannon"   *Nov. 22, 1965*
Deputy Warren captures two thieves attempting a robbery in Mayberry. His and Goober's bumbling attempt to fire the old town cannon leads to the criminals' arrest. (Episode 172)

171. "A Man's Best Friend"   *Nov. 29, 1965*
Opie and a smart-aleck friend plant a walkie-talkie under the collar of Goober's new dog and make Goober think that he has a talking dog. Goober dreams of show business until he learns that the dog won't talk when he is around other people. Andy discovers the boys' trick and persuades Goober to play a practical joke back on them. (Episode 170)

172. "Aunt Bee Takes a Job"   *Dec. 6, 1965*
Aunt Bee gets a job with a greeting card company, but the new proprietors are really counterfeiters. The merchants of Mayberry alert Andy to the appearance of false currency, and while he becomes suspicious of Aunt Bee's new employers, he refrains from investigation to protect Aunt Bee until the evidence becomes overwhelming. Andy nabs the two men just as they are about to leave town, and Aunt Bee happily returns to her domestic duties in the Taylor home. (Episode 171)

173. "The Church Organ"   *Dec. 13, 1965*
Andy struggles with the financial challenge of helping his impoverished church congregation obtain a new organ. But Clara Edwards saves the day by playing a heart-felt song for a local widower, who is so moved by her sincerity that he donates his organ to the church. (Episode 174)

174. "Girl-shy"   *Dec. 20, 1965*
Normally shy with girls, Warren becomes aggressive after watching a love story on television. He goes to sleep, and when

Helen comes to the courthouse, he becomes a Casanova while sleepwalking. Helen is shocked at his behavior, but Warren has no recollection of his actions the next morning. He does everything to combat his night-time activities, including trying to stay up all night, but finally ends up chaining himself to the bed. (Episode 173)

175. "Otis, the Artist" *Jan. 3, 1966*
Warren attempts to rehabilitate Otis, the town drunk, by starting him on a therapeutic career in art, and Andy is faced with the problem of whether or not to display one of Otis's horrible paintings in his living room. Otis's artist career proves to be short-lived. (Episode 175)

176. "The Return of Barney Fife" *Jan. 10, 1966*
Barney returns to Mayberry from Raleigh, where he has become a detective with the police force. He and Andy enjoy talking over old times, and while the two are preparing for their high school reunion, Barney expresses interest in his old sweetheart, Thelma Lou. He is sure that she still loves him. At the reunion Barney is crushed when he finds out that Thelma Lou is married. Andy consoles him, and the two have a good time with other ladies, one of whom informs Barney that she has always admired him. (Episode 176)

177. "The Legend of Barney Fife" *Jan. 17, 1966*
Warren idolizes Barney, whom he has replaced, as he has heard stories from Andy and others of Barney's past "heroism." When the state police inform Andy and Warren about an escaped convict near Mayberry, Warren assumes that Barney will be anxious to accompany them. Of course, Barney is afraid, but Warren all but shames him into going. Andy makes it look as if Barney is responsible for capturing the criminal, and Warren's hero-worship is justified. (Episode 177)

178. "Lost and Found" *Jan. 24, 1966*
Aunt Bee collects insurance for the loss of an antique jeweled pin, and after she spends the money, she finds the missing heirloom. Jack Dodson, playing the insurance agent, makes his first appearance in this episode. (Episode 178)

179. "Wyatt Earp" *Jan. 31, 1966*
Mayberry residents are impressed when an imposter, accompanied by his promoter (played by Pat Hinkle), comes to May-

berry claiming to be a descendant of Wyatt Earp. The promoter in actuality is using the boy to get rich, though he in fact means no harm. In the end, Andy exposes the promoter and convinces Clarence Earp that he must search for his identity and that he shouldn't live his life for or through others. (Episode 179)

180. "Aunt Bee Learns to Drive" *Feb. 7, 1966*
Andy is at his wit's end when Aunt Bee buys a secondhand car and begins taking driving lessons. She accidentally damages the car by backing it into a tree, and afraid that Andy will not allow her to drive anymore, she lets Andy think that he damaged the car when he pulled up behind it in his squad car. When he finally discovers the truth, he reassures Aunt Bee and allows her to continue driving. (Episode 180)

181. "Look Paw, I'm Dancing" *Feb. 14, 1966*
Opie is dreading the upcoming school dance because he is too shy to dance in public. Helen and Andy, who are chaperons at the annual event, join in the dance with the young people. Seeing his father on the dance floor, Opie overcomes his fear and asks a young girl to dance. (Episode 181)

182. "The Gypsies" *Feb. 21, 1966*
A band of gypsies sets up camp just outside of Mayberry, where they practice their magic on the townspeople. They sell various "precious" pieces of jewelry to Aunt Bee and her friends, claiming that these jewels were worn by famous people. When Andy tries to evict them, they come into Mayberry and convince many people that they have put a curse on the town. They make people believe in their powers when they correctly predict rain, but Andy reveals that their power of prediction derives from the local weather report. Jamie Farr, who plays Corporal Klinger on M*A*S*H, is featured as one of the gypsies. (Episode 183)

183. "Eat Your Heart Out" *Feb. 28, 1966*
Goober becomes infatuated with Flora, the new waitress at the diner, and he talks Andy into going with him for a meal. Flora, however, becomes interested in Andy, and the sheriff finds himself in a dilemma. By teaching Goober to play hard to get, Andy enables him to win Flora's interest. (Episode 182)

184. "A Baby in the House" *March 7, 1966*
Aunt Bee is upset when she discovers that her niece's baby cries

every time she tries to hold or feed it. So she solicits help from Andy, Opie, or whoever happens to be available—all of whom are successful in feeding the infant. Aunt Bee doesn't realize that her fear of holding the baby is causing it to be upset until— in a moment of danger to the child—she clutches it to her. When the baby doesn't cry, Aunt Bee realizes that it is because the infant senses her sincere feelings. (Episode 184)

185. "The County Clerk" *March 14, 1966*
The shy, retiring bachelor, Howard Sprague, appears for the first time in this episode. When Andy and Helen attempt to get Howard involved in the social life of Mayberry by introducing him to the county nurse, they must endure the wrath of Howard's overprotective mother. (Episode 185)

186. "The Foster Lady" *March 21, 1966*
An advertising agency is looking for someone who will appeal to the small-town audience. So to advertise Foster Furniture Polish, they plan to use Aunt Bee in a commercial. The creator of the product encourages her and approves of her natural appeal. The situation becomes complicated, however, when Aunt Bee proves to be too nervous in front of the camera. Her initial excitement fades when she realizes stardom isn't for her. (Episode 187)

187. "Goober's Replacement" *March 28, 1966*
Goober is excited about his forthcoming fishing vacation. However, he is not sure he will be able to go because Wally, the station owner, can't find a replacement. When Flora, the waitress at the diner, volunteers to fill in for him, Goober is amused but agrees. Upon his return from his trip, he finds that business at the station is booming because of Flora's sexy appearance. Andy steps in and explains to Wally and Flora that Goober is without a job and is miserable, and Wally gives him back his job. (Episode 186)

188. "The Battle of Mayberry" *April 4, 1966*
In a paper for his history class, Opie uncovers proof that one of Mayberry's sacred moments of the past, the Battle of Mayberry, held in the 1700s, was simply a feud that was settled over a jug of corn liquor. Those Mayberry residents—Clara Edwards among them—whose ancestors participated in the "war" become incensed, and chaos results. Opie comes to realize that legends and facts do not necessarily mix. (Episode 188)

189. "A Singer in Town"   *April 11, 1966*
Aunt Bee and Clara Edwards are excited when rock 'n' roll star
Keevy Hazelton plans to sing their song honoring Mayberry,
"My Home Town," on his television show. The two ladies, with
Andy and Opie, attend the show's rehearsal, and when they
hear the "jazzed up" version of their ballad, they refuse to let
their song be performed. The show's producer and Hazelton
agree to slow the song a bit, and the result proves satisfactory to
Aunt Bee and Clara. (Episode 189)

End of 1965–66 season

190. "Opie's Girlfriend"   *Sept. 12, 1966*
Helen's niece is interested in Opie but succeeds in isolating him
when she proves herself to be athletically superior in a game of
football. Opie's pride is hurt and he tries to get her to fight, but
even here she gets the best of him. Helen advises the girl to
boost Opie's ego by feigning inferiority in all activities. She pretends to be impressed by anything Opie does, and his self-confidence is restored and their friendship blossoms. (Episode 190)

191. "The Lodge"   *Sept. 19, 1966*
Howard is anxious to join the local men's lodge after attending
on a trial basis. During the election to approve him, however,
Goober blackballs him. Howard's mother, not wanting Howard
to leave her at night, convinces Goober that Howard's father
had met his ruin in such an organization. When Andy uncovers
the problem, he persuades Goober to change his vote, and Howard is allowed to join the lodge. (Episode 192)

192. "The Barbershop Quartet"   *Sept. 26, 1966*
Howard Sprague, the Mayberry Quartet's tenor, contracts laryngitis. Andy begins auditions for a new tenor, but his search
proves futile until he overhears a prisoner's beautiful voice.
Andy is reluctant to let the prisoner go to the concert until another sheriff, whose quartet has won earlier contests, boasts that
his group will win again this year. The prisoner attempts to escape, but his conscience prevails and he returns just in time to
enable the Mayberry Quartet to win the contest. (Episode 191)

193. "The Ball Game"   *Oct. 3, 1966*
Andy is persuaded to umpire a little-league baseball game be-

tween Mayberry and Mt. Pilot. He tries to prove his impartiality and calls Opie out in the final inning with the run that would have tied the game. The play was close, and a later photograph proves that Opie was safe. Andy is kept from learning of this by Helen and Aunt Bee, but in the meantime Andy becomes the town pariah. Rance Howard, Ronny's father, co-authored this script with Sid Morse. (Episode 195)

194. "Aunt Bee's Crowning Glory" *Oct. 10, 1966*
Aunt Bee shocks Mayberry and especially Andy when she buys a blonde wig. Thinking that everyone is impressed with the wig, Aunt Bee, though she dislikes it herself, continues to wear it. Finally the truth comes out that Aunt Bee's friends and family prefer her as herself, and she is glad, to everyone's surprise, to abandon her "crowning glory." (Episode 194)

195. "The Darling Fortune" *Oct. 17, 1966*
Andy and the town of Mayberry undergo a trying experience when the Darling family comes into a fortune of three hundred dollars. This is the last episode in which the Darlings appeared. (Episode 193)

196. "Mind over Matter" *Oct. 31, 1966*
When Goober sustains a minor jolt, friends convince him that he has a severe case of whiplash. Goober stays with the Taylors and has Andy constantly attending him. Andy is sure that Goober is a victim of hypochondria and finally tricks him into revealing that his aches and pains are, in fact, imagined. (Episode 199)

197. "Politics Begin at Home" *Nov. 7, 1966*
The town is divided when both Aunt Bee and Howard decide to run for town councilman. Andy, unaware that Aunt Bee has decided to run, pledges his support to Howard. He is of two minds when he finds that Aunt Bee is a candidate but feels that he must maintain his allegiance to Howard. Howard wins, and Aunt Bee proves to be a gracious loser. (Episode 200)

198. "The Senior Play" *Nov. 14, 1966*
When Helen Crump and her senior class decide to depart from tradition in putting on the class play, they are opposed by the old-fashioned principal, who disdains rock 'n' roll music. Helen's idea to fuse new styles with old traditions proves suc-

cessful and satisfies the principal's high standards. He is made to see that the younger generation is not so different from past youth, and applauds Helen's production. (Episode 197)

199. "Opie Finds a Baby"   *Nov. 21, 1966*

Opie and Arnold find a baby and take it upon themselves to find the infant new parents. Jack Nicholson guest stars as the child's father. The couple who abandoned the baby return to Mayberry to claim the child, and Andy severely reprimands them for being so irresponsible. Convinced that the couple's problems are solved, Andy allows them to take their baby. (Episode 202)

200. "Big Fish in a Small Town"   *Nov. 28, 1966*

Before the fishing season begins, Mayberry's fishermen enjoy talking about the legendary silver carp, "Old Sam." When Howard, a novice, catches "Old Sam" on his first fishing trip, the town's sportsmen are a bit perturbed, especially when Howard decides to donate "Old Sam" to an aquarium in another city. Howard detects disapproval among the townspeople and is lauded when he decides to return "Old Sam" to Tucker's Lake. (Episode 198)

201. "Only a Rose"   *Dec. 5, 1966*

Aunt Bee feels that she has a prize rose, one that can compete with those of Clara Edwards—the perennial champion at the Mayberry flower show. However, Opie destroys the rose when he accidentally hits it with a football. He tries to tape the flower together to no avail. Aunt Bee is crushed and must endure the boasts of Clara when she wins once again. However, Andy had taken a picture of Aunt Bee's beautiful rose, and when he shows it to Clara she acknowledges the superiority of Aunt Bee's flower, which will appear on the cover of a local garden periodical. (Episode 203)

202. "Otis the Deputy"   *Dec. 12, 1966*

Otis and Howard attempt to rescue Andy, who has been taken prisoner by a pair of desperate bank robbers. Howard carelessly walks into the hands of the criminals, and they tie him and Andy to chairs. Otis, meanwhile, falls asleep in a drunken stupor outside the window where his friends are held captive. His snoring alerts Andy and Howard to his presence, so they pretend to be thirsty and ask for glasses of water, which they manage to throw onto Otis, thereby waking him up so that he can help them escape and capture the criminals. (Episode 204)

203. "Goober Makes History" *Dec. 19, 1966*
Goober's lack of confidence in his mental abilities changes when he grows a beard and is told that the addition makes him look more intelligent. During the night class in history that he, Andy, Helen, and others are enrolled in, Goober begins to dominate the class with his verbose, often nonsensical speeches. His arrogance carries over into his social life, and he becomes even more of a nuisance. Finally, Andy confronts Goober, tells him how obnoxious he has become, and Goober, realizing his mistake, shaves off his beard and becomes his old self again. (Episode 196)

204. "A New Doctor in Town" *Dec. 26, 1966*
Traditional Mayberry is unwilling to accept the "new-fangled" methods of its new, young doctor. When the doctor (played by M*A*S*H's William Christopher) explains that Opie should have his tonsils out, Andy very reluctantly shows his faith in the young doctor by letting him remove them. The operation is a success, and the townspeople place their confidence in the new doctor. (Episode 201)

205. "Don't Miss a Good Bet" *Jan. 2, 1967*
Andy, Goober, and Floyd are taken in by a con man's get-rich-quick scheme to uncover oil or minerals from a tract of land. The con man leaves town, and Andy and his friends learn that good honest work is the best investment. (Episode 205)

206. "Dinner at Eight" *Jan. 9, 1967*
With Aunt Bee and Opie out for the evening, Andy looks forward to a relaxing night. Unfortunately, Goober forgets to give him two phone messages: a dinner invitation from Helen and an invitation from Howard to stop by after dinner. During a spaghetti dinner with Andy, Goober recalls but jumbles the messages. As a result of the confusion, Andy arrives at Howard's early and at Helen's late and has to endure two more spaghetti dinners. (Episode 206)

207. "A Visit to Barney Fife" *Jan. 16, 1967*
Andy visits Barney in Raleigh and discovers that his former deputy, now a detective with the police department, is really no

more than an errand boy. Further, he is in danger of losing his
job. Andy makes a hero out of Barney when he arranges for
him to get credit for capturing a band of criminals who are responsible for a series of grocery store robberies. Barney is
shocked to learn that the criminals are, in fact, the "nice family"
he has been living with and that they have been getting their
information on police stakeouts from him. After the arrest, Barney wins the respect of his colleagues and keeps his job. (Episode 211)

208. "Barney Comes to Mayberry"   *Jan 23, 1967*
Barney's visit to Mayberry coincides with the return of a hometown girl who has become a Hollywood star. Coincidentally, Barney had dated Teena Andrews in high school and imagines that
she still "has it for him." Barney is flattered and Mayberry residents are impressed when Teena asks Barney to escort her
through the day's activities. Barney jumps to conclusions about
her intentions when she invites him to her hotel room, and his
feeble passes are interrupted by the entrance of Teena's husband. (Episode 212)

209. "Andy's Old Girlfriend"   *Jan. 30, 1967*
Andy's romance with Helen is temporarily disrupted when
Andy's old high school sweetheart moves back to town. Andy
must deal with Helen's obvious jealousy, but their time-tested
romance holds up to the test provided by his old flame. (Episode 207)

210. "Aunt Bee's Restaurant"   *Feb. 6, 1967*
Aunt Bee opens a Chinese restaurant with some oriental ac-
quaintances and makes a go of it. The townspeople are impressed, but Aunt Bee decides that she shouldn't ignore Andy
and Opie and that the job requires too much time away from
home. So she sells her share of the restaurant to her partners
and happily returns to the Taylor kitchen. (Episode 209)

211. "Floyd's Barbershop"   *Feb. 13, 1967*
Howard Sprague dabbles in real estate when he decides to buy
the building that houses Floyd's barbershop, a Mayberry fixture.
In order to pay increased property taxes, Howard must raise
Floyd's rent. But Floyd, in an act of protest, decides to leave
Mayberry despite pleas from his friends not to. Andy tries to
make him understand Howard's situation. Finally, Howard gives

in, agrees to take a loss, and Floyd returns. Once again the sense of permanence in Mayberry is reestablished. (Episode 210)

212. "The Statue" *Feb. 20, 1967*
Mayberry plans to honor its most illustrious ancestor by dedicating a statue of that person. There is much dispute as to who this ancestor should be, Seth Taylor or an ancestor of Clara Edwards. The committee, led by the logical Howard Sprague, chooses Seth Taylor, and Andy and Aunt Bee are thrilled until they learn, just before the unveiling of the statue, that he was the state's biggest swindler. (Episode 208)

213. "Helen, the Authoress" *Feb. 27, 1967*
Both Helen and Andy are excited when her children's book is accepted for publication. Andy accompanies Helen to her publisher in Raleigh and is treated rudely. Andy wonders how he will cope with the idea of being the fiancé of "Helene Alexion Dubois"—Helen's suggested pen name—when he realizes that she will become a celebrity. Helen resists the publisher's efforts to change her image, and Andy is reassured in his relationship with her. (Episode 213)

214. "Goodbye Dolly" *March 6, 1967*
Mayberry's milkman is forced to retire his milkwagon horse, Dolly, who has been replaced by a more efficient milk truck. She misses her job, and the milkman observes her backing up to the old milkwagon, waiting to make her deliveries. Andy solves the problem by suggesting that the milkman tie Dolly to the milk truck, thereby allowing her to accompany him on his daily rounds. (Episode 214)

215. "Opie's Piano Lesson" *March 13, 1967*
Opie is excited about learning to play the piano until he realizes that football practice seems to be more important to him. When Andy strongly suggests that he give up the football, Opie realizes that he is capable of making time for both activities and that a proper amount of each sort of activity is necessary. (Episode 215)

216. "Howard, the Comedian" *March 20, 1967*
Howard becomes a popular comedian on a Raleigh television show, but when he begins to use the names of his fellows in Mayberry as part of his old jokes, his friends become irate.

When they later discover that they have become "famous" because of Howard's humor, they not only lose their anger but supply Howard with more comic stories about themselves. (Episode 216)

217. "Big Brothers"   *March 27, 1967*
Howard Sprague volunteers to become the Big Brother of a high school boy and falls in love with his sister. (Episode 217)

218. "Opie's Most Unforgettable Character"   *April 3, 1967*
Andy is distressed when Opie chooses someone else to write about as his "Most Unforgettable Character" for a school composition. Another boy, however, chooses to write about Sheriff Taylor, and Andy learns that Opie was simply too close to him to be able to deal successfully with him as a subject for his essay. (Episode 218)

219. "Goober's Contest"   *April 10, 1967*
Goober's "great gas giveaway" results in catastrophe for him when a printing error awards Floyd a large cash prize. When Goober cannot honor the award, Floyd insists that Andy arrest him for fraud. Later, however, Floyd feels sorry for Goober and drops charges against him. (Episode 219)

End of 1966–67 season

220. "Opie's First Love"   *Sept. 11, 1967*
Opie develops a crush on Mary Alice Carter and is finally able to bring himself to invite her to a party. She accepts, but when an older boy asks her, she throws Opie over at the last minute. Opie goes to the party anyway and sees her there. When Mary Alice is ignored by her date, she apologizes to Opie, who understands, and they enjoy the party. (Episode 220)

221. "Howard the Bowler"   *Sept. 18, 1967*
Howard is a last-minute substitution for Emmett's bowling team and remarkably almost rolls a perfect game. The electricity goes off in the building just before Howard rolls the final ball, and he must come back the following day to complete his game. Howard spends a sleepless night but astonishes everyone the next day when he responds to the pressure and throws a strike. (Episode 224)

222. "A Trip to Mexico" *Sept. 25, 1967*
Aunt Bee, Clara, and another friend go to Mexico and return
to Mayberry bitter enemies. Everyone tries to get them back together, and when the photographs they took on the trip are developed, Andy gets the idea of bringing the ladies together to
view them. Their differences are quickly forgotten amid the re-
vived memories of their vacation. (Episode 227)

223. "Andy's Trip to Raleigh" *Oct. 2, 1967*
Andy finds himself in trouble when he cancels a date with Helen
to meet with a lawyer in Raleigh. The lawyer proves to be a very
attractive woman, and Andy spends the day with her by a swimming pool. Despite the fact that he has not done anything
wrong, he fears what Helen may think and thus seeks to hide
the fact that the lawyer is a beautiful woman. When Helen finds
out, Andy has to work hard to explain himself and soothe
Helen's suspicions. (Episode 226)

224. "Opie Steps Up in Class" *Oct. 9, 1967*
Andy becomes involved in Opie's stay at a swank boys' camp
when he is invited for Father's Sunday. Andy finds himself in
the company of very rich men who talk of yachts and swimming
pools. In an attempt to fit in, Andy brags about his own boat
until Opie overhears and reminds him that the "oars" need to
be fixed. Andy is humiliated, especially since he warned Opie
not to put on airs, but he then openly describes his small-town
heritage, and the wealthy men express interest in joining Andy
in some good old lake fishing. (Episode 225)

225. "Howard's Main Event" *Oct. 16, 1967*
Howard is threatened by Millie's former boyfriend, a muscular
fellow who is trying to resume his courtship of her. Andy advises
Howard to stand up to him. When he does, the boyfriend backs
down. Howard later tries this approach again when he sees another man flirting with Millie, but this time he gets punched in
the stomach. Andy advises Howard that this method doesn't
work every time. (Episode 222)

226. "Aunt Bee the Juror" *Oct. 23, 1967*
Aunt Bee is summoned for jury duty and trusts her intuition in
deciding the verdict of a thief (played by Jack Nicholson). The
other jurors, all men, become furious when Aunt Bee continues
to maintain the criminal's innocence. It turns out that the man
is innocent, and Aunt Bee ends up the hero. (Episode 223)

227. "Tape Recorder"   *Oct. 20, 1967*
Opie and his friend Arnold use a tape recorder to eavesdrop on a prisoner and his lawyer, despite Andy's warning that such action is illegal. The tape reveals to the boys the location of the stolen money. Andy, refusing to listen to them, solves the case in his own way, keeping the law intact. (Episode 228)

228. "Opie's Group"   *Nov. 6, 1967*
When Opie is asked to join a rock 'n' roll band, he is excited, but when his grades suffer, Andy and Aunt Bee become worried. They ask Clara Edwards if she will have a talk with the band about classical music. She agrees, but Andy and Aunt Bee return to find that Clara has become the group's manager and pianist. (Episode 229)

229. "Aunt Bee and the Lecturer"   *Nov. 13, 1967*
Aunt Bee goes picnicking and dining out with a charming visiting lecturer. Impressed by his broad knowledge and urbanity, Bee enjoys being seen in his company and making Clara and the other women jealous.(Episode 230)

230. "Andy's Investment"   *Nov. 20, 1967*
In an attempt to earn more money for Opie's college education, Andy opens a coin laundry in Mayberry. He soon learns that the laundry business is much more trouble than he anticipated, for his time is dominated by overflowing washers and customers' complaints. Driven nearly to distraction, he gives up the laundry and trusts that Opie's future education can be funded by careful planning and faith in Opie's abilities. (Episode 231)

231. "Howard and Millie"   *Nov. 27, 1967*
Howard decides to propose to Millie at the bakery where she works. His proposal is typically a nervous one, but Millie accepts, and they take a train to her home in West Virginia to meet the folks. En route Howard and Millie have several disagreements and decide that they should wait until they are more certain that marriage is right for them. (Episode 233)

232. "Aunt Bee's Cousin"   *Dec. 4, 1967*
To protect Aunt Bee, Andy doesn't tell her that he saw their cousin Bradford alight from a freight train when he comes to visit. Aunt Bee thinks that he is a wealthy relative and never finds out the truth. Andy bribes Bradford into leaving when it

appears that he is going to stay in Mayberry to "live off" the Taylors. (Episode 234)

233. "Suppose Andy Gets Sick"   Dec. 11, 1967
Andy catches the flu and is confined to bed for a few days. He hires Goober to act as a temporary deputy to take care of necessary duties around the town, but Goober constantly disturbs Andy with trivial questions. Disgusted and unable to rest, Andy gets out of bed and goes back to work. (Episode 232)

234. "Howard's New Life"   Dec. 18, 1967
Howard's attempt to break out of his boring job as county clerk lands him on a Caribbean island, where he expects to enjoy the life of a beachcomber. However, he finds that life here is just as boring and certainly more lonely than city life. He encounters several islanders whose only activity is to make ships in bottles, and Howard is shocked into returning to Mayberry. (Episode 235)

235. "Goober the Executive"   Dec. 25, 1967
Goober is interested in buying Wally's gas station but needs some financial backing from Andy and Emmett. Although Emmett is reluctant to support Goober, Andy helps him to get established in the business. (Episode 221)

236. "The Mayberry Chef"   Jan. 1, 1968
Aunt Bee's reputation as a cook lands her a job as a television chef. Initially Andy and Opie are excited for her, but she has to be away at night, and meal after meal of burnt food causes the Taylor men to regret Aunt Bee's taking the job. Aunt Bee senses their feelings and returns to her household duties. (Episode 237)

237. "Emmett's Brother-in-Law"   Jan. 8, 1968
Emmett is shamed by his successful brother-in-law into joining him in the "more lucrative, more prestigious" insurance business. But Emmett is not a successful insurance man because he doesn't fit the mold, and he longs to return to his casual life as a fix-it-man. (Episode 236)

238. "Opie's Drugstore Job"   Jan. 15, 1968
Opie is happy to get a job at the drugstore but is not sure how long that job will last when he breaks a bottle of expensive per-

fume. Rather than endanger his job, Opie replaces the bottle with a less expensive brand. Later, he is faced with a dilemma when a customer wants to buy the perfume. He confesses his accident, and the druggist, who admires his honesty, doesn't make him pay for the perfume. (Episode 239)

239. "The Church Benefactors"   *Jan. 22, 1968*
The Mayberry church receives a $500 gift, and the congregation is undecided as to how to spend the money. The church almost divides over whether to spend the money for new choir robes or for strengthening the church's crumbling foundation. Andy's common sense finally rules the day when he convinces the congregation that they must be practical. (Episode 238)

240. "Barney Hosts a Summit Meeting"   *Jan. 29, 1968*
Andy allows Barney to arrange an East-West summit meeting at the Taylor household because he feels this will boost Barney's reputation with his superiors in the Raleigh Police Force. Confusion at the Taylors' house at first prevents the two diplomats from making any decisions. But the two reach an agreement at midnight when they meet in the kitchen and talk while enjoying Aunt Bee's cooking. Aaron Ruben wrote the script for this episode. (Episode 240)

241. "Goober Goes to an Auto Show"   *Feb. 5, 1968*
Goober's attempt to impress an old mechanics' school friend by taking him out to dinner and bragging that he owns a chain of gas stations backfires. However, he learns a valuable lesson of telling the truth and being himself when later in the episode he discovers that his friend has also been lying about the importance and prestige of his job. (Episode 242)

242. "Aunt Bee's Big Moment"   *Feb. 12, 1968*
Hearing her friends talk about the things they are proud of, Aunt Bee longs to have something to boast about, so she signs up for flying lessons. She is terrified when the time comes for her to solo, but she is determined to make the flight. It is a successful one, of course, but Aunt Bee decides to quit flying. The thrill of the flight remains with her, but most importantly she has something to be proud of, something to boast about to her friends. (Episode 243)

243. "Helen's Past" *Feb. 19, 1968*
Andy and the Mayberry School Board are shocked about Helen's past when they find a photograph of Helen in the company of a hoodlum and learn that she was once arrested for carrying a gun and gambling. The school board considers suspending her until the truth is uncovered that Helen was a reporter who had gone undercover to expose a gambling ring and got arrested by mistake. (Episode 244)

244. "Emmett's Anniversary" *Feb. 26, 1968*
Emmett gets his wife a coat from a wholesale fur dealer, and his wife finds it before their anniversary. Only after she discovers it does Emmett see the price tag. His dilemma is that he doesn't want to disappoint her and at the same time he doesn't have the money to pay for the coat. He decides to give her the coat, but when she finds out how expensive it is, she has him return it. (Episode 245)

245. "The Wedding" *March 4, 1968*
When Howard's mother remarries and moves away, he abandons his conservative ways and remodels their home into a bachelor pad complete with throw pillows, a bar (including ginger ale and grapefruit juice), a stereo, and beads hanging from doors. His attempt to throw a swinging party results in fiasco when only Goober, Emmett, Andy, and Helen show up, and the entire party consists of Goober and Emmett dancing with Helen. (Episode 246)

246. "Sam for Town Council" *March 11, 1968*
Sam Jones (Ken Berry) is established as a respectable citizen in this episode when Andy and other friends talk him into running for town council. (Episode 247)

247. "Opie and Mike" *March 18, 1968*
Andy and Opie pitch in to help Sam Jones solve a delicate social problem faced by Sam's son, Mike. (Episode 248)

248. "A Girl for Goober" *March 25, 1968*
Andy and Sam talk Goober into filling out a questionnaire for a computer dating service. Goober misinterprets the questions by answering that he reads thirty books a month (comic books) and enjoys painting (he once painted a barn). Goober's date turns

out to be a woman with a Ph.D., and they soon realize that they
have nothing in common. The lady, however, sees something
special in Goober and agrees to go out with him again. (Episode
249)

249. "Mayberry, R.F.D." *April 1, 1968*
Sam Jones takes on an immigrant Italian family to work on his
farm, and the family learns that it's not entirely suited to the
American way of life. Nevertheless, they prove to be hard workers (the old man's daughter cooks for the Joneses), and Sam
hates to see them return to their homeland. The last episode to
be aired, "Mayberry, R.F.D." prepared the audience for next
season's series of the same name. (Episode 241)

Index

The preface, the actual script of "The Sermon for Today," the unfilmed script of "The Wandering Minstrel," and the 249 brief summaries have not been indexed.

CPSIA information can be obtained at www.ICGtesting.com
Printed in the USA
BVOW08s0309010915

415211BV00001B/3/P